THE
FISHERMAN'S
HANDBOOK

THE
FISHERMAN'S
HANDBOOK

How to find, identify and catch the top Australian angling fish

STEVE
STARLING

SANDSTONE BOOKS

First Published in Australia in 1992

This Edition Published for Sandstone Books Australia 1998

Revised and reprinted 1999

ISBN: 1 86505 1187

Printed in Hong Kong through
Colourcraft Ltd

A SANDSTONE PRODUCTION

CONTENTS

PREFACE

Well over 2000 species of fish have been recorded and scientifically described from Australia's fresh, brackish and salt waters during this island continent's two centuries of European settlement. Without doubt, many more still await discovery and classification. However, the vast majority of these 2000-plus fish are of little more than academic interest to most recreational anglers. Many of them either live in very deep water far from shore, or never grow to more than a few centimetres in length. Only about 200 types of fish are taken by Australian anglers with anything approaching regularity, and even fewer are commonly targeted on hook and line.

In this book I have chosen to look at around 100 different fish species which, in my opinion, constitute our favourite or most sought-after angling targets. Certainly, I will have omitted some types of fish that enjoy a specialist or regional following, and just as surely, I have included a few that appeal to only a tiny band of devotees. However, I believe that the 100 or so species covered here account for close to 95 per cent of the fishing effort expended by recreational anglers in this country.

When you stop to think about it, 100 species is quite a long list of potential angling targets! Few of us will account for more than half that number in a lifetime of keen angling, and only a very lucky—and very skilful—handful of travelling fisher-folk could ever hope to approach a 'full house' of 100 species. Although, it certainly would be a lot of fun trying!

I sincerely hope this book makes identifying your catch a great deal easier, but I also hope it helps you to add a few new fish to your personal tally of species. This is, after all, more than a standard fish identification guide. It is, first and foremost, a book about recreational angling and, as such, it is intended to increase your fishing success rate by teaching you more about the habits, the diet and the distribution of the fish you pursue.

Finally, may I suggest that as you learn more about the fish we all rely on for our angling enjoyment, you share that knowledge with others and also help to promote a modern, ethical and conservation-conscious attitude toward the sport we love? By all means, keep a few legal-size fish for the table, but also consider joining the growing swing toward catch-and-release that is now sweeping this country. Please fish not only for today, but for the future, and remember that wonderful angling axiom; 'limit your kill, don't kill your limit!'

Tight Lines,
Steve Starling
1999

ACKNOWLEDGEMENTS

'We are fortunate indeed to live on an island continent that offers such a diversity of fishing opportunities, and we owe it to ourselves to learn as much as we can about the creatures that provide us with so much challenge and sport.' With those words I launched the first edition of this little book onto the Australian market, more than a decade ago. Since then it has been reprinted several times, and has proven to be my most popular title.

Sitting down to thoroughly revise and update *The Fisherman's Handbook* in time for a new century has brought back a great many fond memories, and I'd like to take this opportunity to once again thank all the people who have helped me over the years by willingly sharing their vast stores of knowledge on matters piscatorial. Not surprisingly, that list has grown somewhat since 1988!

Writing a book such as this in the first place would have been simply impossible without the accumulated wisdom, passed freely to me over many years, of learned laymen like John Prosser and Mark Hanlon, and of approachable scientists such as Dr Julian Pepperell (formerly of New South Wales Fisheries, and now an independent fisheries consultant of international standing) and John Gunn, of the CSIRO.

Thanks must also go to all my fellow anglers, especially those who supplied the photographs I didn't have in my own collection. Major contributors in this regard included Roger Apperley, Bill Classon, Mark Hanlon, Fred Jobson, Alex Julius, David Lockwood, Shane Mensforth and Warren Steptoe.

I owe another thank you to Angela Newman, who typed so much of the original manuscript back in the late 1980s, and to Jenni Muller, whose expertise at the computer keyboard has played such an important role in all subsequent updates and revisions.

Finally, my greatest debt of gratitude is to my wife, Julia, and my two children, Tom and Amy, to whom I dedicate this book. They not only put up with my seemingly endless 'field trips', but are always there with a helping hand or a word of encouragement when the going gets tough. I couldn't do any of it without them!

NOTES ON
FISH IDENTIFICATION

As stated in the preface, this book is first and foremost a fishing guide. Its secondary purpose is to make identification of the fish species easy.

In my experience, the average angler is only really interested in identifying major species and being able to put a name to his catch. The ability to identify accurately the many almost identical types of wrasse and parrot fish, or to pick the western sub-species of salmon from its eastern counterpart is less important.

Similarly, not too many laymen are overly interested in scientific names or toxonomic classifications. They certainly want to know whether the silvery fish they've just pulled from the surf is a black bream or a tarwhine, but they'll be less than fascinated to learn that the former is an *Acanthopagrus australis,* while the latter is a *Rhabdosargus sarba!*

There are excellent books on the market — most of them written by scientists — with the specific intention of identifying Australasian fish accurately. However, few of these scholarly works address the subject of catching fish. That is where I come in!

Having said that, it should be noted that scientific names are given for all fish mentioned and every effort has been made to ensure the accuracy of these names and of the descriptions given for each species. This may be a guide for the common man, but it is nonetheless a useful and correct one.

VARIATIONS AND IRREGULARITIES

The photographs and descriptions in this book are intended to portray each species in its most common or typical form and colour.

Every fish is capable of altering its colouring to adapt to environmental demands, and some of them perform this feat quite rapidly. In addition, almost all species look slightly different when viewed underwater, and most change colour or fade after capture and death.

Wherever possible, such colour variations have been mentioned in the description of each fish, though allowances must be made for more unusual irregularities, as well as for rare instances of albinism (lack of pigment), xanthochromism (yellow pigmentation) and colour reversal (light for dark). Hardly surprising, then, that fisheries biologists place so little credence on colouration when it comes to distinguishing similar species!

Variations in body shape and fin structure are less common, but can occur as a result of deformity, injury or even differences in physiognomy between isolated populations and individuals. The presence or absence of 'humps' on the heads of adult snapper is an obvious example.

HELP FROM THE BOFFINS

Should you catch a fish which defies identification, wrap it in plastic or cling wrap and freeze it whole. Your nearest museum, fisheries inspector or even a knowledgeable layman such as the recorder or weighmaster of a local fishing club should be able to help to identify it.

Colour photographs or slides are also useful in identifying fish, particularly those that are too big to freeze, or are intended for live release. The photo should show the entire length of the fish and be as clear and well focussed as possible.

ALBACORE

Thunnus alalunga

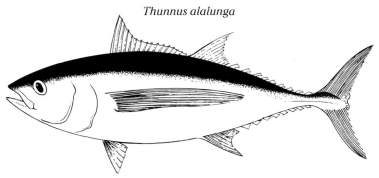

COMMON NAMES

This member of the tuna family is usually called albacore, but is also known as longfin tuna, white meat tuna or 'chicken of the sea', and as with so many of the tunas, may be erroneously tagged tunny, skipjack, bonito or horse mackerel. The fish is also sometimes confused with the yellowfin and bluefin tunas, though the albacore's elongated pectoral fins easily distinguish it from these related species.

DESCRIPTION

The fish has long, strap-like pectoral or side fins which, when pressed flat against its flanks, extend beyond the base of the second dorsal and anal fins.

The albacore has big, dark eyes. When fresh from the water it is dark metallic blue, but the colour changes quite suddenly along a somewhat irregular line, to silvery-blue on the flanks and fades more gradually to silvery-white on the belly. An iridescent band of electric blue is sometimes present along the sides just below the line of demarcation between the dark back and lighter flanks.

SIZE

In some parts of the world, albacore have been recorded at weights in excess of 35 kg. Here in Australia and New Zealand the species rarely tops 22 kg and is more common at weights of between 4 and 12 kg. At times, large schools of very small juveniles weighing from 0.5 to 2 kg are encountered in cooler southern waters off Tasmania, western Victoria, South Australia and New Zealand.

DISTRIBUTION

Along with the striped tuna or skipjack, they are among the most prolific of the tunas and are found throughout the oceans of the world.

Although reasonably temperature tolerant, albacore prefer clean, bluewater currents of between 14^0 and 18^0C. They are more at home in deep water, and adult fish are rarely found in areas less than 150 metres deep.

HABITS AND FEEDING

Albacore are a schooling fish and swim anywhere between the seabed and the surface, though unlike many of the other tunas, they rarely break through the surface when travelling or feeding.

Albacore make rapid, vertical movement through the water column in pursuit of the small fish, large planktonic organisms and squid, which make up the bulk of their diet. They will also scavenge dead fish, flesh pieces and the refuse from trawler nets or other fishing operations.

FISHING TECHNIQUES

Albacore respond to lure trolling, live baiting and dead baiting. They may also be taken by casting and retrieving lures, or allowing lures to sink deep beneath the

Left: Albacore are characterised by their long, strap-like pectoral or side fins. These are significantly longer than the pectoral fins of any other fish in the tuna family.
Below: Most Australasian albacore are taken in deep water over the continental shelf.

school before a rapid retrieval to the surface.

Favoured lures for albacore include rubber and vinyl squid patterns, feather jigs, small pushers, hexheads and Konahead-style skirted trolling models. Timber or plastic swimming minnows, chrome slices and alloy slugs or fish-shaped jigs also work well. Lures should measure between 7 and 20 cm overall, though larger artificials are occasionally taken. Favoured colours include black, blue, dark green, pink and red.

Live baits of yellowtail scad, slimy mackerel, garfish or mullet are also readily accepted by feeding albacore, as are dead baits of the same species, whole or cut pilchards, herring and anchovy, or cut strips and slabs of fish flesh especially from oily, pink or red-fleshed species.

When drift fishing or fishing at anchor for albacore, a berley or chum trail of minced fish flesh, oil and chopped fish scraps will quickly attract and concentrate the fish.

EATING QUALITIES

Albacore are regarded by many as the best tasting of all the tunas. They have finely textured pink flesh which cooks up white and firm and is also well suited to raw fish or sashimi recipes.

As with all the tunas, captured albacore should be killed, bled, cleaned and iced down promptly to preserve the quality of their flesh.

AMBERJACK

Seriola dumerilii

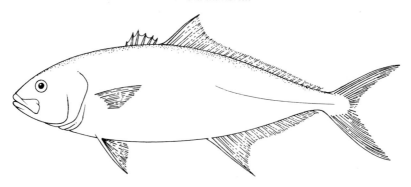

COMMON NAMES

In Australia, amberjack or greater amberjack is often confused with its more common local relatives, the yellowtail kingfish and the samson fish.

DESCRIPTION

The amberjack is best distinguished from the yellowtail kingfish by body shape and fin colouration. Its body is deeper and its fins are much darker and less yellowish than those of the kingfish. In addition, live or freshly killed amberjack usually have a dark, diagonal stripe running from the top of the head through the eyes to the snout area.

Distinguishing the amberjack from its close cousin the samson fish is more difficult, and is best done by counting the rays or soft spines in the second dorsal fin. Amberjack have between 29 and 35; samson fish have from 23 to 25.

Amberjack are usually blue-green or blue-black on the back, silvery-blue or green on the flanks and silvery-white on the belly. A yellowish band along the centre of each flank may be noticeable in live specimens.

The fins are dusky amber with tinges of yellow or rust-red. The teeth and mouth lining may be dark red, but this is not a diagnostic feature.

SIZE

Overseas, amberjack have been recorded at weights in excess of 60 kg. Australian specimens are rarely half that and are more common in the 2 to 15 kg range.

DISTRIBUTION

Found mainly in the sub-tropical and warmer temperate oceans of the world, they are most prolific in the western Atlantic around Florida, the waters of the Bahamas and the Caribbean.

Amberjack are widely found around Australia, but are not particularly common in any one region; the best concentrations are off the far north coast of New South Wales and over the offshore reefs of southern Queensland.

HABITS AND FEEDING

Like the kingfish and samson fish, amberjack relate strongly to significant structures such as reef pinnacles, drop-offs, floating debris, marker buoys, mooring lines and drilling rigs.

Australian amberjack prefer water temperatures between 18⁰ and 24⁰C.

They range further offshore than either kingfish or samsons, and are more truly pelagic or free-roaming in their habits. However, a school will take up semi-

permanent residence over a deep reef complex.

Amberjack feed mainly on smaller fish, including reef-dwelling species. They take crustacea, are particularly fond of squid, and will scavenge dead fish and fish scraps.

FISHING TECHNIQUES

Amberjack are rarely targeted by Australian anglers. They are more likely to be incidental catches taken during sport and game fishing for kingfish, cobia and mackerel, or during reef fishing for snapper, cod, pearl perch, coral trout and the like.

Amberjack respond to all of the techniques which take kingfish, especially trolling with deep-running minnows,

jigging, slow trolling live baits, casting near structures such as marker buoys, and free lining live or dead fish baits and squid in a berley trail.

When fished for over a reef they are particularly responsive to live baits of 0.5 to 1 kg snapper, large yellowtail, slimy mackerel and even bream or tarwhine which should be weighted for deep presentation. Sturdy tackle is needed as, once hooked, a large amberjack will race for the sanctuary of the nearby reef and attempt to sever the line on the sharp coral.

EATING QUALITIES

Small amberjack are generally tastier than their larger brethren which tend to be dry-fleshed and somewhat coarse.

ARCHER FISH

Toxotes chatareus, Toxotes jaculator

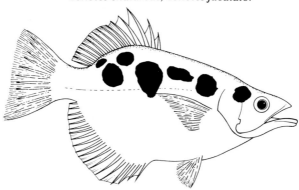

COMMON NAMES

These two closely related species are usually called archer fish or rifle fish. A third, more distantly related member of the family *(Protoxotes lorentzi),* is known as the primitive archer fish.

DESCRIPTION

A deep-bodied, laterally-compressed fish with moderately large scales and a large, upturned mouth.

Archer fish are characteristically coloured and marked. The base colour is creamy or creamy-yellow, the back a dark olive-brown. Several large, dark blotches extend downwards over the pale flanks.

Fins are variable in colour, though the tail is usually dark.

SIZE

Exceptional specimens may weigh 1 kg or slightly more, but they are much more common at weights of less than 0.5 kg and lengths of between 8 and 20 cm.

DISTRIBUTION

Archer fish live in our tropical estuaries, rivers, billabongs and lakes. Their normal range extends from central Queensland, around the northern half of Australia to the north west of Western Australia.

In all but monsoonal flood conditions they are found from the saline, tidal, lower reaches of tropical estuaries, far up into freshwater tributaries and headwaters, and in isolated billabongs and waterholes cut off from the main river system.

HABITS AND FEEDING

Archer fish feed on insects, shrimp and very small fish, most of which they find close to the bank of a stream or waterhole, under the shadows of overhanging vegetation.

The fish has the fascinating habit of squirting a jet of water from its mouth to knock down flying or crawling insects. This skill, combined with the ability to move just beneath the surface without causing a swirl or ripple, enables it to sneak very close to a spider, beetle or moth resting on a piece of bankside foliage and to blast the unsuspecting quarry into the water.

FISHING TECHNIQUES

Archer fish are rarely special targets but are usually taken incidentally by lure fishermen casting for barramundi, mangrove jack, saratoga or sooty grunter. The can surprise anglers by taking lures almost as long as themselves.

Large numbers can be caught if very small lures on light tackle are cast close to bankside cover. Artificials such as trout spinners and spoons, small bass plugs, mini

The handsome little archer fish is often encountered by tropical anglers casting small lures in estuaries and freshwater. It is usually released.

jigs and flies are particularly successful.

Even more effective is the use of a natural live bait such as a grasshopper, beetle, cricket, moth or march fly, rigged on a small hook and 'dapped' or dangled on the surface of the water under overhanging branches. A bunch of worms, a prawn or a live shrimp, cast, unweighted, towards fish holding areas also work well.

EATING QUALITIES

Archer fish are not often eaten because they are so small and more desirable table fish can be found in the same areas. Nonetheless, their flesh is sweet and white, if a little bony.

Most are returned to the water alive, or are kept as aquarium fish. Young archer fish make a fine live bait for barramundi.

BARRACOUTA

Leionura atun

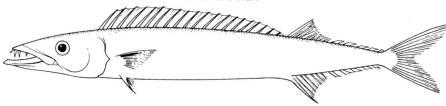

COMMON NAMES

The barracouta is frequently referred to by the shortened version of its name, 'couta'. This fish has several other colloquial names including 'pickhandle', 'axehandle' and 'hammer-handle', all of which refer to its shape. In some areas its South African name, snoek, is used.

Barracouta are sometimes confused with barracuda. Beyond vague similarities in body shape and dental equipment, the two have little in common.

DESCRIPTION

This slim, needle-toothed fish is usually dark steely-blue or dark green along the top of the back and bright, metallic silver on the flanks and belly.

There is a distinct black patch near the front or leading edge of the long, relatively high dorsal fin. The forked tail is dark.

The related gemfish, 'hake' or 'king barracouta' *(Rexea solandri)* is very similar in appearance, though shorter and deeper in the body, weighing a good deal more for a given length. The gemfish's teeth are even sharper and more dangerous than those of the barracouta. Gemfish inhabit deep water near the continental shelf and are rarely taken by anglers.

SIZE

Although often measuring between 50 and 140 cm, barracouta are very lightly built. Even exceptional specimens in excess of 150 cm rarely weigh more than 4 or 5 kg. A typical barracouta measures under a metre in length and weighs between 0.8 and 1.5 kg.

DISTRIBUTION

A cold-water fish, it is most numerous in the seas around Tasmania, Victoria, parts of South Australia and southern Western Australia and is reasonably common in New Zealand and South Africa.

Barracouta spend their early years in cold southern estuaries and bays, moving out to sea as they reach maturity.

Small fish are prolific in southern waters, fewer, larger individuals make forays north into warmer areas, especially in winter. Some exceptionally large specimens have been recorded in New Zealand's Northland region.

Schools of barracouta undertake extensive migrations northwards in winter and spring, occasionally reaching the central and north coasts of New South Wales.

Adults prefer reasonably clean, cool water and may be found anywhere between the shoreline and the continental shelf.

HABITS AND FEEDING

The barracouta is a schooling fish and hunts voraciously for small fish and squid. Their schools are often found in association with abundant southern baitfish species such as pilchards and cowanyoung.

Although usually found feeding at or near the surface, barracouta utilise the entire water column, from surface to seabed.

FISHING TECHNIQUES

Barracouta are specifically fished for in southern states, but are regarded as a pest in New South Wales.

They respond to a range of techniques,

Barracouta have a fearsome set of sharp fangs and should be handled with great care at all times. They are taken on a wide variety of baits and lures, and although despised in New South Wales, are held in reasonably high regard through the southern states.

but are best caught by casting or trolling a lure such as a flashy, chrome spoon or silver or white jig. Their teeth make short work of the tails of feather, vinyl, rubber or plastic trolling lures. They are partial to swimming minnow-type lures and plugs. The addition of a diving paravane to the rig ahead of the lure can improve trolling results.

Strips of fish flesh or whole pilchards and garfish on ganged hook rigs are the best bait. Live baits make for plenty of action, though many strikes are missed due to the barracouta's habit of running with the bait held crosswise between the jaws.

A wire trace is practically essential in all forms of barracouta fishing. Many fish are landed on lures or ganged hooks without wire, but eventually one of the school will take in the bait or lure beyond the metal, and make short work of even heavy nylon line.

EATING QUALITIES

Though generally despised in New South Wales, barracouta have tasty, pinkish-coloured flesh which cooks up firm and white and is ideally suited to smoking. After cooking, the many long, flexible bones are easily removed.

The flesh of barracouta can be infested, to varying degrees, with a parasitic worm. Cooking destroys these worms and they appear to have no effect on the eating quality of the fish. However, barracouta should never be eaten raw.

Barracouta flesh is regarded as a top bait, especially for snapper, by many southern anglers.

BARRACUDA

Sphyraena barracuda

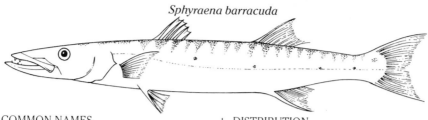

COMMON NAMES

Mainly known as barracuda or 'cuda', this fish is occasionally called the great barracuda, giant sea pike, dingo fish or 'pickhandle'.

Although barracuda are sometimes confused with the southern barracouta, the two are unrelated and have little in common beyond superficial physical similarities.

Several related species are found in Australian tropical and sub-tropical waters; all are smaller than the great barracuda described here, but otherwise have very similar habits and characteristics.

DESCRIPTION

A long, almost cylindrical fish with a large mouth full of fearsome-looking canine teeth.

They usually have steely-grey-or dark green backs and their silvery flanks carry between 18 and 24 faint vertical stripes or bars when fresh. There are often irregular dark blotches on the fish's sides, mainly towards the tail.

The tail fin can be strongly tinged with yellow.

SIZE

In parts of the Atlantic and Caribbean, barracuda are reputed to exceed 220 cm (2.2 metres) in length.

In Australian waters, barracuda over 170 cm and 25 kg are considered exceptional, though isolated specimens may occasionally top 30 kg.

The majority of barracuda encountered by anglers will be about a metre long and weigh from 4 to 8 kg.

DISTRIBUTION

This tropical and sub-tropical fish is found in all the warm oceans of the world.

While stray specimens have been caught as far south as Sydney and Perth, barracuda are mainly confined to waters north of the Tropic of Capricorn.

Their habitat ranges from the bluewater currents of the open ocean to the tidal reaches of mangrove-lined estuaries. Small fish are generally found inshore and larger ones offshore. However, the odd 8 kg-plus 'cuda' is likely to turn up in an estuary and cause much alarm and excitement!

HABITS AND FEEDING

Small barracuda are schooling fish. Groups are often seen drifting, or gliding almost motionless, across offshore reefs or through tropical lagoons.

They make a sudden, fast burst to seize their prey which is mostly small fish, especially fusiliers, banana fish, mullet, gar and long tom. Smaller barracuda, living in inshore or estuarine locations, may sometimes include prawns and other invertebrates in their diet.

Very large barracuda weighing more than about 15 kg tend to be more solitary and haunt a particular reef, drop-off, pass, bombora or hole. They prey on small tuna, mackerel, trevally and even younger members of their own species.

FISHING TECHNIQUES

Barracuda are rarely fished for specifically or exclusively. Small fish tend to be taken by estuary anglers working baits and lures for barramundi, mangrove jack

Left: A fine specimen of a barracuda.
Below: A large 'cuda performs near the boat
after being hooked on light lure casting tackle
in a north Queensland estuary.

and the like; offshore fishermen chasing mackerel, trevally, cobia and even marlin and sailfish, take most of the bigger specimens.

'Cuda' are particularly partial to a trolled bait of garfish, mullet or scad and respond enthusiastically to swimming minnow lures, trolling heads and metal spoons. Live bait is rarely passed up.

A wire trace is helpful, but some big ones have been landed on heavy nylon traces.

EATING QUALITIES

Barracuda flesh is not held in particularly high regard in Australia, since it is somewhat grey and strong smelling. The species is a definite ciguatera poisoning risk and should not be eaten in known ciguatera locations.

BARRAMUNDI

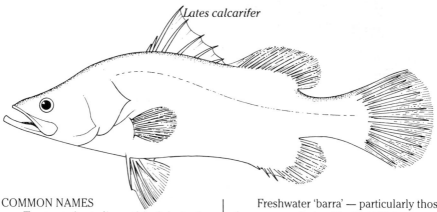

Lates calcarifer

COMMON NAMES

To most Australians this fish is the barramundi or, more frequently, just plain 'barra'. In some fishing books and magazines the fish is referred to as the 'giant perch', 'palmer' or 'cock-up', though these names are almost never used by fishermen.

Some confusion seems to exist between the name of this fish and the two species of saratoga *(Scleropages leichardti* and *S. jardini)* found in our tropical fresh waters. These saratoga were once known in certain circles as spotted barramundi or, in the case of *S. leichardti,* as the Dawson River barramundi.

It seems possible that in some Aboriginal dialects the word barramundi or something like it did once refer to the saratoga. These days it is so firmly associated with *Lates calcarifer* that there is no point in clouding the issue. In any event, nowadays few people ever call *S. leichardti* and *S. jardini* anything other than saratoga.

DESCRIPTION

The barramundi is a handsome fish with big scales, a large mouth, humped shoulders, a deeply scooped forehead and characteristic close-set eyes, which shine ruby-red in artificial light or at certain angles in sunlight.

The colouration of individual barramundi varies considerably depending on environment.

Freshwater 'barra' — particularly those from seasonally land-locked billabongs and waterholes — are usually dark bronze to chocolate-brown on the back with brassy flanks and very dark fins. The tail, in particular, may be almost black.

At the opposite extreme, saltwater 'barra' from reasonably clean water appear to wear suits of chrome-plated armour. Each scale is a metallic mirror, and there is very little pigmentation apart from a mauvish or purple sheen along the top of the back. The fins are very lightly coloured and the tail is often tinged with yellow.

Exceptions occur, and silvery barra are occasionally taken from fresh water, though even these fish usually have darker tails and fins than their salt water brethren.

Juvenile barramundi sometimes show faint bars on the body, and a dark stripe down the forehead between the eyes. This stripe intensifies when the fish is excited or alarmed. It is occassionally found in large fish.

SIZE

Exceptional specimens in excess of 120 kg have been taken in nets in the Bay of Bengal, near the Indian coast.

It appears likely that Australian waters once held a few monster barramundi of 50 kg or more, but today there would be almost no chance of a fish escaping capture long enough to grow to such dimensions.

Left: The barramundi or 'barra'.
Below: Barramundi water near the upper tidal limits of a Queensland estuary.

Still, commercial netters in the Northern Territory continue to take an occasional specimen of 35 kg or more, and it is just possible that somewhere, in a remote region of the Kimberley coast or Arnhem Land, a 40 kg 'barra' lives on, even today.

More realistically, anglers who trek to the tropics each year in search of barra can hope to find fish in the 1 to 10 kg range, with an outside chance of a 15 kg-plus specimen, particularly in the Territory.

DISTRIBUTION

Barramundi are found as far afield as the Bay of Bengal, Thailand and parts of Indonesia. They are reasonably prolific along the southern coast of Irian Jaya and Nuigini, though not on the northern side.

In Australia, 'barra' range roughly from the Mary River in southern central Queensland to the Ashburton River,. near Onslow, in Western Australia, but the species is not commonly found at either extremity of the range.

Barramundi numbers have been seriously depleted on the east coast of Queensland, and, apart from pockets around Shoalwater Bay in the south and Princess Charlotte Bay in the far north, the fish is now something of a rarity. Today, visitors to the once-renowned stretches of coastline and estuary between Townsville and Port Douglas can fish hard for a week or more without even sighting a 'barra'.

Happily, the situation is somewhat better on the western side of Cape York,

through the Gulf and into Arnhem Land, although even here numbers of 'barra' are lower than in the past.

Darwin anglers still have access to some of Australia's best 'barra' water, though they too must now work harder for their fish.

Fine 'barra' fishing still exists in remote and barely accessible parts of the Kimberleys.

Barramundi utilise environments from the inshore waters around rocky headlands and shore-fringing reefs, through tidal estuaries to freshwater creeks and rivers, billabongs and waterholes. They will inhabit bodies of water cut off from river systems for a year or two at a time, but, because of their breeding requirements, the fish must ultimately have access to tidal, brackish waters in order to complete their life cycle and reproduce.

HABITS AND FEEDING

One of the most fascinating aspects of barramundi biology is that all are born male, and, given the chance, mature into females after becoming fathers several times! The age and size at which this transition occurs varies between geographically isolated populations. It takes place at weights of between about 5 and 8 kg in most areas, but in certain specific locales sexually mature or 'precocious' females as small as 2 kg are often found.

Because of their ability to move easily from saline to fresh water, barramundi travel from areas several kilometres outside the river mouth to tiny holes in the upper watershed which may only join up with the system in years of exceptional monsoonal rains.

Despite this mobility, fish from one river system rarely move to a different one.

It appears likely that the stock in each river system is unique; its genetic structure varying ever so slightly from its neighbours.

The diet of the 'barra' is almost as variable as its choice of habitat though it concentrates mainly on small fish, prawns and freshwater shrimp.

In a saltwater bay or around an inshore island, barramundi feed on whiting, mullet, garfish, small javelin fish and the like, as well as prawns and even the occasional crab and squid. Further into the river system, mullet and prawns are the main food supply, while higher upstream still, archer fish, freshwater mullet, small catfish and the *macrobrachium* or freshwater prawn are all important. In waterholes and billabongs the 'barra' preys upon mullet, rainbow fish, various perchlets, archer fish, yabbies, shrimp and *macrobrachium* along with frogs, lizards, large insects and other terrestrial organisms which fall into or swim through the water.

The barramundi has no obvious teeth. It feeds by racing up to its prey, snapping open its cavernous mouth and sucking in the victim and copious quantities of water. The great, round maw slams shut like a trap, the water is expelled through the gills while the prey is held in the back of the mouth, juggled around and swallowed.

FISHING TECHNIQUES

There is surely no more exciting and rewarding way of fishing for barramundi than casting and retrieving artificial lures around snags, mangrove roots, rock bars, fallen trees and other cover. This method accounts for a good percentage of the fish taken each year.

At certain times and in certain places, slow trolling lures behind a boat works even better than casting.

The lures used for both casting and trolling tend to be swimming minnows with timber or hollow plastic bodies; they are available in a wide range of styles, sizes and colours, both from overseas manufacturers and local cottage-industry craftsmen.

Opposite: a dark-hued freshwater barramundi taken in a Northern Territory billabong.
Below: Muddy run-off channels such as this one on the Top End's East Alligator River fish particularly well at the end of the wet season.
Bottom: A fine 'barra' taken on fly casting tackle.

This silvery saltwater 'barra'. took a Cotton Cordell Rattlin' Spot.

Famous brands include Nilsmaster, Rebel, ABU, Killalures, Elliots, Nautilus and Barra King.

Rubber-tailed jigs, surface lures and even metal spoons and jigs all attract barra, too, though most are taken on floating/ diving or slow-sinking minnows.

One relatively new form of lure-fishing for 'barra' which has produced excellent results is jigging a sinking, hollow plastic 'sonic' style lure, such as a Cotton Cordell Rattlin' Spot, among snags and sunken timber. These lures have built-in rattles and a tight, shimmying action which obviously appeals to the fish. In addition, this style of fishing allows access to water not easily worked by standard cast-and-retrieve or troll tactics.

Bait fishing for 'barra' faded into virtual obscurity during the sportfishing boom of the '70s and early '80s. Today, however, it is coming back into vogue, especially along the Queensland east coast.

Best baits are small live mullet, live prawns or live *macrobrachium*. These may be cast unweighted, rigged with a small running sinker, or suspended beneath a cork or float, depending on the terrain,

water depth and strength of the current.

Fine barra are occassionally taken on dead baits of prawn or cut fish flesh, but these are the exception rather than the rule.

EATING QUALITIES

The 'barra' has a reputation as one of our finest eating fish — and a market price to match!

Many would argue that this reputation is somewhat undeserved, but there is no denying the quality of a well-cooked fillet of saltwater or tidal river barramundi. The meat is white, firm, fine-grained and delicious.

'Barra' which have spent weeks or months in a turbid billabong are another story altogether. Freshwater barra can range from good to almost inedible.

Any 'barra' under a kilo should be released; it has too little flesh to warrant killing it.

Many sport fishermen choose to release the majority of the 'barra' they land, and this trend is to be encouraged, even where there is no bag-limit or closed season on this valuable and diminishing fisheries resource.

Above: a small lagoon 'barra' taken on a fly.
Below: The author landing a small Top End 'barra'.

BASS, AUSTRALIAN

Macquaria novemaculeata

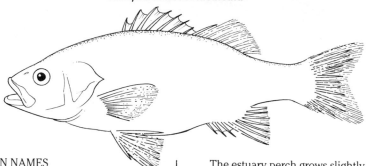

COMMON NAMES

The Australian bass is known through much of its range, especially by older fishermen, as 'perch'. This tends to cause some confusion between it and two other native species taken in the same waters: the Macquarie perch *(Macquaria australasica),* and the estuary perch *(Macquaria colonorum),* which is a close relative of the bass.

DESCRIPTION

This small native fish is usually found in fresh and brackish water. It has moderately large scales, large dark eyes, a scooped forehead and a capacious mouth.

Colouration varies with the environment. They can be almost black on the back, with dark bronzy flanks and a creamy belly tinged with yellow, to bright coppery-gold on the back and silver belly. The tail is usually relatively dark.

Bass have a very fine, but defined, white leading edge on each pelvic fin. In many cases this is the only feature allowing the species to be distinguished from the nearly identical estuary perch, which has no such colouration.

SIZE

Any bass weighing more than 1.5 kg can be regarded as a big fish; specimens in excess of 2 kg are exceptional. The maximum growth-potential is probably in excess of 4 kg, but bass of this size are almost unknown today.

The estuary perch grows slightly larger than the bass, and commercial prawn netters still snare the odd 5 kg fish.

DISTRIBUTION

Our bass is unique to the south eastern corner of Australia, from the Mary River system in southern central Queensland to the Gippsland Lakes area of eastern Victoria.

The estuary perch extends this range westwards to the Hopkins River in western Victoria and was also once found on the northern coast of Tasmania. It is not known if this Tasmanian population still survives.

HABITS AND FEEDING

Bass live their lives within a single river system.They range from the brackish tidal waters where they spawn, to the first major obstruction in the freshwater reaches of the river. This obstruction may be a high waterfall, dam or weir. If such a barrier is inundated by floodwaters, bass will almost certainly seize the opportunity to forge further upstream.

The diet of the bass varies with the seasons and the fish's location within the river system.

During winter, when most of the sexually mature fish move downstream to spawn, prawns, marine worms and small fish play a vital role in the food intake.

In the summer, terrestrial insects, frogs, lizards, spiders and even small snakes and mice are taken, along with fish,

shrimps and yabbies. Earthworms washed from riverbanks by heavy rainfall provide a bonus.

FISHING TECHNIQUES

Traditionally, bass or 'perch' were taken on baits of live black crickets, grasshoppers, cicadas or shrimps dangled or 'dapped' on the surface of the water close to the bank. Practitioners of this syle of fishing often used a long cane pole with the line fixed to the end, rather than a rod and reel.

Bass still respond enthusiastically to a live cricket or shrimp, but today most devotees prefer to cast and retrieve lures off a light, single-handed spin or baitcaster (plug) outfit.

Lure casting is generally held to be more exciting and challenging than bait fishing, and as a bonus, most lure-caught fish are hooked in the mouth, allowing them to be released without undue injury should the angler desire to do so.

A bag-limit of five bass per person per day is now in force in New South Wales, though few true sport fishermen would kill as many as five of these unique and sadly depleted fish in an entire season, let alone a day.

Best lures for bass are the squat-bodied diving plugs or 'crank baits' built for the North American large and smallmouth bass.

Surface lures, poppers, crawlers, and fizzers or plugs fitted with little propellers and swimming arms, all work well on bass, particularly in high summer. This type of topwater fishing is often at its best around dusk and into the night, and provides unmatched excitement in the still, warm gloom of a summer's evening.

Bass also respond to metal spoons and trout spinners, and are avid takers of soft-bodied surface flies and flyrod poppers.

EATING QUALITIES

Bass are superb to eat, rating with the best of our freshwater species.

Despite their eating quality, sport fishermen mainly choose to release bass, in recognition of their much reduced numbers and degraded habitat.

BONITO

Sarda australis, Sarda orientalis

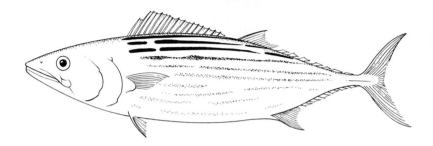

COMMON NAMES

These two very similar and closely related fish are generally called bonito or Australian bonito, although this is often shortened to the colloquial 'bonny'. In certain areas the fish are known as 'horse mackerel'.

In some fishing books *S. orientalis* is called Oriental bonito, though this name is not in common useage among fishermen.

There are superficial similarities between bonito and striped or skipjack tuna *(Katsuwonus pelamis)* though the pattern of stripes on each is quite different and the striped tuna does not have the prominent teeth of the bonitos.

It should be noted that in certain areas, most notably north Queensland, 'bonito' is erroneously used as a general term to cover several small to mid-range tunas, including mackerel tuna and striped or skipjack tuna.

DESCRIPTION

Bonito have relatively large, strong jaws which carry a single row of small but distinct conical teeth.

Bonito are generally dark green on the back and silvery-green on the flanks fading to silvery-white on the belly. A series of dark, longitudinal stripes are evident along the fish's upper flanks. When fresh, these stripes may be broken into separate dashes by lighter vertical bars; a particularly common colour variation in small bonito.

The stripes of the bonito are limited to the upper flanks, while those of the striped tuna are found on the lower flanks and belly.

SIZE

Bonito commonly weigh from 1 to 3 kg; fish over 4.5 kg are uncommon, though off certain parts of the south coast of New South Wales, bonito of about 7 kg are sometimes taken. Conversely, schools of juvenile bonito weighing a few hundred grams are found off the north. They should not be confused with a similar sub-tropical species of small tuna: the Watson's leaping bonito.

DISTRIBUTION

These inshore predatory pelagics, rarely venture outside the continental shelf and range from southern Queensland to about Mallacoota in Victoria, with a similar sub-tropical to temperate distribution on the west coast.

HABITS AND FEEDING

Bonito are a schooling fish which can be much more plentiful in some years than others.

They feed within a few hundred metres of the shoreline or around inshore islands and over reef complexes, and will often mix in with feeding schools of Australian salmon, striped tuna and juvenile kingfish.

Bonito often seek out areas of wave-agitated whitewater around rock ledges and reef breaks.

They prey primarily on small fish, particularly pilchards, anchovies and whitebait, but also on yellowtail, slimy mackerel, garfish and mullet.

FISHING TECHNIQUES

Bonito respond to the same techniques which take striped and mackerel tuna, and also fall for those employed to target salmon, tailor and kingfish.

Boat fishermen take good hauls of bonito by trolling diving minnows parallel with the shore close to headlands and rock ledges, or by casting and retrieving lures around the sudsy washes of broken water adjacent to these areas.

Land-based anglers do well by casting and retrieving lures from ocean rocks.

Bonito attack pilchards and garfish rigged on ganged hooks, live baits and strip baits or cubes of fish flesh free-lined in a berley trail.

They are generally less fickle in their feeding than striped or mackerel tuna, and will strike at larger bait.

EATING QUALITIES

While bonito have long been regarded as fit only for bait or berley (for which purposes they are excellent), their flesh is very tasty. Many of the prejudices concerning these fish could stem from confusing them with the much less palatable striped tuna.

Bonito flesh is pink and flaky, and all the better if the fish is bled immediately after capture. It should be handled and stored carefully as it is particularly susceptible to bruising. Generally speaking, it should be eaten fresh rather than frozen.

BREAM, BLACK

Acanthopagrus australis

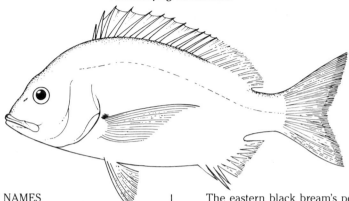

COMMON NAMES

This vitally important angling species is known as bream by most fishermen, though it is also referred to as the eastern black bream, black bream or silver bream. On rare occasions it may also be dubbed yellowfin bream, though this name more correctly belongs to a closely related but less prolific fish of Western Australian waters *(A. latus)*.

Very large eastern black bream, in common with other members of the family, often exhibit a blue tinge around the nose and upper jaw, which earns them the nickname 'blue-nose bream'.

DESCRIPTION

A deep-bodied, laterally-compressed fish with moderately large scales, a forked tail and smallish mouth lined with strong, peg-like teeth.

Colouration varies considerably depending on habitat and water clarity. Fish from the headwaters of tidal estuaries or land-locked lagoons are usually black on the back and bronze on the flanks. At the opposite extreme, bream taken from the surf are usually bright silver.

The most common colour pattern is greenish or purple-blue on the back, silver on the flanks, and silvery-white on the belly. Large fish have a strong blue tinge to the nose and upper jaw area.

The eastern black bream's pelvic and anal fins are usually yellow; the tail is dusky-yellow with a black trailing edge. There is small black blotch at the base of each pectoral fin.

SIZE

Most bream landed by recreational anglers weigh between 0.2 and 1.2 kg; fish over that weight are prize catches. An isolated specimen may top 2 kg and records for the species stand at weights in excess of 4 kg.

DISTRIBUTION

The eastern black bream's range extends from the central northern coastline of Queensland south through New South Wales to about Eden on the far south coast, although occasional stragglers are found as far south as Mallacoota and even the Gippsland Lakes, where the range of this fish overlaps with that of the southern bream *(A. butcherii)*.

Eastern black bream occupy a wide range of environmental niches, from the drinkable freshwater reaches well above the upper tidal limits in coastal rivers, down through the estuaries and into harbours, inlets, bays and tidal lakes, and land-locked lagoons which only open to the sea or to tidal estuaries at times of flood.

Bream also range along ocean surf

The eastern black bream is one of our most popular angling species, and is taken in a wide range of environments.

beaches, rocky foreshores, around headlands and on to near-shore reefs and gravel patches. They are also found around some offshore islands inside the continental shelf, and on reefs out to the 50 metre depth mark and beyond.

HABITS AND FEEDING

A relatively slow-growing fish, the bream may take from four to six years to reach legal length, and any weighing more than a kilo are usually well into their 'teens'.

Bream are cautious and have a tendency to take flight at any suggestion of danger; a tactic essential for survival in clear, shallow waters where predators are not only larger fish, but birds such as cormorants and sea eagles.

The eastern black bream's diet varies according to location, but is largely based on prawns, shrimp, yabbies, worms, crabs and octopi, supplemented at times with small fish such as sandy sprat, whitebait, anchovies and juvenile mullet. Bream occasionally graze on algae and filamentous green weed.

They travel both in schools and individually, though typical aggregations are of between six and 50 fish. There is evidence that adult bream migrate along the north coast of New South Wales and in southern Queensland most years, mainly during winter.

FISHING TECHNIQUES

The most productive techniques for taking estuary bream are based around the use of light, sensitive tackle and live or fresh baits of yabbies (nippers), crabs or prawns. The fish also succumb to an array

Bream are taken in estuaries and also from beaches and rock ledges.

of less conventional offerings such as bullock's heart, tripe, steak, chicken intestines and various 'pudding' mixtures of flour, water, cheese, tinned sardines and the like.

Estuary bream are also taken from time to time on lures and jigs, usually by anglers hoping for flathead or tailor.

Tackle for estuary breaming can be as simple as a handline, or as complex as a baitcaster and graphite plug rod. In New South Wales the most popular set-up is a 1.8 to 2.2 metre hollow fibreglass rod with a light, whippy tip, matched to a small threadline (spinning) reel spooled with 3 or 4 kg breaking strain line. In southern Queensland a soft actioned 'Sloppy Joe' rod measuring anywhere between 2.5 and 3.5 metres and a light, shallow-spooled sidecast reel is preferred.

Surf and rock rigs incorporate slightly larger sinkers, bigger hooks and stronger line than those used in the estuaries. Three-metre-plus rods are preferred for casting and line control, and nylon with a breaking strain of 4 or 5 kg is usually employed.

Offshore, boat anglers rarely make bream their target; they are just an incidental catch taken during berleying and fishing lightly weighted 'floaters' of cut pilchard or fish strip for snapper.

EATING QUALITIES

Bream are a much prized and highly rated food — some people, the author included, would argue they are over-rated.

Bream from the open ocean have moist, white flesh with a clean if somewhat bland flavour. Estuary-dwelling fish have slightly softer, moist flesh, and can have a weedy or slightly muddy taste if caught in closed waters or upper tidal reaches.

BREAM, PIKEY

Acanthopagrus berda

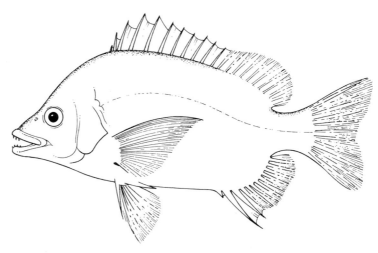

COMMON NAMES

In its native, northern waters the pikey bream is usually known as bream or black bream.

It is a close relative of, and very similar to, the eastern black bream *(A. australis)*. Their range overlaps in central and northern Queensland, though if specimens are laid alongside each other, identification is easy.

DESCRIPTION

This tropical, estuarine bream species is characterised by a relatively deeply-forked tail, which is often a little rounded at the lobe tips, and an overall dark colouring.

The 'pikey' is generally much darker in hue than either the black or southern bream, and the fins (excluding the pectorals) are particularly dark. The tail, anal and pelvic fins are usually dark slate to charcoal and rarely exhibit any of the yellow commonly seen in the fins of the black bream.

SIZE

Pikey bream are a relatively small fish. Most of those taken by anglers weigh between 0.4 and 1 kg, with exceptional examples occasionally topping 1.5 kg.

DISTRIBUTION

In the east the range of this fish of the tropical north overlaps the northern range of the black bream *(A. australis)* and in the west that of the western yellowfin bream *(A. latus)*.

Pikey bream are rarely found outside estuarine or bay mangrove environments, though they will range upstream beyond the tide-limit into near-pure fresh water.

HABITS AND FEEDING

Small to medium size pikey bream form large schools around estuarine snags, rock piles, bars and spits, while larger fish tend to swim alone or in much smaller groups.

Pikey bream are active, opportunistic feeders which prey on prawns, shrimp, crabs, marine worms and small fish.

FISHING TECHNIQUES

Pikey bream respond to all of the techniques which take their southern relatives, but are less finnicky and more

Left: The pikey bream is dark-hued and attractive.
Below: Pikey bream are abundant in tropical mangrove estuaries.

aggressive, particularly in lightly-fished waters.

They are the most avid lure takers of the bream clan, and even small specimens will strike at large lures intended for barramundi and mangrove jack. The use of small diving plugs, spoons, jigs and flies will often provoke exciting action.

Tackle for 'pikeys' is similar to that used for southern and black bream, with more emphasis on single-handed spinning rods or baitcaster (plug) outfits of the type commonly used for lure and bait fishing in mangrove-lined tropical rivers.

EATING QUALITIES

Although tasty members of the bream clan, tropical anglers often overlook pikeys' in favour of glamorous species such as barramundi, fingermark and mangrove jack.

BREAM, SOUTHERN

Acanthopagrus butcherii

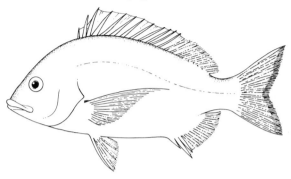

COMMON NAMES

This species is known as southern black bream, black bream, Gippsland bream, southern yellowfin bream, blue-nosed bream and just bream.

The southern bream is closely related to the eastern black bream *(A. australis)*, and is almost identical in appearance. The ranges of the two species can overlap in estuarine systems between Narooma in southern New South Wales and the Gippsland Lakes in Victoria.

DESCRIPTION

The southern bream is almost identical in appearance to the eastern black bream *(A. australis)*, though two specimens laid side by side exhibit minor differences. The more obvious of these are the more distinct lateral line and dark spot at the base of pectoral fins of the eastern black bream.

The southern bream tends to have a more gradually sloping forehead and is often a little less deep in the body for a given length.

Colouration of the southern bream is mostly black or dark grey on the back, grading to silver or silvery-gold on the flanks and white or silvery-white on the belly.

The southern bream's fins are generally dusky, and although the anal and ventral fins may show a tinge of yellow, this is rarely as obvious as that seen on the eastern

black bream, and much less distinct than on the western yellowfin bream *(A. latus)*.

SIZE

Southern bream usually weigh from 0.4 to 1 kg, with fish over 1.5 kg regarded as prize catches. Growth potential is 4 kg, but such record weights are almost never found.

DISTRIBUTION

A fish of our southern estuaries, ranging from the far south coast of New South Wales (rarely north of Merimbula) to about Geraldton in Western Australia, the southern bream is also found in the tidal rivers of Tasmania and the southern islands such as Flinders and Kangaroo.

Southern bream almost never leave the estuary unless flushed out by floodwaters, but will, however, sometimes travel upstream into fresh water.

HABITS AND FEEDING

Southern bream often form large, reasonably loose schools, particularly during the spawning season in late winter and spring. At such times, the fish seek stretches of river or lake bed with reasonably uniform depth and water of a salinity level a little less than their summer and autumn haunts.

They feed on prawns, shrimp, small crabs, marine worms and shellfish such as

Top Left: A kilo-plus southern bream.

Centre Left: Bream fishing in eastern Victoria is often at its best when the wattles bloom in early spring. These fish came from the Tambo River.

Below: A Tambo River fisherman hooked up to a solid southern bream. Long, soft rods and light line are typical of Gippsland Lakes tackle.

When southern bream bite well, large hauls are the norm!

mussels and immature oysters. They will also scavenge scraps and occasionally graze on algae and aquatic weed.

FISHING TECHNIQUES

Southern bream may be fished for in all of the ways previously described for taking black and pikey bream.

In southern estuaries bream specialists usually opt for a relatively long (2.2 to 2.8 metre) rod with a light, soft action, a small threadline or spinning reels and lines of 2 to 4 kg breaking strain.

Hooks are generally a little smaller than those employed for catching eastern black bream in more northerly waters.

These smaller hooks are better suited to the southern bream baits which are sand worms, yabbies (also called bass yabbies), shrimp, small estuarine crabs and the meat of various cockles and small shellfish.

In some areas southern bream will also take chunks and strips of fish flesh and small whole fish such as whitebait, sprat and anchovy.

EATING QUALITIES

Southern bream are arguably the tastiest of all the Australian bream, with moist, white flesh and a slightly higher flesh yield per unit of whole weight than their northern cousins.

CARP

Cyprinus carpio

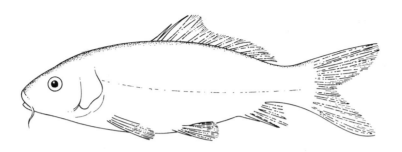

COMMON NAMES

Although originally from Asia, this fish is widely known as the European carp or the common carp.

The partially scaled mirror carp and the completely scaleless leather carp are variations.

Carp are similar in appearance to feral goldfish, although the latter do not have the carp's two pairs of barbels or whiskers around the mouth. Carp and goldfish will interbreed in some waters; the hybrids have a single pair of barbels.

Other members of the carp family found in Australia include the tench *(Tinca tinca)* and roach *(Rutilus rutilus)*. There are occasional reports of Cruscian carp in Australia, but so far these have turned out to be goldfish or goldfish x carp hybrids.

DESCRIPTION

A heavily scaled, small-mouthed fish with rubbery lips, four barbels, and a single dorsal fin with one stout spine at the leading edge.

Colouration varies enormously, from the standard coppery or bronze hue through dark olive-green, gold, orange, mottled or piebald patterning to plain white.

Some are completely scaleless, others have isolated patches of large scales.

SIZE

Carp in Australasia commonly attain weights between 1 and 4 kg, and specimens in excess of 6 kg are often found. The largest carp yet recorded here have weighed from 9 to 12 kg, and it seems likely they could attain 15 kg in very fertile waterways. They do reach this weight in Europe and rare specimens of twice the weight have been taken in North America.

DISTRIBUTION

Originating in Asia, these fresh and brackish water fish with their remarkable range and tolerance of temperature, water quality and food requirements, are now found on every continent except Antarctica.

Carp prefer reasonably still, turbid and generally warm water, but will tolerate cool, fast-running streams, polluted ponds and brackish estuaries.

In Australia, carp are found throughout the Murray/Darling system, in many eastern and southern coastal streams, dams and lakes, and are also common in ornamental ponds, lakes and permanent drains in metropolitan areas south of the tropics.

HABITS AND FEEDING

Carp will eat almost anything. Given a choice, they prefer aquatic weeds, algae,

Common or European carp can vary considerably in colour and even body shape from one individual to another.

insect nymphs and invertebrates such as worms, shrimps and water beetles. They eat the eggs and fry of other fish and, less often, prey on small forage fish such as gudgeons.

Around settled areas, they make the most of sewage, food scraps and refuse.

FISHING TECHNIQUES

Although regarded as a noxious pest in most areas, carp are being fished for deliberately by an increasing number of anglers. They provide good sport when hooked, and, in many regions, are available in far greater quantities than the more desirable freshwater species.

Carp are usually fished for with lightly weighted, unweighted or float-suspended baits of bread, dough, sweet corn kernels, parboiled baby potatoes, earthworms, shrimp, yabby tails or freshwater mussels.

They can be readily attracted and excited by berleying or ground baiting the fishing area with stale bread, soaked chicken-feed pellets or sweet corn.

Carp are also taken on flies and small to medium lures. They are particularly partial to a small brown or orange nymph fly. If you use polarising sunglasses you can spot the path of the fish and use the fly close to the surface of the water.

EATING QUALITIES

Carp are generally regarded as inedible in Australia, except by certain ethnic groups. The flesh is soft, watery, laced with bones and usually tastes of mud. Carp caught in Australia must, by law, be killed, but few are eaten. Their flesh makes a reasonable bait and berley for many saltwater fish.

CATFISH, EEL-TAILED

Tandanus tandanus

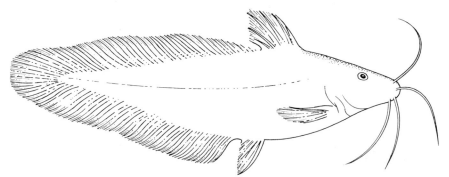

COMMON NAMES

Catfish, 'cattie', tandan, jewfish, dewfish or kenaru. A closely-related Western Australian fish is commonly called 'cobbler'.

DESCRIPTION

A scaleless, whiskered freshwater fish with an eel-like tail.

Catfish are usually black or blue-black to very dark brown on the back, steel-grey or chocolate-brown on the flanks and creamy or creamy-yellow on the belly. The flanks are often darkly mottled.

Eel-tailed catfish have a stout, serrated spine in each pectoral fin and another in the separate first dorsal fin. These spines can lock in the erect position and are coated in a mildly venomous mucus which can cause severe pain and irritation if the spines penetrate the human skin. Allergic reactions can be severe and may necessitate hospitalisation.

SIZE

Catfish usually weigh between 0.5 and 2 kg, with occasional specimens topping 4 kg. A rare specimen may weigh around 6 kg and be 90 cm in length.

DISTRIBUTION

This native Australian species was once found throughout the Murray/Darling system as well as in the upper reaches of some eastern coastal streams.

The range of the catfish has been reduced by dam and weir construction, and their numbers have declined, probably because of competition with the introduced carp.

They prefer relatively slow flowing, warm and turbid water.

HABITS AND FEEDING

Eel-tailed catfish spend most of their lives on or near the bed of a stream or lake floor, nosing through the mud, weed and leaf litter for shrimps, yabbies, insect larvae, freshwater mussels and earthworms and crickets washed into the water.

At spawning time, during the warmer months of the year, catfish clear a large nesting area on the river or lake bottom and actively protect it against all intruders.

FISHING TECHNIQUES

Catfish are mainly fished on or very near the bottom. Earthworms or scrubworms are favourite baits, but many are taken on baits of shrimps, whole small yabbies, yabby tails, mussels or pieces of steak.

Catfish will occasionally grab a lure, particularly a bobber or jig intended for redfin. At spawning time, they become particularly aggressive and are likely to strike at a lure being used to fish for Murray cod and golden perch.

Left: The common eel-tailed catfish or tandan (Tandanus tandanus). *They vary in colour from pale creamy yellow to dark chocolate to blue/black.*
Below: The Glencoe or yellowfin tandan (Neosilurus glencoensis) *lives in tropical areas and the Lake Eyre system.*
Bottom: A mottled or spotted tandan (Neosilurus sp.).

EATING QUALITIES

Though they are ugly, spiny, tough-skinned and slimy, eel-tailed catfish are arguably the tastiest fish available from our outback rivers, rivalling even the highly regarded golden perch. You will need a sharp knife and a pair of long-nosed pliers to skin them before they are cooked.

CATFISH, FORK-TAILED

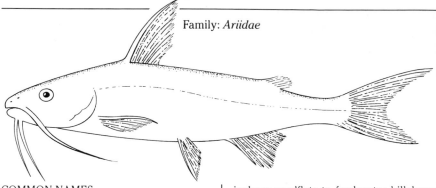

Family: *Ariidae*

COMMON NAMES

Members of this family of ·similar-looking tropical freshwater, estuarine and inshore fish are known by a variety of names including fork-tailed or fork-tail catfish, salmon catfish, blue catfish, gold catfish and 'cattie' or 'cat'.

DESCRIPTION

The fork-tailed catfish are characterised by their forked tails, scaleless skins, single dorsal fins, well developed adipose fins and sets of barbels or 'whiskers' around the mouth.

Colouration of the clan varies enormously, from dark blue-black through chocolate-brown to gold, grey or even pale cream and albino pink. Piebald specimens are sometimes found.

Fin colour varies with body hue; the tail is usually dark.

SIZE

Certain types of fork-tailed catfish grow to more than a metre in length and may weigh in excess of 12 or 14 kg, although members of this family more commonly weigh 0.8 to 6 kg.

DISTRIBUTION

The different species are widely distributed throughout the north, from southern Queensland in the east to about Carnarvon in the west.

Catfish are mostly found in coastal rivers and estuaries, but may range from inshore mudflats to freshwater billabongs and marshes far inland.

The family prefers muddy, discoloured water.

HABITS AND FEEDING

Catfish are found both in schools and singly. They eat anything and everything from live fish, prawns and frogs to vegetable matter and decaying animal flesh or fish offal.

They feed right through the day, but are particularly active at night.

FISHING TECHNIQUES

Fork-tailed catfish are rarely fished for deliberately, except in areas with few other fish species.

'Catties' are mainly taken incidentally by anglers bait or lure fishing for barramundi, sooty grunter and other tropical sportfish.

Forktails will take most baits and a wide range of lures and flies. They are particularly susceptible to dead fish flesh bait on the riverbed, and are often hooked on strong actioned minnow-style lures being cast and retrieved, or trolled for barramundi.

EATING QUALITIES

Although denigrated through most of the north, catfish from clean, flowing water are fine table fish, but those from muddy waterholes and swamps have a strong, weedy taint.

Left: A large fork-tailed catfish taken on light lure casting tackle from a Top End billabong. Note the dark mottling.

Below: Catfish are often taken on lures while fishing for barramundi, even in very muddy or discoloured water.

COBIA

Rachycentron canadus

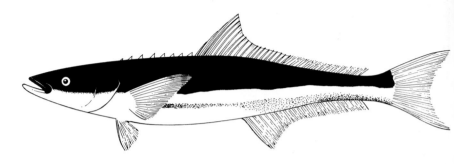

COMMON NAMES

The cobia or 'cobe' is known in many areas as the black kingfish or 'black king'. Other names include sergeant fish, crab-eater, lemon fish and ling.

In the water, cobia are often mistaken for sharks because of their prominent dorsal fins and large, dark pectorals and tail. Once landed they are seen to have more in common with catfish or remoras, but can be identified by the very short, stout spines of their first dorsal fin.

DESCRIPTION

This dark, broad-headed and shark-like fish is the only member of its family and has no close relatives. It is occasionally confused with fork-tailed catfish and remora or suckerfish.

Typical colouration is very dark, chocolate-brown to black on the back fading to cream or creamy-yellow on the belly. The flanks are marked with two light, longitudinal stripes. These stripes are well defined when the fish is small, but fade as it grows.

All the fins are dark brown to black; the eyes are large and dark.

SIZE

Cobia may occasionally reach 1.8 metres in length and weigh close to 70 kg, but are more commonly caught at weights of 3 to 20 kg, with 25 to 35 kg fish being reasonably common in some areas.

DISTRIBUTION

The cobia is a cosmopolitan species, found throughout the tropical and sub-tropical areas of the Pacific, Indian and Atlantic Oceans.

Although not especially prolific in Australian waters, cobia are likely to be found singly or in small groups anywhere between Geraldton in Western Australia and Port Stephens in New South Wales, although summer and autumn stragglers occasionally extend their range much further southwards on both coasts. Rare examples have turned up as far south as Batemans Bay and Cape Leeuwin. Cobia have yet to be recorded in New Zealand or Tasmania.

They are at home in the clear, oceanic waters of offshore coral reefs, the more turbid expanses of big bays and inlets, and even the lower reaches of estuary systems.

HABITS AND FEEDING

Cobia are a somewhat enigmatic pelagic fish rarely found in large numbers, although a few locations have a history of producing quantities of them.

Cobia tend to congregate around 'structures'. Reef pinnacles, bomboras, islands, mooring buoys, wharves, wrecks

Left: A 7 kg cobia or black kingfish.

Bottom Left: A fish aggregation device (FAD) and large manta ray; two of cobia's favourite things!

Below: Cobia are strong, determined fighters, and almost always save some fireworks for boatside antics.

and breakwalls are all likely holding areas, especially if expanses of mud or sand with healthy crab populations lie nearby.

They travel in the company of manta rays, whale sharks and even big tiger sharks, and at such times form schools, but, more typically, they travel singly or in small packs of 2 to 10.

They eat live fish, crabs, prawn, squid, octopi, and sometimes dead fish and the refuse from trawling operations.

FISHING TECHNIQUES

An opportunistic feeder, cobia take such diverse prey as sand crabs, reef fish, squid and small tuna.

The species responds to live and dead baits, lures and flies, but can be frustratingly difficult to tempt, particularly in clear water.

Deep-bodied, flashy live baits such as bream, tarwhine, snapper and sweep, or strongly-worked, surface-running 'popper' lures will sometimes turn the trick when all else fails.

Once hooked, the cobia will test angler and tackle to the limit, especially at boatside. The fish's shark-like gyrations have broken many a gaff or landing net.

Tackle needs to be sturdy and well maintained.

EATING QUALITIES

Cobia are a superb eating fish with firm, sweet white flesh that cooks up beautifully in any number of ways.

COD, ESTUARY

Epinophelus suillus

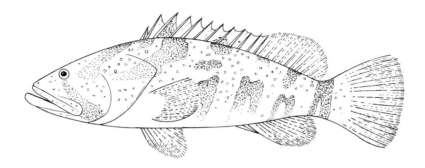

COMMON NAMES

The estuary cod or estuary rock cod is known as brown-spotted rock cod, north-west groper, spotted cod and greasy cod.

Large adult estuary cod may be confused with Queensland groper *(Promicrops lanceolatus)* although the groper has a more rounded gill plate and blunter head profile.

DESCRIPTION

The estuary cod is a large mouthed, predatory fish with a typically cod-shaped body. It belongs to the family *Serranidae.*

The large mouth is lined with rows of small, fine teeth.

Colouration is variable, but usually consists of a series of dark brown or gold spots and blotches over a vaguely barred creamy-grey or light brown background. Larger fish may be quite dark.

SIZE

Estuary cod grow to about 1.8 metres in length and weights well in excess of 100 kg, though they cannot rival the growth potential of the related Queensland groper, which has been known to reach a weight of 400 kg or more.

Most cod taken in estuaries weigh between 0.8 and 6 kg, though offshore and around reefs and headlands, 10 to 25 kg cod are far from uncommon.

DISTRIBUTION

A fish of tropical and sub-tropical estuaries, inshore waters and offshore reefs, estuary cod occasionally stray south to northern New South Wales and central Western Australia.

Estuary or spotted cod are found in a wide range of habitats, extending from the highest limits of tidal movement in rivers, down through the estuaries and on out to the deep coral reefs of the continental shelf.

They are attracted to snag piles, mangrove roots, rock bars, drop-offs and coral bombies.

HABITS AND FEEDING

Cod are rarely found far from cover.

Although they rarely school in the true sense of the word, one good snag pile or rock bar may be home to several cod.

Estuary cod eat prawns, crab, octopi, squid a wide range of small to medium size fish, and even lizards and snakes.

FISHING TECHNIQUES

Within estuaries small cod up to about 6 or 8 kg in weight respond very well to lures of the type used for barramundi and mangrove jacks. They also bite strongly on dead and live baits.

Larger, reef-dwelling cod will take most types of cut, whole and live fish baits, as well as jigs and deep-running troll lures.

Left: The author with a handsome marked estuary cod taken on a cast-and-retrieved lure in north Queensland.

Below: This 4 kg estuary cod took a jigged sonic lure. Note the variation in colour and patterning between this cod and the one above. Scientists are yet to agree on whether they represent different species.

In the estuaries, cod are usually hooked on single or double-handed casting tackle and lines of 4 to 12 kg breaking strain.

Most of the larger fish landed offshore succumb to heavy handlines or robust jigging and reef fishing outfits spooled with 15 to 50 kg breaking strain line.

EATING QUALITIES

Small to medium sized estuary cod are very good to excellent table fish; the flesh of large reef-dwelling specimens tends to be coarse.

Reef-caught cod weighing more than 8 or 9 kg are potential ciguatera toxin carriers in areas where this poisoning is common.

CORAL TROUT

Plectropoma maculatum, Family: *Plectropoma*

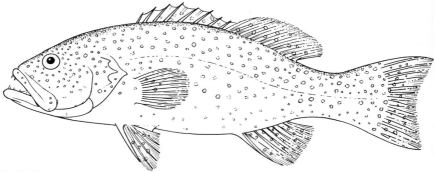

COMMON NAMES

There are several closely related and very similar members of the family *Plectropoma* in Australian waters, the most common being *P. maculatum.*

Coral trout are known simply as 'trout' in northern waters, though they are totally unrelated and dissimilar to the freshwater fish of the same name.

Juvenile coral trout may be confused with the distantly related coral cod *(Cephalopholis miniatus)*, but this much smaller tropical reef fish has a convex or outwardly curving tail, while the coral trout has a slightly concave tail.

DESCRIPTION

The coral trout is a beautifully marked, robust, predatory reef fish of tropical waters, and belongs to the same large group of fish as the Australian saltwater cods *(Serranidae).*

Colouration varies greatly between species and locations, from greenish-brown in shallow water, through brick-red to bright red in deep water, but always with an overlay of blue or red spots. The eye is red around the elongated pupil.

The fins usually carry the body colours of the fish and are spotted or marbled.

SIZE

Most coral trout caught in Australian waters weigh between 1 and 6 kg, although the larger, oceanic ones found on outer reefs and around offshore islands may weigh 10 or 12 kg and very rarely top 20 kg.

Maximum growth potential of the largest members of this family may be from 30 to 35 kg.

DISTRIBUTION

The coral trout is a tropical, reef-dwelling species which occasionally strays into sub-tropical waters and ranges from near-shore reefs and rock piles to deep, continental shelf drop-offs. The biggest trout are generally found well offshore.

Although basically a bottom-dwelling fish, coral trout can cruise and hunt many metres clear of the seabed and are capable of bursts of surprising speed.

They prefer warm, clear water and avoid turbid or discoloured areas.

HABITS AND FEEDING

Coral trout are fierce, territorial predators which feed mainly on smaller reef fish, but will hunt prawns, crayfish, crabs, squid, octopi and cuttlefish.

Other than at spawning time, they rarely school in the true sense of the word, although a particularly suitable area of reef may contain many resident fish.

FISHING TECHNIQUES

The bulk of coral trout taken by anglers fall to traditional bottom-fishing techniques

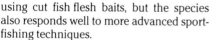

Left: A coral trout in typical shallow water colouration. Those from even shallower areas tend to be greenish.

Bottom left: A big coral trout from deep water. They're definitely a ciguatera poisoning risk at this size.

Below: A jig-caught trout in deep water livery.

using cut fish flesh baits, but the species also responds well to more advanced sport-fishing techniques.

Coral trout strike savagely at all types of cast, jigged and trolled lures, live baits and rigged dead-fish baits.

Large commercial catches are still taken in isolated areas on a rudimentary lure called a 'wog', which is made from a sinker and strips of black rubber from the inner tube of a car tyre.

Tackle for catching coral trout ranges from relatively heavy handlines in the 15 to 50 kg breaking strain class, to jig outfits and double or single-handed casting gear and 6 to 10 kg breaking strain line.

EATING QUALITIES

The coral trout is a superb table fish considered by most reef fishermen to be tastier than the sweetlip, and only a little way behind the red emperor and the barramundi cod in flavour.

However, in some areas, large coral trout are a ciguatera poison risk, and eating more than one meal from trout over 8 kg is unwise. It is best to heed local advice in this regard.

DART, SWALLOWTAIL

Trachinotus coppingeri

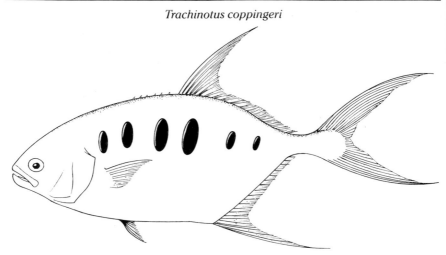

COMMON NAMES

The dart, swallowtail dart or swallow-tailed dart has several relatives in Australian waters, including the larger but less frequently caught common dart *(T. botla)* and the black spotted dart *(T. bailloni)*.

The more distantly related snub-nosed dart or oyster cracker *(T. blochii)* — a near-identical fish to the permit of the Atlantic ocean — is also taken in our waters.

DESCRIPTION

Swallowtail dart are members of the family *Carangidae*, to which various trevally and kingfish species also belong.

Dart are characterised by a deep, laterally-compressed body, well-forked tails and a series of fairly large dark blotches along the lateral line.

Their colouring is usually bluish to greenish-silver on the back, bright, metallic silver on the flanks and silvery-white on the belly. The line of dark grey 'thumbprints' along the lateral line varies in intensity between individuals.

The fins — especially the long second dorsal and anal fins — are often dark tipped or margined and quite striking in freshly caught specimens.

SIZE

Swallowtail dart are relatively small fish, and most of those taken by anglers weigh less than 0.8 kg. One of more than 1 kg is an exceptional catch.

The common dart *(T. botla)* of tropical waters grows to about 3 kg, while the shy snub-nosed dart *(T. blochii)* rarely exceeds 9 kg.

DISTRIBUTION

Swallowtail dart are a fish of tropical and sub-tropical waters, and come about as far south as Sydney and Perth.

These fish are mainly found along ocean beaches, around sand cays and inside gravel-bottomed lagoons.

The dart favours clean, well-oxygenated slightly turbulent water.

HABITS AND FEEDING

Swallowtails travel in small, loose schools or — more rarely — in isolation.

The species feeds on small marine invertebrates such as crabs, prawns, shrimp, sandhoppers, sea lice, worms and the like, and on small fish.

FISHING TECHNIQUES

Swallowtail dart are mostly taken

Dart are a lightweight fish often taken incidentally by surf and sandflat anglers chasing whiting, bream and other species in tropical or sub-tropical areas.

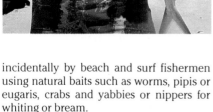

incidentally by beach and surf fishermen using natural baits such as worms, pipis or eugaris, crabs and yabbies or nippers for whiting or bream.

Dart will also take cut fish flesh baits, whole whitebait or small pilchards and strips of squid.

Dart can sometimes be taken on small lures, jigs and flies and provide fast and furious sport on ultra-light tackle.

These fish are usually caught on the long casting rods and relatively heavy rigs and lines employed by surf casters. They give a much better account of themselves on lighter tackle.

EATING QUALITIES

Dart are tasty, white-fleshed fish, but are often overlooked by beach fishermen targeting more desirable species such as bream, whiting, flathead and mulloway.

Dart should be bled promptly.

DOLPHIN FISH

Coryphaena hippurus, Coryphaena equiselis

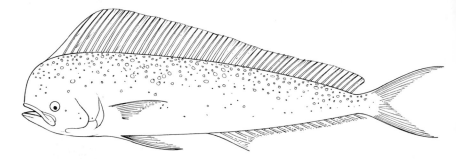

COMMON NAMES

The two similar and closely related types of dolphin fish — the more common *C. hippurus* and the much smaller and less abundant *C. equiselis* — are also known as mahi mahi, dorado, dolphin and dolphinfish.

DESCRIPTION

These two closely related species are renowned the world over as being among the most colourful, spectacular and sought-after pelagic fish.

Despite their name, dolphin fish have nothing at all in common with the marine mammal, the dolphin. Confusion arising from this shared name has led non-anglers to shy away from dolphin fish on restaurant menus and to accuse fishermen of cruelty for catching them. For this reason, many record-keeping bodies call them mahi mahi (pronounced 'mar-he mar-he') — their Hawaiian name.

The larger and more common dolphin fish, *C. hippurus*, is characterised by the disparate appearance of the sexes. The female, or 'cow', has a low, rounded head profile; the male or 'bull' develops a high, steep forehead with age.

Colouration ranges from electric blue with numerous dark or gold speckles through intense green and gold to silver, depending on size, location and behaviour patterns. A hooked specimen may change colour several times while being landed.

The tail is nearly always yellow, but may be tinged with blue or even silver.

SIZE

Dolphin fish grow to almost 2 metres in length and weights of close to 45 kg, although any specimen over 25 kg is an exceptional fish.

Large schools of juvenile dolphin fish in the 0.7 to 3.5 kg range are seasonally abundant under floating debris and fish trap marker buoys in warm currents off our east and west coasts.

DISTRIBUTION

The dolphin fish is a world-wide species found in tropical, sub-tropical and, more rarely, in temperate waters. In Australasia it ranges as far south as Eden, Albany and New Zealand's Bay of Islands.

A true oceanic wanderer, the mahi mahi rarely ventures into waters shallower than 60 metres, and is much more at home in continental shelf drop-off areas between 150 and 400 metres deep.

Dolphin fish prefer clean, cobalt-blue water with a temperature in excess of 20°C but juveniles, in particular, will occasionally be found in cooler currents.

HABITS AND FEEDING

This fast-growing and relatively short-lived fish forms large schools when

juvenile, smaller packs as a young adult, and is likely to be solitary when fully grown.

Dolphin fish gather around flotsam and jetsam, and a large log or floating piece of ship's cargo may attract and hold hundreds of dolphin.

Man-made fish aggregation devices (FADs) anchored in deep, warm water are a magnet for dolphin fish.

Their diet varies with size and location.

Small dolphins eat plankton, krill, and tiny fish, while larger specimens prey on flying fish, sauries, gar, pilchards, small tuna and squid.

FISHING TECHNIQUES

Dolphin fish caught in Australasian waters are usually taken on small to medium size trolling lures being used to catch tuna or other pelagics.

They will attack live baits, rigged dead

As the photographs on these pages so graphically show, the colouring of dolphin fish is highly variable. In fact, an individual specimen may change colour several times while being fought, landed and killed. Note also the difference in forehead profiles between the females or 'cows' (this page) and male or 'bull' (opposite).

baits, fresh fish strips, bottle squid, cast jigs and plugs, poppers and flies.

A keen-eyed and intelligent fish, the mahi mahi will shy away from clumsy rigs or unnatural baits unless competing strongly with fellow school members. Often, the school will cease biting after one or two fish have been caught.

Once hooked, dolphin fish leap high out of the water and run hard and long, providing thrills not easily forgotten by those lucky enough to encounter this living jewel of the ocean.

Tackle needed ranges from single-handed casting outfits and 2 to 4 kg breaking strain line for small dolphins, through to light 6 to 15 kg trolling tackle for bigger fish.

A trace of some sort — either light wire or heavy nylon — is advisable when pursuing large dolphin fish.

EATING QUALITIES

The dolphin fish is arguably the tastiest of all the pelagics. Pink fleshed and delicious, it is regarded as a delicacy in many parts of the world and commands high market prices.

Dolphin fish should be killed and bled immediately after capture. They must be handled carefully, as they frequently thrash wildly and throw themselves about when brought into the boat.

Small dolphin fish make excellent live and dead baits for bigger game fish.

DRUMMER, BLACK

Girella elevata

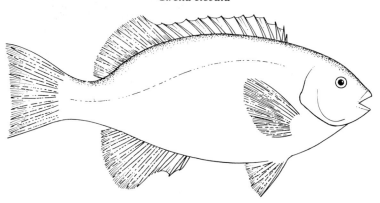

COMMON NAMES

The officially sanctioned name is 'eastern rock blackfish' but since fishermen hardly ever use it and considering the confusion the name causes between this fish and its close relation the luderick or blackfish *(G. tricuspidata)* the time may have come to stick to the popularly used one — black drummer. East coast anglers call it 'pig'.

An almost identical fish, which is practically never fished for in the West Australian waters it frequents, is the western rock blackfish. There is also a distant relation *Kyphosus sydneyanus* called the silver drummer.

DESCRIPTION

The black drummer is a robust, deep-bodied marine fish with a relatively small mouth and head.

Its colour can vary from black to blue-black to dark grey or slate-grey. The belly is only slightly paler than the rest of the body. Young ones sometimes have indistinct bars and patches. The fins are uniformly dark.

SIZE

The most common weight is from 0.4 to 3 kg. but can sometimes exceed 5 kg. Specimens of around 9 kg have been reported.

DISTRIBUTION

These fish frequent the cool and temperate shorelines from around Noosa Heads in southern Queensland to western Victoria and south-east South Australia. They have also been taken along the northern and eastern Tasmanian coast.

Juveniles and sub-adults sometimes enter estuaries and harbours.

HABITS AND FEEDING

The black drummer is a schooling fish which stays close to shallow turbulent water inshore and is rearly found more than 100 metres out, unless around an island, reef or bombora. They are omnivorous; eating crabs, prawns and shrimps — large fish may take octopi, and they also graze on marine algae and kelp.

Tagging and research has shown that the drummer grows rapidly and tends to stay in the same general vicinity throughout its life.

FISHING TECHNIQUES

Lightly weighted baits of cunji, crab, bread, abalone gut and peeled prawn-tail have proved most successful, particularly when used with a berley of soaked bread or bran and chopped green weed or cabbage weed.

The drummer will often take weed

Left: An adult black drummer or rock blackfish. The fish's colour is somewhat variable.

Below: Black drummer habitat. Fish will move over these cunjevoi encrusted rocks to feed at high tide, particularly during the night.

baits used by luderick anglers, but their light tackle is not strong enough to land drummer of more than about 2 kg.

Most drummers are taken from the shore but there are small-boat specialists who have success by anchoring close to the rocks, inshore bomboras, reefs or islands and casting towards the shoreline.

'Pot-holing' or 'puddle-holing' — a specialised way of angling mainly used at night or in wet, overcast weather in large rock pools which are connected with the ocean at high tide — involves berleying and seems to work quite well with drummer.

Since the fish is a strong fighter and will dive for the seabed or make a run for a cave when it feels the hook bite, double-strength hooks and lines from 6 to 15 kg breaking-strain are mandatory.

The most popular tackle is based around a 3 to 4 metre rod and a side-cast reel. Some fishermen prefer a large threadline (spinning) reel or an overhead or centrepin model.

EATING QUALITIES

Black drummer are very tasty, particularly if cleaned, skinned and filletted soon after being caught. Small fish from 0.8 to 3 kg are better for the table than very large ones.

EMPEROR, RED

Lutjanus sebae

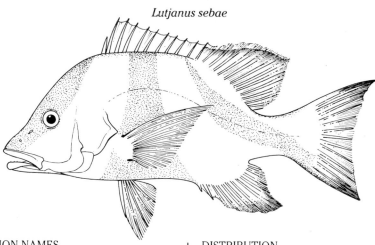

COMMON NAMES

The highly prized red emperor or emperor is also known as government bream, king snapper, red kelp or 'red'.

DESCRIPTION

The largest, best looking and most sought after of all the emperor clan, the red emperor is a very deep-bodied fish with strong jaws and a large, powerful tail.

Red emperor colouration varies with age. The arrowhead pattern or stripes are darker and more clearly defined when the fish is young.

Adults are salmon-pink to pale or bright red with three vertical bands of darker red, one sloping back from the snout through the eye, a broader one running up through the pectoral fin area, and another slanting back down into the lower tail fin.

The fins are all reddish, particularly the first dorsal, which is often very bright along its upper edge.

SIZE

Red emperor grow to well over a metre in length and as much as 20 or 22 kg in weight, though such giants are uncommon. Weights of between 1 and 8 kg are the most common, though runs of 6 to 12 kg fish are far from unknown.

DISTRIBUTION

The red emperor frequents tropical and sub-tropical waters, and occasionally wander as far south as northern New South Wales.

They prefer deep coral reef areas, especially over gravel or 'marl' patches between hard outcrops.

They are schooling fish, and once located, action can be fast and furious.

As with most desirable reef fish, the best specimens come from deep reefs far offshore.

HABITS AND FEEDING

Red emperers feed on prawns, crabs, squid, octopi, cuttlefish and various invertebrates, and small, live fish.

Although they feed at any time, particularly in deep water, large fish are far more active at night.

FISHING TECHNIQUES

Most emperor are taken on bottom-fished baits of cut fish flesh or squid, particularly by night anglers operating from boats moored over coral reefs and gravel patches.

Small live fish and rigged live squid will take trophy-sized emperor if other methods fail.

Left: An adult red emperor in all its glory.
Below: The best red emperor fishing normally occurs from sunset through the hours of darkness and around first light.

Red emperor occasionally strike at jigged lures, but such captures tend to be the exception rather than the rule.

The most common tackle is a heavy handline in the 25 to 80 kg breaking strain range, though some reef anglers prefer a short, stout rod and centrepin or sidecast reel filled with slightly lighter line of 18 to 35 kg breaking strain.

'Reds' may also be taken on more sporting tackle of a medium overhead or large threadline reel and a 1.7 to 2.2 metre jig-style rod and 10 or 15 kg line., though a large one is likely to sever the line on the coral.

EATING QUALITIES

Red emperor of all sizes are among the very best of the many fine table fish available in northern reef waters. They are second only to the delectable barramundi cod *(Cromileptes altivelis)*.

There have been no reported instances of ciguatera poisoning in connection with the red emperor in Australian waters to date.

EMPEROR, SPANGLED

Lethrinus nebulosus

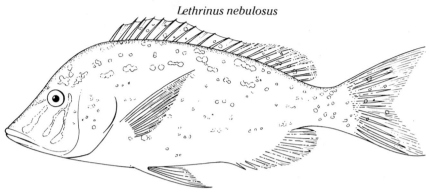

COMMON NAMES

The spangled emperor or 'spangled' is also known as the nor'west snapper or 'nor'wester', particularly in Western Australia, and also as sand emperor, sand bream and yellow-spotted sweetlip or yellow-spotted 'lipper' (YSL).

DESCRIPTION

The spangled emperor is a very attractive, deep-bodied fish with a steep forehead profile and powerful jaws.

Colouration is golden or yellowish to silvery-blue, overlaid with pale blue spots — one on each scale on the back and flanks — the fish looks faintly striped. Brilliant blue lines and markings are usually evident around the head and gill covers. The upper lip is yellow.

The fins are yellow with blue specks.

SIZE

Most spangled emperor caught by anglers weigh between 0.8 and 6 kg, although exceptional ones may occasionally top 10 kg.

DISTRIBUTION

The spangled emperor is a fish of tropical and sub-tropical seas, although isolated specimens wander as far south as Sydney or Jervis Bay in the east and Perth in the west.

The 'spangled' prefers sand, gravel or broken coral 'marl' bottoms in 1 to 10 metres of water, particularly in lagoons or around cays and islands.

Spangled emperor are also found over deeper reef areas further offshore.

HABITS AND FEEDING

Small to mid-size spangled emperor form schools, although larger fish are less gregarious.

The species feeds mainly on crustacea and molluscs nuzzled from the sand and gravel, and will chase prawns, crabs, octopi, squid and small fish.

FISHING TECHNIQUES

Spangled emperor are often taken while anglers are bottom-fishing with cut baits over broken reef and sand or gravel beds.

They bite best on fresh baits of whole or cut fish, crabs, prawns and squid and will sometimes strike at lures, jigs and flies worked close to the bottom.

Tackle needed ranges from moderately heavy handlines to jig outfits and single or double-handed casting rigs.

A berley trail of bait scraps and crushed shellfish or prawn heads often works well.

EATING QUALITIES

The spangled emperor is a very good table fish, though not in the same class as the red emperor, which is superb.

Left: A spangled emperor.
The mottled patterning is not always evident.

Below: Spangled emperor or 'nor' westers' are regularly taken from the rocks in Western Australia.

FINGERMARK

Lutjanus johnii

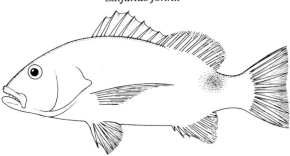

COMMON NAMES

The fingermark or fingermark bream is also known as the spotted scale seaperch in some literature. In the Northern Territory this species is known almost exclusively as the golden snapper or snapper, while in parts of north Queensland it is called a red chopper, though this title may also be applied to the closely related mangrove jack *(L. argentimaculatus)* at times.

Another closely related and similar looking fish, the Moses perch *(L. russelli)* is also taken by anglers, but rarely grows larger than 0.8 kg in weight.

DESCRIPTION

A deep-bodied, particularly attractive member of the *Lutjanidae* family, the fingermark bream is characterised by its golden lustre, spotted scales and the large, dark blotch high on the back ahead of the tail wrist on each side. In common with the other *Lutjanid* fishes, the fingermark has powerful jaws with sharp, canine teeth. The eye is large and dark.

When freshly caught, the fingermark glows like a newly minted copper coin, particularly around the head. The base colour is coppery-gold to purple-gold, and each scale has a darker centre to give a chequered effect. There is a large, dark irregular patch on the back under the second dorsal fin.

The fins of the fingermark are mainly dark, especially the tail, although in some specimens the pelvic fins are much lighter.

SIZE

Fingermark may rarely top 10 kg in weight, though any specimen over 6 or 7 kg is a real prize. Most of those taken by anglers weigh between 0.6 and 4 kg.

DISTRIBUTION

Fingermark are confined to tropical waters, rarely wandering south of Rockhampton in the east and Carnarvon in the west.

Fingermark are mainly encountered in tropical, mangrove lined estuaries, but they also inhabit bays and inshore reefs. At times they are prolific around rocky headlands and islands.

Fingermark favour drop-offs with at least three metres of water on the deeper side. Unlike the closely related mangrove jack, fingermark operate close to the bottom and do not often take up a defined territory among snag cover. Instead, they move with the tides, adopting different feeding stations at different states or heights of the tidal cycle.

HABITS AND FEEDING

Fingermark are a schooling species, the number of fish in the school being largely dictated by the size of the individual fingermark. Smaller fish tend to form much denser aggregation.

Fingermark are opportunistic predators and foragers. They will eat a wide range of small fish such as herring, mullet, gar, archer fish and the like, as well as prawns,

Left: Fingermark are characterised by the dark blotch ahead of the tail wrist.
Below: Queensland fingermark.

shrimp, crabs, octopi and worms. However, they are particularly partial to squid, and will seek out these cephalopods in preference to all other prey.

FISHING TECHNIQUES

Most fingermark taken by anglers are caught on well-presented baits of small, live fish such as mullet, herring or whiting, or on live or fresh prawns.

They will also take cut fish flesh, dead squid and whole dead baitfish, although larger specimens prefer live bait. If a small live squid can be obtained, it will rarely be passed up.

Fingermark sometimes provide superb action for the lure caster or troller, but 'artificials' should be worked as close to the bottom as practical. Deep-diving minnow-style lures such as Rapalas, Rebels, Newells and the like are best.

Tackle used for catching fingermark ranges from heavy handlines to light, single or double-handed casting outfits with 3 to 8 kg breaking strain line.

A trace of heavy nylon with a breaking strain at least two or three times that of the main line is advisable when using tackle lighter than about 10 kg.

EATING QUALITIES

The fingermark is a superb table fish and is often rated ahead of many other tropical glamour species, including the barramundi. Its flesh is white, sweet and moist, even in very large specimens.

FLATHEAD, DUSKY

Platycephalus fuscus

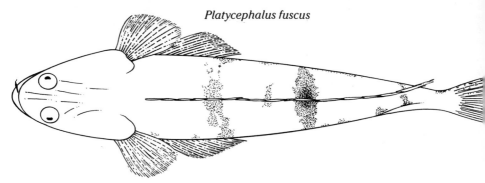

COMMON NAMES

The dusky flathead or dusky is also known as the estuary flathead, flattie and lizard.

The dusky is the largest member of the family *Platycephalidae*, which contains more than 30 species, at least 14 of which are taken by anglers from time to time. Most of the more common flathead may be separated and identified by examining the colouration and markings on the tail or caudal fin.

DESCRIPTION

The dusky is the largest and most sought after of all the flatheads. It has the characteristic flattened body, broad, spade-like head, large mouth and fine teeth common to all members of the family. Sets of sharp spines covered in mildly venomous mucus are located on the gill covers.

Dusky flathead colouration is extremely variable, ranging from very light sandy or fawn with darker bars and blue 'stars' to almost jet black. The fish's belly is always creamy, creamy-yellow or white.

The dusky flathead's fins are sometimes tipped or bordered in blue, and the tail or caudal fin features a dark spot or blotch in the top, trailing corner and a patch of blue on the lower half.

The closely related and very similar bar-tailed flathead *(P. endrachtensis)* of Western Australia lives in the same range of environments as the dusky and shares very similar habits. However, the bar-tailed flathead rarely tops 2.2 kg in weight and is more common at less than half that size.

SIZE

Duskies are the giants of the flathead clan, very occasionally topping 1.5 metres and 10 kg in weight. However, most of those taken by anglers weigh between 0.5 and 6 kg, with fish towards the upper end of that range being regarded as real prizes.

DISTRIBUTION

The dusky is an estuarine and inshore species of the east coast, ranging southwards from about Rockhampton or Mackay to Wilsons Promontory in Victoria.

A fish of our tidal rivers, estuaries, saltwater lakes, bays and inshore sand patches, dusky flathead will sometimes travel upstream well into the fresh, and at other times—may be encountered several kilometres out to sea.

They favour mud or sand bottom strata, but will occasionally be found over rock and gravel.

HABITS AND FEEDING

Dusky flathead rarely form schools in the manner of the various sand flathead. However, a productive stretch of river may hold quite a concentration of these fish, giving the same effect as a school.

Dusky flathead are ambush predators

Left: A dusky flathead taken on a soft plastic jig.

Below: An angler working a sandflat drop-off in a New South Wales estuary. Such locations are prime holding areas for dusky flathead.

and occasional scavengers. They lie camouflaged on the seabed and make lightning fast, short range bursts to take prawns, shrimp, crabs, octopi, squid and a wide range of small fish.

FISHING TECHNIQUES

Dusky flathead may be fished for in a variety of ways.

Many are taken on bottom-fished baits of small, live poddy mullet or herring, dead mullet, pilchards, whitebait, sprat, anchovy or garfish, and strips of mullet, tailor, yellowtail, tuna or garfish.

When using dead baits and cut fish flesh strips, results are often improved by retrieving the bait slowly over the seabed, or by using the tide and current to keep the rig moving.

Many flathead, especially smaller fish, are also taken on prawns, yabbies, nippers, pipis and the like.

Drifting in a boat with weighted lines trailing behind is a popular and productive method for catching dusky flathead, and many anglers believe that results are improved by bouncing or 'yo-yoing' the bait up and down a few centimetres at a time while drifting.

Dusky flathead are also a recognised lure fishing target. They respond particularly well to small and medium sized metal

While dusky flathead average a kilo or so, exceptional specimens may top 6 kg.

spoons such as Wonder Wobblers, ABU Tobies, Pegron Tiger Minnows and the like. Many are also taken on rubber-tailed jigs like the Mister Twister and Scrounger ranges, and on floating/diving or sinking bibbed minnows including models from Rapala, Nilsmaster, Rebel, Cotton Cordell, Shakespeare and Australian makers such as Killalure, Elliot, Newell and Nautilus.

Tackle for flathead fishing in the estuaries ranges from a simple handline to sophisticated rods and reels. However, a trace of some kind should be employed when using light lines.

Flathead use tides and currents to their advantage when feeding and will usually choose a lie close to abundant food supplies. Drop-offs and gutters adjacent to sandflats and weedbeds are top flathead areas.

EATING QUALITIES

Dusky flathead are highly rated table fish with firm, white and flaky flesh which tends towards dryness in larger fish.

Flathead are best suited to recipes which help to maintain moisture content in the flesh while cooking.

FLATHEAD, SAND

Platycephalus arenarius, Platycephalus caeruleopunctatus, Platycephalus speculator, Platycephalus bassensis

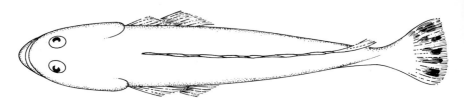

COMMON NAMES

These four related sand flathead have near identical habits and occupy very similar environmental niches along various parts of the coastline, and are therefore best dealt with together.

Other names for fish in this group include southern blue – spotted or Castelnau's flathead *(P. speculator)*, eastern blue-spotted flathead *(P. caeruleopunctatus)*, northern sand flathead *(P. arenarius)* and southern sand flathead *(P. bassensis)*. Other titles and colloquial names for all of these fish include spiky flathead, slimy flathead, flattie, lizard, frog, spiky and yank.

DESCRIPTION

All four sand flathead are very similar in appearance to each other, and also to the previously described dusky flathead.

Most of the sand flatheads are a light sandy-fawn to light brick-red, overlaid with small blue spots or 'stars' and sometimes mottled with rusty-red to brown patterns.

Markings on the tail or caudal fin help to separate these fish. *P. arenarius* has a pattern of long, horizontal black stripes on its tail. *P. caeruleopunctatus* has three or four thick black ovals or bars on the lower part of the tail fin. *P. speculator* has three to five black spots on the lower tail margin, and *P. bassensis* has two squared-off black patches on the lower half of the tail fin.

SIZE

The largest of the four species covered here under the general heading of sand flathead is the southern blue-spotted *(P. speculator)*, which on rare occasions approaches 80 cm and 3.5 kg. The other three have top weights of around 2.5 kg.

In some areas, such as Melbourne's Port Phillip Bay, the average sand flathead caught is quite small, weighing from 0.2 to 0.5 kg. In other locations, such as Flinders Island and parts of Tasmania, fish in the 0.5 to 1.2 kg range are more common.

DISTRIBUTION

All of the flathead described here inhabit inshore bays and offshore sand or gravel beds, mainly in water between 10 and 80 metres deep. All four also enter estuaries, but are mainly confined to the lower reaches.

The four species described take in almost the entire Australian coastline, though sand flathead are more prolific and more often fished for in southern waters, from about Moreton Bay to Shark Bay, as well as in Tasmania and Bass Strait.

HABITS AND FEEDING

The actual feeding styles of all the sand flathead are not unlike those described for the dusky. These fish are opportunistic short-range ambushers and occasional scavengers.

Unlike duskies, sand flathead often form large but fairly loose schools on sandy or muddy bottom strata.

Sand flathead feed on all types of small fish, as well as prawns, crabs, squid, octopi and cuttlefish. They will also scavenge.

Left: An eastern blue-spotted flathead
(Platycephalus caeruleopunctatus).
*Below: Most sand flathead are taken by boat
anglers working inshore grounds, bays and
large estuaries.*

FISHING TECHNIQUES

The methods and tackle described for dusky flathead may also be employed for taking sand flathead, although heavier lines and sinkers may be needed in deeper water to overcome the current and drift rate of the boat, for most sand flatties are taken from boats operating in big estuary mouths, bays, harbours and on offshore drifting grounds.

The most popular gear for those targeting sand flathead consists of a handline in the 10 to 20 kg breaking strain class. The usual terminal rig involves a relatively heavy sinker with two, three or even four hooks on short droppers above. Baits usually take the form of small whole fish or, more commonly, strips of fish flesh. Fillets of small flathead make excellent baits for this cannibalistic species.

EATING QUALITIES

Sand flathead are delicious and highly regarded table fish with white, flaky and slightly dry flesh.

FLOUNDER

Pseudorhombus arsius, Pseudorhombus jenynsii

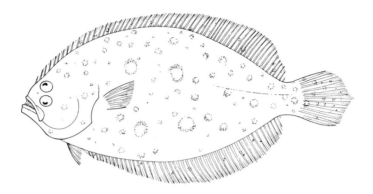

COMMON NAMES

The large-toothed flounder *(P. arsius)* and small-toothed flounder *(P. jenynsii)* are the most common of the flounder species taken by anglers in Australasian waters. Less abundant flounder species include the greenback flounder *(Rhombosolea tapirina)* and long-snouted flounder *(Ammotretis rostratus).*

Flounder are occasionally confused with another group of flatfish called sole. However, sole have no separate tail, unlike flounder, which have a distinct tail

DESCRIPTION

The flounder are all relatively small, very compressed, bottom-dwelling fish with both eyes on the same side of the body (in adults). There are many species of flounder in Australasian waters, but only a few are large enough, and common enough to be of interest to anglers.

Flounder alter their colour to suit the bottom strata on which they are lying. Most are brown, fawn, sandy or light khaki to green, usually overlaid with darker spots, blotches and halos.

The underside of an adult flounder is almost always white, cream or creamy-yellow, although rare specimens are coloured or partially coloured on both sides.

SIZE

The largest of the flounders — small-toothed and large-toothed — grow to about 50 cm in length and 1.2 kg in weight, though fish over 0.9 kg are exceptional. The average, line-caught flounder measures about 30 to 35 cm and weighs from 0.3 to 0.8 kg.

DISTRIBUTION

Flounder of one sort or another are found right around Australasia, but these fish are more commonly caught in the southern half of Australia.

They prefer mud, sand or fine gravel-bottomed areas in tidal rivers and estuaries. They are also found in bays and on inshore grounds.

Flounder occasionally penetrate upriver into fresh water, but are more common in the lower stretches of estuaries.

HABITS AND FEEDING

Flounder are opportunistic predators and scavengers, feeding on small fish, prawns, shrimp, crabs, marine worms, octopi and small squid.

Flounder vary enormously in colouration, and individuals can actually alter their patterning to adapt to different environments.

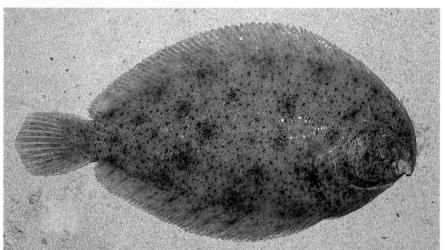

These flatfish rely on camouflage to ambush their prey, and make a short burst off the sand or mud to seize their quarry in their large, tooth-lined jaws.

Juvenile flounder are very different looking; they swim upright in the manner of a normal fish. However, as they grow, one eye begins to 'migrate' around the head until both are on the same side. At this stage the fish turns on its side and adopts a bottom-dwelling lifestyle.

FISHING TECHNIQUES

Voracious little hunters, flounder will take surprisingly large baits into their tooth-lined mouths.

Most are caught on baits of prawn, worm, yabby or nipper, fish flesh or squid strip. They are usually an incidental catch by anglers fishing for flathead, bream and whiting.

Flounder feed on or close to the bottom and prefer natural baits, although they succumb to small leadhead jigs, spoons or flies fished on or near the seabed.

EATING QUALITIES

The flounder are excellent and highly prized table fish often given star billing on restaurant menus. However, fine bones can be something of a problem in smaller specimens.

The flesh is white, moist and sweet and has a delicate flavour. It should not be overcooked.

GARFISH

Family: *Hemiramphidae*

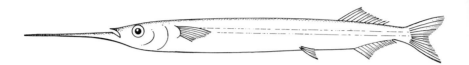

COMMON NAMES

This large family of world-wide fish species is well represented in Australasia. The more common types found here include the near identical eastern and southern sea garfish *(Hyporhamphus australis* and *H. melanochir)*, the river garfish *(H. regularis)*, the robust garfish or 'three-by-two' *(Hemiramphus robustus)* and the snub-nosed garfish *(Arrhamphus sclerolepis)*.

All garfish are commonly called 'gars', 'gardies' and 'beakies'. The New Zealand name is 'piper', while in other parts of the world they are known as needlefish and 'balao'or 'ballyhoo'.

DESCRIPTION

Garfish are a diverse and widespread group of small, slender fish, most of which have a bottom jaw which extends into a bill or beak.

Body colour varies between species, from bright, metallic silver to silvery-green or silvery-blue. Some have dark blotches, bands or bars. The belly is pale-coloured and a red tip on the bill is common.

SIZE

The southern sea garfish and the robust or 'three-by-two' gar are our largest representatives of this family. Both can be more than 45 cm in length and approach weights of 0.35 kg, and the southern sea gar may very rarely reach 52 cm and weigh 0.4 kg.

Garfish are more common at lengths of 25 to 35 cm and weights of 0.1 to 0.2 kg.

Very small garfish, popular as bait, are called 'pencil' or 'splinter' gar.

DISTRIBUTION

Depending on the exact species, garfish are found from the surface layers of oceanic waters far offshore, through inshore reef areas to bays and estuaries, and into freshwater reaches far up river.

One type of garfish or another is present in practically every Australasian estuary, harbour, bay and inshore area.

HABITS AND FEEDING

Gars are a schooling fish which feed on the surface on plankton and floating debris such as leaf litter from mangrove forests. They prefer calm, reasonably clear water.

FISHING TECHNIQUES

Garfish are mainly taken on float-suspended baits of bread, dough, 'pudding' mix, fish strips, prawn pieces, cut squid or maggots.

Hooks should be small and long-shanked.

They respond well to a berley of pollard, crushed wheat or breadcrumbs, especially if a little fish oil is added.

For best sport and results, fine line and light tackle should be used. A very light 2.5 to 3 metre rod, a small threadline, sidecast or centrepin reel and line of 1 to 3 kg breaking strain make a perfect set-up.

Rigs utilising light quill floats, small bobby corks or bubble floats are best.

Garfish are usually caught in shallow water over sand or mud, and may be taken with whiting, mullet and other inshore species.

Garfish will take small flies and tiny jigs or lures, especially when berleyed into a feeding frenzy.

EATING QUALITIES

Garfish — particularly the larger varieties — are delectable table fish with sweet, moist flesh, but unfortunately have many fine bones.

After capture garfish should be squeezed from the head towards the tail to expel the semi-digested vegetable matter and berley in the stomach, then kept cool until cleaned. Their scales dislodge easily, and those not rubbed off at the time of capture are easily removed during cleaning.

Garfish of all species and sizes make superb bait for a wide range of predatory species. They can be used alive, as whole dead-bait, or cut into strips, chunks and cubes.

GROPER, BLUE

Achoerodus viridis, Achoerodus gouldii

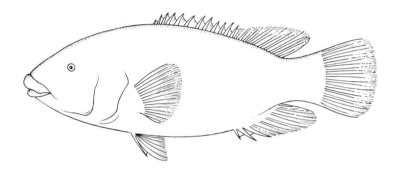

COMMON NAMES

These two very closely related species, the eastern blue groper *(A. viridis)* and western blue groper *(A. gouldii)* are also known as groper, brown groper and red groper, the last two names referring to the colours of the female fish.

DESCRIPTION

These two near-identical, heavily scaled, barrel-bodied and peg-toothed members of the wrasse family *(Labridae)* exhibit well-defined colour differences between the small female and the large male.

Juvenile and female colouring ranges from green to brown to orange-red, often with a darker reddish spot on each scale. Males are brilliant blue, with darker blue and sometimes reddish lines or spots around their small, pig-like eyes.

The fins are much the same colour as the body.

SIZE

The western species *(A. gouldii)* is the larger of the two, growing to 1.6 metres in length and weighing at least 40 kg, while the eastern fish, rare at weights in excess of 15 kg, can approach 20 kg in isolated instances.

Groper taken by anglers in eastern states mainly weigh from 1.8 to 10 kg.

DISTRIBUTION

The eastern blue ranges from about Hervey Bay in southern Queensland to Wilsons Promontory in Victoria, while the western blue extends from west of Melbourne to the Houtman Abrolhos .

Groper frequent reefy, rock-lined stretches of coast and stay in close proximity to the shore, or to islands and bomboras.

The species prefers turbulent areas with heavy weed-growth and plenty of crabs and other crustacea among the rocks.

Most groper are landed by shore-based anglers, but smart boat operators who work the near-shore reefs can do very well.

HABITS AND FEEDING

Blue groper have an interesting life cycle. All begin life as green, brown or red females, but can change sex and become blue males.

There is usually only one large male in each 'pack' or school of groper. Should this fish be caught or killed, the largest female in the group will transform into a male, changing from brown or red to blue in a few days or weeks. Because of this trait, browns and reds are rarely seen at weights of more than 5 or 6 kg, while blues are practically unknown at sizes less than 5 kg.

Blue groper feed on crabs, shellfish, marine worms, octopi and cuttlefish. Their

Left: A brown groper (top) and blue (below). The brown and red colour variations are exhibited by females. After the fish change sex and become males, they take on blue colouration.
Below: An 8 kg-plus blue groper.

powerful jaws and peg-like teeth allow them to crack open large molluscs such as mussels and even abalone.

FISHING TECHNIQUES

Strong line, heavy tackle and fresh crab baits are the tools of the groper specialist.

Crabs are by far the best bait for groper, particularly the large, red crabs found close to the water's edge among short, red weed growth.

Groper will also take other species of crabs, shellfish, cunji and sometimes prawns.

This powerful fish will dive for cover among the rocks when hooked so very strong tackle is required.

Land-based groper tackle consists of a stout 2.5 to 3.5 metre rod, large sidecast, centrepin or overhead reel and line of 15 to 40 kg breaking strain.

A bag limit of two groper per angler per day applies in New South Wales, and varying closures and restrictions apply to divers and fishermen in other states.

EATING QUALITIES

The groper is a delicious eating fish, particularly in the 3 to 8 kg range. Smaller fish can be soft and tasteless, and very large specimens a little coarse.

Groper are best filleted and skinned as their large scales are tough and difficult to remove.

HAIRTAIL

Trichiurus lepturus

COMMON NAMES

Hairtail or 'hairy', and, more rarely, Australian hairtail or Cox's hairtail.

The hairtail is occasionally confused with the related frostfish *(Lepidopus caudatus)*. The latter has a tiny, forked tail, in contrast to the hairtail's whip-like one.

Hairtail bear a superficial resemblance to barracouta and to some eels, particularly the pike eel.

DESCRIPTION

It is a long, silvery, eel-like fish with no tail fin and a large mouth, full of sharp fangs. Colouration is bright, reflective, metallic-silver with a tinge of blue or green along the top of the back. The fins are almost transparent.

SIZE

Hairtail commonly reach lengths of between 1 and 1.7 metres and weigh a little over 2 kg, though outstanding examples may exceed 2 metres and weigh as much as 5 or 6 kg.

DISTRIBUTION

Hairtail or closely related fish appear sporadically in many parts of the world, and are an important commercial catch in parts of South East Asia and India.

In Australia they turn up just about anywhere at times, but are common only in a few select estuarine and harbour environments between Newcastle and Wollongong on the New South Wales coast. Good quantities are occasionally reported in localities as widely separated as Townsville in Queensland and Bunbury in Western Australia.

HABITS AND FEEDING

The hairtail is something of a mystery fish.

They are taken in deep, continental shelf waters by trawlers and, at times, in bays and large estuaries by anglers.

In general they prefer deep, cool water with some current flow, but exceptions abound.

They feed mainly on small, live fish, but will also prey on prawns and squid, and scavenge on dead fish.

Hairtail must be very capable hunters, as they have been found with speedy pelagics such as frigate mackerel in their stomachs.

FISHING TECHNIQUES

Hairtail taken outside their few common haunts are incidental captures. However, in the Hawkesbury and — to a lesser extent — Sydney Harbour, Botany Bay and Newcastle Harbour, the species has attracted a dedicated band of specialist anglers.

Left: The hairtail has a truly fearsome set of fangs.
Below: When alive, hairtail gleam as if chrome plated. This specimen was taken from Newcastle Harbour, NSW.

The best hairtail fishing occurs at night or in deeper holes during the day. Most fish are caught in the cooler winter months.

Small to medium live baits such as yellowtail, slimy mackerel and mullet, whole dead fish such as pilchards or garfish and cut flesh strips account for most hairtail caught on hook and line.

When biting well, hairtail will strike savagely at lures, but their toothy mouth makes hookup difficult.

Wire traces or ganged hooks should be used to prevent them biting off.

EATING QUALITIES

The hairtail has delicious, delicate flesh which should not be over cooked. Many people believe rubbing the fish with a piece of rough cloth to remove the skin before cooking commences will improve its flavour.

GIANT HERRING

Elops machnata

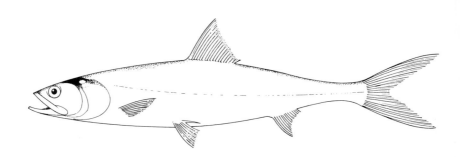

COMMON NAMES

The giant herring or 'GH' is also known simply as herring or, more rarely, by the names 'pincushion fish', 'lady fish', 'banana fish' and 'ten-pounder'.

Although occasionally confused with two other herrings, the bonefish *(Albula neoguinaica)* and the milkfish *(Chanos chanos)*, the giant herring's slender body and large mouth are diagnostic.

DESCRIPTION

The giant herring is a long, slender fish with a huge, forked tail, single dorsal fin and big, upturned mouth.

The moderately large, easily displaced scales are bright metallic silver, although the fish is gun-metal blue to dark grey along the very top of the back.

The fins are dark, the tail sometimes showing a black border on the trailing edge.

SIZE

Giant herring most commonly weigh from 0.4 to 2 kg, although the species is known to occasionally weigh as much as 10 kg and exceed 1.5 metres in length.

DISTRIBUTION

Giant herring are a highly rated and sought after sport fish with a sporadic distribution through the tropical north, and the habit of occasionally turning up in southern waterways such as Perth's Swan River or Sydney's Queenscliff Lagoon and Port Hacking, either singly or in small schools.

Mainly a fish of the tidal estuaries, bays and saltwater lagoons, herring favour shallow, warm areas with plenty of prawns and small baitfish for food. They are rarely found far offshore, unless the location is an island or sand cay.

HABITS AND FEEDING

Giant herring feed extensively on small fish such as mullet, gar, hardihead and sprat, as well as preying on prawns, small crabs, large planktonic organisms and bottle squid.

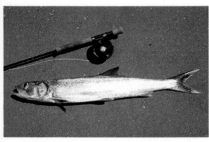

Left: Giant herring.
Below: This premier sportfish frequents tropical estuaries and flats. Its distribution appears to be sporadic and discontinuous.

FISHING TECHNIQUES

Specifically fished for in just a few locations — such as Mornington Island in the Gulf of Carpentaria — herring are more likely to be encountered incidentally during a hunt for mackerel, queenfish, trevally or the like.

Giant herring are taken on small live baits, fresh fish strips, prawns, small crabs, many different small lures, and flies.

Perhaps the most effective ploy is to use a small, cup-faced popper-style lure or fly.

Herring, with their lightning strikes, incredible bursts of speed and acrobatic leaps and gyrations, always provide the fisherman with a real thrill.

EATING QUALITIES

The giant herring is a poor to fair table fish. The flesh is full of fine bones — a trait common to the herring family.

JAVELIN FISH

Pomadasys hasta

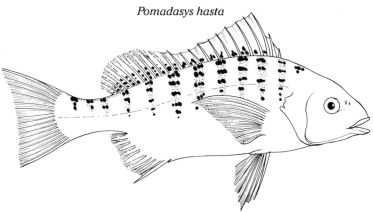

COMMON NAMES

There are three main species of javelin fish, though *P. hasta* is the best known. It is also called the spotted javelin or grunter.

DESCRIPTION

The javelin fish or grunter is a handsome, speckled, deep-bodied fish named because of the stout spine at the front edge of its anal fin.

Typical colouration is purple-silver to dark silvery-grey on the back, silver on the flanks and silver-white on the belly, overlaid by darker vertical bands and dark speckles.

The fins often have a yellowish tinge.

SIZE

Spotted javelin fish are commonly caught at weights of between 0.4 and 2 kg, although trophy size specimens may reach 6 or even 8 kg. The other two species are generally smaller.

DISTRIBUTION

A fish of tropical estuaries and inshore waters, javelin fish range from the central coast of Queensland to at least Exmouth in the west; most are found in estuaries.

HABITS AND FEEDING

Javelin fish frequent estuaries and bays in our tropical north, often forming small to medium-sized schools. They prefer hard-bottomed gravel, rock or coral 'marl' channels with a reasonably strong tidal flow.

They are in many ways the 'bream of the north', and feed in similar areas to bream.

The javelin's diet is mainly comprised of prawns, shrimp, small crabs, marine worms, squid, octopi and various invertebrates.

FISHING TECHNIQUES

Live prawns, fresh dead prawns, crabs, yabbies and fresh fish strips are the best baits for this sometimes shy biter.

Tackle should be kept light and sinker weights minimised when pursuing javelin fish. The fish often runs with the bait held lightly in its mouth before swallowing it.

Slightly beefed-up bream tackle is ideal for catching javelin fish, with light-tipped 2 to 2.5 metre rods, threadline, sidecast or baitcaster reels and lines of 4 to 6 kg breaking strain being best suited to catching this desirable northern species.

EATING QUALITIES

The javelin fish is a fine table species held in high regard by tropical anglers. The flesh is firm, white and slightly moist. The fish handles well and can be frozen without significant loss of quality.

In many ways, javelin fish are the 'bream of the tropics'. They may be fished for with beefed up bream tackle and respond to similar baits. They often feed over flats on a rising tide.

– JEWFISH, WEST AUSTRALIAN –

Glaucosoma hebraicum

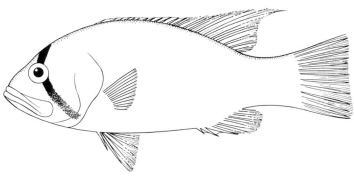

COMMON NAMES

The West Australian or Westralian jewfish is commonly known just as jewfish or dhufish. This species should not be confused with the mulloway, an unrelated fish frequenting the same waters and known in the eastern states as jewfish.

The only known relative of the West Australian jewfish in our waters is the much smaller pearl perch *(G. scapulare)* of northern New South Wales and southern Queensland.

DESCRIPTION

A big, deep-bodied and strikingly attractive fish found only in the offshore waters of southern Western Australia, it has large eyes and a big, slightly undershot mouth.

Typical colouring is purplish-silver to metallic-grey, overlaid with vague, length-wise stripes of darker purple. Juveniles have a distinct, black, diagonal stripe through the eyes, but this fades as the fish approaches maturity. It remains fairly obvious in freshly-caught adults but fades after death.

SIZE

The average size of jewfish taken by anglers has fallen in recent years, due to overharvesting. Most of those caught weigh from 2 to 8 kg, but many over 10 kg are still taken by fishermen working deeper or less fished reefs. Any jewfish over 20 kg is a real trophy, though weights up to 25 kg have been recorded.

DISTRIBUTION

This fish is confined to south Western Australia, ranging from about the Recherche Archipelago off the southern coastline to Shark Bay in the north.

HABITS AND FEEDING

The Westralian jewfish is an offshore species favouring deep reefs beyond the 40 metre mark, although stray jewfish are encountered closer inshore, particularly in their juvenile stages.

Jewfish are mostly found over hard, but relatively flat, bottom strata, especially limestone shelf country.

They also frequent wrecks and submarine rockpiles.

In a few areas of the south west where deep water is found close to shore, jewfish are occasionally caught from the rocks.

They sometimes travel in small schools, though larger individuals tend to swim alone, usually close to the cover of ledges, caves or wrecks.

The fish feeds on small fish, crustacea — including crayfish — octopi, squid and flesh scraps. It is both hunter and scavenger.

Left: A 5 kg male jewfish taken off Perth.
Below: Most West Australian jewfish are
taken by boat anglers operating well offshore,
although a few deepwater rock spots in the
south of the state offer land-based fishermen a
chance to tangle with this species.

FISHING TECHNIQUES

Bottom bouncing with strong hand-lines, heavy sinkers, big hooks and baits of octopus, squid, cut fish flesh or whole small fish is the favourite method for taking Westralian jewfish.

The species also responds well to live baits fished close to the bottom and even jigs or other deep-fished lures.

Although not regarded as an outstanding sportfish on the tackle usually employed, jewfish hooked on lighter line, or encountered in the shallows, give a fine account of themselves.

Jewfish anglers use thick handlines with breaking strains of 25 to 50 kg, or slightly lighter lines on short, stiff rods and large centrepin or sidecast reels. However, overhead or magnum threadline tackle and 15 kg line will suffice for most 'jewie' fishing Since there is less water-drag, lighter sinkers can be used.

EATING QUALITIES

The West Australian jewfish is a highly acclaimed delicacy and among the country's short list of best table species. All sizes are delicious and may be cooked in any way. The flavour should not be masked by a strong tasting sauce.

JOBFISH, GREEN

Aprion virescens

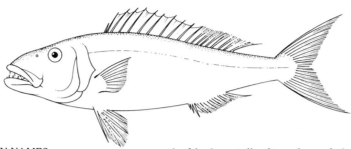

COMMON NAMES

Jobfish, green jobfish or 'samurai salmon'. The closely related rosy jobfish or king snapper *(A. microlepis)* is a less common deep water species with a range extending south of that of the green jobfish.

DESCRIPTION

The green jobfish is a robust, heavily scaled fish with a long, almost cylindrical body, a powerful, forked tail, heavy jaws and large canine teeth.

Colouration is normally greenish-grey to purple-grey on the back, shading to lighter purple-green or grassy-green on the sides and belly. The fish sometimes has a 'brassy' look around the head. Each scale carries a slightly darker centre.

The fins are coloured much like the body, although the pelvics and ventral fin are sometimes edged with off-white.

SIZE

Most jobfish caught by tropical anglers weigh between 1.4 and 5 kg, although the species occasionally approaches 12 kg and a metre in length. The rosy jobfish may grow slightly larger.

DISTRIBUTION

The green jobfish is a fish of tropical offshore waters with a somewhat sporadic range extending from north Queensland to the nor'west of Western Australia.

Its habitat extends from the deeper shorelines to the outer reef drop-offs and fringing atolls. It prefers relatively deep water over and around coral and rock bottom strata.

HABITS AND FEEDING

Green jobfish frequent the coral reefs and drop-offs in water depths between about 10 and 50 metres.

Although spending most of their time close to the bottom, they range quite high in the water column chasing small fish, squid and the like.

Jobfish form loose schools, though larger examples tend to be more solitary.

FISHING TECHNIQUES

Jobfish are rarely encountered in heavy enough concentrations to be specifically targeted. Most are picked up by anglers bottom fishing with bait or trolling deep-running, minnow-style lures.

Baits of whole or cut fish flesh and squid will tempt them as will small to medium live baits such as juvenile trevally, scad and banana fish or fusiliers.

Once located, a patch of jobfish will respond very well to cast or jigged lures and deep-diving minnows or plugs.

When hooked, they fight strongly and will attempt to sever the line on a coral ledge

EATING QUALITIES

The jobfish has firm, white and delicious flesh. Larger specimens may cause ciguatera poisoning, though no cases have yet been attributed to this species.

Left: A lure-caught green jobfish
Below: This large jobfish was taken on a deep fished live bait near a coral drop-off.

JOHN DORY

Zeus faber

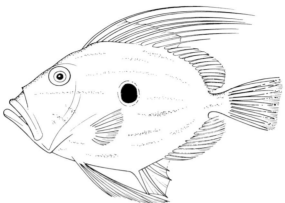

COMMON NAMES

In Australasia John dory is the common name for this fish, though it is occasionally called Peter's fish, Peter's dory or simply, dory.

Several related species with a common body shape are found in our waters. The most common are the silver dory and the mirror dory, though both are deepwater trawl-fish rarely taken by anglers.

DESCRIPTION

An unusual looking, scaleless, plate-like fish with a deep, circular and laterally-compressed body, a big head, huge protrusible mouth, and long, filamentous dorsal fin.

The fish exhibit varying colouration depending on environment. Usually, they are greenish-brown to olive or grey on the back, lighter on the flanks and belly, sometimes with dark patches or even a golden sheen. A large black spot or blotch bordered by a light edge is prominent on each flank.

The dory's fins, particularly the dorsal one, have dusky rays, but are almost transparent between the rays.

SIZE

John dory commonly weigh between 0.6 and 1.4 kg; occasionally up to 2 kg; rare giants approaching 4 kg in weight have been reported.

DISTRIBUTION

John dory are found in cool and temperate waters all over the world. In Australasia they seem to be confined to the southern coastline from about South Queensland to South Australia, with sporadic appearances in Tasmania and the south of Western Australia. They are also found in New Zealand, particularly on the eastern seaboard of the North Island.

They frequent shallow bays and large estuaries, and are found far offshore over deep reefs close to the edge of the continental shelf. There appears to be some sort of seasonal or size-related migration from the inshore to the offshore grounds.

Near the shore, where they are most often caught by anglers, John dory favour areas of mud or sand with seagrass or ribbon weed cover. They also frequent the shadows between the pilings of wharves.

HABITS AND FEEDING

The John dory is a predator. It will drift slowly into the midst of a school of small fish and suddenly shoot out its telescopic mouth to take in the hapless prey.

They mostly feed on live yellowtail, slimy mackerel or mullet when hunting

Although slow moving, the John Dory is a superb predator, relying on stealth and the sudden projection of its oversize, protractile mouth to snare its prey. These fish will take surprisingly large live baits at times.

shallow, inshore waters, where they are most common during the winter months.

FISHING TECHNIQUES

Many of the John dory taken by anglers are incidental captures landed while fishing with live baits for flathead, mulloway or kingfish. If slightly smaller baits are used, the chance of taking a dory increases.

Estuary and harbour anglers specifically targeting John dory mostly use handlines and small live baits, sometimes trimming the tail of the bait with scissors to slow it down.

Over the deep reefs, John dory take cut-flesh strips and whole small fish such as pilchards, as well as deep-fished live baits.

In New Zealand John dory have been caught on rubber-tailed jigs, but this is rare in Australia.

EATING QUALITIES

The John dory is rated as one of our very best table fish. The flesh is pearly-white, firm and extremely fine-grained. Once filleted, there are no bones in the flesh.

Because of its quality it commands a high price at market, despite a fair degree of wastage due to the size of its head.

JUNGLE PERCH

Kuhlia rupestris

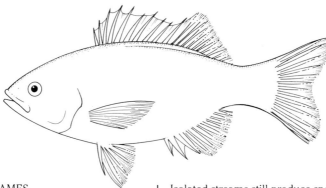

COMMON NAMES

The jungle perch, 'JP' or 'junglie' is also known as the flagtail or rocky flagtail in some areas.

This beautiful and possibly endangered fish is unlikely to be confused with any other species in its native streams, where it is mainly found alongside sooty grunter, archer fish and barramundi.

DESCRIPTION

The jungle perch is a small, handsome perch of the tropical freshwater and upper estuaries characterised by its spotted appearance and dark 'flags' on each tail lobe. Jungle perch are sometimes confused with a small, related fish found in the saltwater and estuaries, but the two are rarely found in the same area.

The jungle perch's colouration is silvery-green above, silver or copper on the flanks and silvery-white on the belly. Each scale carries a dark patch or centre which gives an overall chequerboard effect.

The fins are lightly coloured, with a vague dark blotch on the second dorsal and a distinct black patch bordered in white on each tail lobe tip. The anal fin may be tinged with yellow.

SIZE

These days jungle perch caught by fishermen mostly weigh from 0.3 to 0.9 kg.

Isolated streams still produce specimens in the 1 to 1.6 kg range. Any over 2 kg are extremely rare, though the species may once have topped 3 kg.

DISTRIBUTION

Jungle perch are found only in clear flowing rainforest streams on the east coast of north Queensland and on some larger Barrier Reef islands. Distribution is sporadic, with the species occurring in one river system, but not necessarily the next.

A small pocket of jungle perch also exists on Fraser Island, well south of the fish's 'standard' range.

Jungle perch are found upstream only as far as the first insurmountable barrier: waterfall, dam or weir. They favour rocky streams with plenty of bankside vegetation.

HABITS AND FEEDING

Small to medium-sized jungle perch will form loose, competitive schools, while bigger fish may tend to 'hole up' adjacent to a snag or dominate part of a pool. In areas where stocks are relatively healthy, each likely hole and pocket will contain several fish. Sadly, such areas are rare these days.

These perch feed on terrestrial and aquatic insects and their larvae, small fish, shrimp, freshwater prawns or *macrobrachium*, yabbies and small land creatures which fall into or swim through the water.

Left: The jungle perch is one of our most attractive freshwater natives. Sadly, it is also one of the most threatened.
Bottom left: Jungle perch habitat
Below: Two at once! A pair of juvenile jungle perch taken on the same lure.

FISHING TECHNIQUES

The sportfisherman seeks jungle perch with short, light rods, lines of 2 to 4 kg breaking strain and small lures.

Spoons, spinners and diving plugs of the kind used for trout and bass are best, though surface poppers and flies can also be very successful.

Jungle perch will take natural baits such as insects and live shrimps. A large, live march fly on a small hook is deadly to them. However, most thinking anglers prefer lure fishing, as it makes live release of the fish much easier.

EATING QUALITIES

Jungle perch are a delicious table fish, though nowadays most are released alive in deference to shrinking stocks and degraded habitats. If jungle perch were native to any state other than Queensland, they'd most likely be protected by law.

KINGFISH, YELLOWTAIL

Seriola lalandi

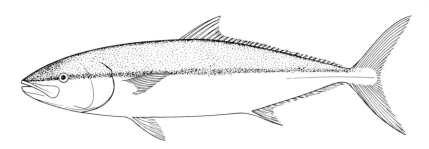

COMMON NAMES

This species is commonly called kingfish, yellowtail kingfish, yellow-tailed kingfish, yellowtail, 'king' or 'kingy'. Colloquial titles include 'hoodlum' and 'bandit', while smaller specimens are often nicknamed 'rats' or 'north headers'.

Some confusion exists between the kingfish and two of its relatives, the amberjack and the samson fish.

An unrelated species, the cobia *(Rachycentron canadus)* is commonly called black kingfish; the mulloway *(Argyrosomus hololepidatus)* is sometimes known as kingfish or 'river king' in Western Australia.

DESCRIPTION

A powerful, pelagic fish characterised by its bright-yellow tail.

Kingfish need not be confused with the less common amberjack, as they are readily distinguished by body shape, colouration and fin ray or gill raker counts.

Kingfish colouration varies slightly between individuals, it is usually dark green or blue on the back, shading through metallic blue-green to silver, to white on the belly. A distinct gold or yellow stripe runs along each flank of a freshly caught fish.

The dorsal fin is dark green or blue, tinged with yellow. The tail varies between dusky-yellow and bright canary-gold. Other fins are off-white or yellowish.

SIZE

Large schools of 'rat' kings in the 1 to 4 kg range are often encountered, and school fish of 6 to 12 kg fish are relatively common, too. Big fish in the 15 to 30 kg range tend to form much smaller schools. The maximum growth potential of the fish is in excess of 60 kg.

DISTRIBUTION

Kingfish are found in the cool, temperate and sub-tropical waters of Australia, New Zealand and nearby islands, including Lord Howe and Norfolk. A similar or identical fish is found off the south-western coast of North America from about Los Angeles to the Baja Peninsula.

Kingfish mainly frequent the waters around offshore reefs, pinnacles and islands, inshore reef systems, large bays and even deep estuaries.

They prefer fairly clean water with a temperature of 18ºC or more, but will occasionally stray into cooler areas.

HABITS AND FEEDING

Kingfish are drawn to structures such as submarine mountains, drop-offs, marker buoys, wrecks, wharves and bridge pylons.

They normally school and feed between the seabed and mid-water, but will chase baitfish to the surface and break the water in the manner of tuna.

They prey on small to medium fish

Left: A 7 kg kingfish.
Below: The eastern side of
Jervis Bay, NSW is prime kingfish habitat.

such as slimy mackerel, garfish, mullet, pilchards, sauries and frigate mackerel, but are particularly fond of squid — which make up a large part of their diet.

Smaller kings will take prawns, crabs and other invertebrates, small fish, squid and octopi.

FISHING TECHNIQUES

The kingfish is a strong, exciting gamefish that strikes savagely at a wide range of lures, live baits and dead or cut-flesh offerings.

Perhaps the most successful way to take them is to present a live bait such as a

Big 'kings' are an extremely exciting catch; from a boat or the shore.

slimy mackerel or yellowtail (no relation to the kingfish) at the depth at which they are schooling. This may involve the use of a running sinker on the line.

Slow trolled live baits, large, deep-diving minnow lures and metal jigs worked vertically over the seabed are also readily taken by the fish.

Land-based anglers enjoy excellent sport with kingfish, especially when using high-speed metal lures, live baits, pilchards or garfish on ganged hooks.

When all else fails, kingfish are particularly susceptible to a bait of whole, fresh squid.

EATING QUALITIES

The flavour and taste of kingfish flesh is good to very good in smaller fish, but tends towards dryness in large specimens.

In some warmer areas kingfish are infested with parasites and suffer from a disease which causes the flesh to turn soft and milky when cooked.

All yellowtail kingfish should be bled and iced as soon as caught.

LEATHERJACKETS

Family: *Monacanthidae*

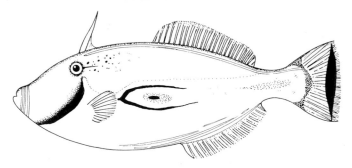

COMMON NAMES

There are at least 60 types of leatherjacket in Australian and New Zealand waters, 20 or more of which are sometimes taken by anglers, and at least 10 of them are often taken.

The more frequently captured species include: the rough leatherjacket *(Scobinichthys granulatus)*, six-spined leatherjacket *(Meuschenia freycineti)*, horseshoe leatherjacket *(M. hippocrepis)*, yellow-finned leatherjacket *(M. trachylepis)*, Chinaman leatherjacket *(Nelusetta ayraudi)*, mosaic leatherjacket *(Eubalichthys mosaicus)*, and the estuary–dwelling fan-bellied leatherjacket *(Monacanthus chinensis)*.

DESCRIPTION

This diverse and extensive group of relatively small, scaleless, rough-skinned fish have tiny mouths, beak-like teeth and a stout, serrated dorsal spine behind the head.

Identifying the different species is a difficult task, and not overly important to the average angler. The habits and feeding patterns of this large clan are much the same, and the majority of fishermen are happy to call them all 'leatherjackets', without attempting to nominate specific types.

Colouration varies enormously, from the brightly-hued and attractive six-spined, mosaic and horseshoe varieties to the more drab and camouflaged rough and fan-bellied leatherjackets.

SIZE

Most of the species of leatherjackets are quite small. The estuarine fan-bellied leatherjacket rarely tops 0.5 kg, while the six-spined and horseshoe varieties occasionally approach 2 kg, but are more common at half that weight. The 'giants' of the family are the mosaic leatherjacket and the Chinaman, both of which may exceed 3 kg. The Chinaman sometimes reaches 3.5 kg.

DISTRIBUTION

Leatherjackets of one type or another are found right around the coastline, although they tend to be replaced by the allied and rather similar trigger fishes (Family *Balistidae*) in tropical latitudes.

Apart from the fan-bellied leatherjacket, which is almost solely an estuarine fish, the leatherjackets are found in a wide variety of habitats ranging from deep, offshore reefs ' to inshore bays, rocky foreshores, harbours and estuaries.

They prefer areas with cover, provided by rocks, weed growth, wharf pilings and wrecks. They are slow-swimming creatures and rely on camouflage, concealment and their lockable dorsal spines to escape predation from larger fish.

Broken sand, gravel and rock strata

Leatherjackets come in a huge range of shapes, sizes and colours. The Chinaman leatherjacket Nelusetta ayraudi *(left) and the scaber leatherjacket* Parika scaber *(below) are good examples of the range of types of leatherjacket.*

with plenty of caves and a dense covering of kelp or seaweed, provide the ideal location for anglers seeking leatherjackets of all types.

HABITS AND FEEDING

Leatherjackets often form large, loose schools, though some species — particularly the offshore, reef-dwelling varieties — are more commonly found in small groups or alone.

They forage on marine algae, tube worms, small shellfish, shrimp, prawns, worms, ascidians, coral and the like. They are active scavengers, and are one of the first fish to move in on a dead or dying creature to feed on it.

Their sharp, fused teeth and powerful little jaws allow them to chomp through shells and tough skin. The beak-like jaws of large fish are capable of severing bones — and fingers!

Kids of all ages love catching leatherjackets!

FISHING TECHNIQUES

These fish can be taken on almost any type of tackle. Most are caught on light handlines or rod and reel outfits used to catch bream, flathead, inshore snapper and the like.

When present in good numbers, leatherjackets are quite easy to hook, especially if a relatively small hook is used in conjunction with soft baits such as peeled prawn, worms, yabbies, cunji, mussels, abalone gut or strips of fish flesh. Pieces of squid also make an excellent bait.

Long-shanked hooks should be used to prevent bite-offs, but even then a determined fish will snip through the line, or even sever the hook shank itself. This usually happens while the fish are being lifted from the water, so a landing net is good insurance.

Leatherjackets bite softly and their struggle, once hooked, could hardly be described as exciting, but they more than make up for any sporting deficiencies when cleaned, skinned and cooked.

EATING QUALITIES

All of the mentioned leatherjacket species have white, sweet and slightly moist flesh and are very good to excellent food-fish. They are easily prepared. Slice off the head, pull it and the insides away in one movement, and peel off the sandpaper-like skin.

There have been occasional reports of mild poisoning after eating leatherjackets, particularly the Chinaman 'jacket'. This appears to be caused by the diet of the fish. If you have made a large catch of Chinaman leatherjackets, just cook and eat small portions of several different fish. If any nausea or dizziness is experienced, the remainder of the catch should be thrown away. It must be stressed that this is rare.

LONG TOM

Family: *Belonidae*

COMMON NAMES

This group of very similar fish, all members of the family *Belonidae*, are usually called long tom or alligator gar or, more rarely, needlefish.

Individual family members are stout long tom *(Tylosurus gavialoides)*, slender long tom *(Strongylura leiura)*, crocodilian long tom *(Tylosurus crocodilus)* and barred long tom *(Ablennes hians)*.

DESCRIPTION

These long, slender fish with elongated jaws armed with fine, sharp teeth are similar in appearance to garfish, but are distinguishable by their two long jaws, and prominent teeth. Longtom grow much larger than garfish, which have a single lower-jaw beak.

Longtom colouration varies between species, and ranges from green through blue to steely-black on the back. Most are bright, metallic silver on the flanks and belly. Some species are barred or marked with dark 'thumbprints' along the flanks.

Interestingly, the bones of most longtom are blue-green, like those of some wrasse and parrotfish.

SIZE

Depending on the species, longtom may be long and slender or shorter and stouter. Some grow to 1.7 metres in length and may weigh more than 5 kg, though most measure a metre or less and weigh less than 2 kg.

DISTRIBUTION

Long tom are widespread through the tropical, sub-tropical and warm, temperate seas of the world.

A species of long tom is found only in tropical freshwater, although it is not particularly common.

Long tom will enter estuaries, particularly on a rising tide, although they prefer fairly clear, warm water.

Travelling with the ocean currents, long tom sometimes migrate far down the coast and are taken seasonally around Newcastle, Sydney, and even Jervis Bay in southern New South Wales.

HABITS AND FEEDING

Long tom are mainly surface-hunting predators of inshore tropical and sub-tropical seas. They hunt schools of baitfish over sand or seagrass beds. Larger specimens haunt the passes and channels between coral reefs.

Some species form schools, while others feed in small groups, or alone.

Long tom of all species are characterised by their slender, silvery bodies and elongated jaws filled with fine, sharp teeth.

FISHING TECHNIQUES

Long tom are rarely fished for specifically, and are usually taken on cast baits or lures intended for other tropical and subtropical species.

Because of their long, tooth-filled jaws, they are difficult to hook, especially on lures, which they often chase and strike at enthusiastically.

Baits of fish strip, squid, pink nippers (yabbies) or prawns used on sharp, long-shanked hooks or a ganged flight of hooks provide the best chance of a hookup.

Lures dressed with wool or a fibre called FisHair give better results, as the long tom's teeth become tangled in the material.

Once hooked long tom may make spectacular leaps and fast dashes, but they tire quickly, even on light line.

EATING QUALITIES

Long tom are reasonable table fare, though there is little flesh on the more lightly-built species.

They make good to very good baits. Smaller ones may be used alive, and are popular among land-based anglers targeting big Spanish mackerel and sailfish from the ocean rocks of Western Australia.

LUDERICK

Girella tricuspidata

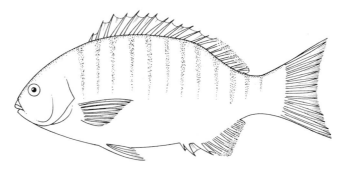

COMMON NAMES

This fish is rarely called by its 'official' name anywhere outside Victoria. In New South Wales and southern Queensland, where most are caught, it is known as blackfish, 'nigger' or 'darky'. Big, sea-going luderick are sometimes nicknamed 'bronzies', while on Queensland's Gold and Sunshine Coasts the species is often erroneously referred to as black bream.

In New Zealand, the luderick is known by its Maori name: parore. The luderick's closest relatives are the black drummer or rock blackfish *(G. elevata)* and the zebra fish *(G. zebra)* and larger luderick are sometimes confused with them.

A closely allied species, the bluefish *(G. cyanea)* was once quite common along the New South Wales and Victorian coasts, but is now so rare as to be a novelty. They are still fairly abundant in waters around Lord Howe Island and New Zealand. The bluefish grows larger than the luderick and is a superb table fish.

DESCRIPTION

A small to medium-sized omnivorous fish of the ocean and estuaries, characterised by a small, square mouth and comb-like teeth.

The luderick's colour varies with its habitat. Estuary fish are usually a dark to purplish-brown, overlaid by nine or more darker vertical stripes. The belly is creamy.

Ocean fish take on a brassy or bronze hue over the purple-brown and may also be a light blue-grey which shows up the stripes clearly.

The luderick's fins, especially the tail, are darker than its body.

SIZE

Most luderick taken by anglers weigh between 0.4 and 1.2 kg. A rare specimen may reach about 3 kg. The fish have the potential to exceed 4 kg.

DISTRIBUTION

Luderick are found around the south-eastern seaboard of Australia from about Fraser Island or Maryborough in Queensland to western Victoria and Tasmania, and are also reasonably prolific in New Zealand waters, particularly around the North Island.

They range into tidal rivers and even venture a little way into freshwater, but their most favoured haunts are the areas from the brackish headwaters, down through the estuaries and out along the rocky foreshores of the open ocean.

Luderick are rarely found further than 100 metres from shore, and then only if there are shallow reefs and bomboras in the area.

HABITS AND FEEDING

Luderick are a schooling species and

Left: A fine specimen of luderick or blackfish.
Below: Luderick specialists fishing from a low,
wave-washed rock ledge with float tackle and
weed baits.

rarely travel in groups of less than 10 or a dozen individuals. The shoals are often much larger.

Largely vegetarian for much of the year, luderick frequent areas with good growths of weed and algae. Their favourite foods are the filamentous, green, streamer weeds and the luxuriant 'cabbage' weed *(Ulva lactuca)* of the ocean rocks, headlands and breakwalls.

During spring, they appear to abandon their vegetarian habits and feed on marine worms and crustaceans such as prawns, shrimp and yabbies or nippers.

FISHING TECHNIQUES

'Niggering' is the traditional and time-proven method for taking these fish. A centrepin reel, long, fine rod and stemmed float are used to suspend a bait of greenweed or cabbage between 1 and 5 metres beneath the surface.

The line to the hook should be light (1.2 to 3 kg breaking strain), the hook small and sharp and the float weighted so that the softest bite will sink it.

'Niggering' with long rods and floats is almost entirely confined to the coast of New South Wales; a few devotees operate in

Luderick are very popular with east coast rock and estuary anglers.

southern Queensland and the Gippsland Lakes area of north eastern Victoria.

Blackfish are also taken on baits of peeled prawn, sand , squirt or bloodworm, cunji, yabbies (nippers) or hermit crabs. In most areas luderick take these baits best in late winter and spring.

Whatever the chosen fishing method, the gear should be light, and hooks small. Berleying is also a big help.

Luderick or 'niggers' bite best where there is a tidal run or wave action. Under cover of darkness or in the foam generated by breaking seas, they will sometimes school and feed in water less than a metre deep.

EATING QUALITIES

Luderick are regarded as a fair to good eating fish, but should be bled and cleaned promptly for best results.

Those caught around the ocean rocks taste better than those taken 'inside'.

All luderick should be filleted and skinned to help remove the slight taste of weed sometimes present in their flesh.

MACKEREL, SCHOOL & SPOTTED

Scomberomus munroi, Scomberomus queenslandicus,
Scomberomus niphonia

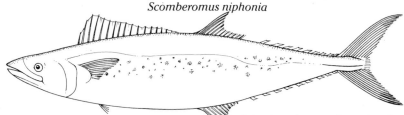

COMMON NAMES

These similar species of small to medium–sized relatives of the Spanish mackerel *(S. commerson)* are known by a variety of names including: spotted mackerel, school mackerel, spotted Spanish mackerel, Queensland school mackerel, Japanese spotted mackerel, 'schooly', 'spotty' and snook.

DESCIRPTION

These closely related, medium-sized members of the mackerel family *(Scombridae)* have a similar body shape to the Spanish mackerel, but are characterised by spots or small blotches instead of the vertical bars of their relation.

Colouration is usually purplish-blue to blue-green on the back, silver on the belly and overlaid with spots. *S. munroi* has four irregular bands of quite distinct spots, while *S. queenslandicus* has fewer, larger but less distinct spots or blotches, which are most noticeable in the area behind the pectoral fin.

SIZE

Spotted and school mackerel are mostly taken at weights ranging from 1.5 to 4 kg, although 6 kg specimens are not unknown, and *S. munroi* may very rarely top 10 kg.

DISTRIBUTION

Spotted and school mackerel are pelagic fish of tropical and sub-tropical inshore areas, which travel well south with summer and autumn currents. They enter bays, harbours and, at times, estuaries.

School and spotted mackerel prefer similar water conditions to Spanish mackerel, but will sometimes tolerate greater levels of turbidity or muddiness.

HABITS AND FEEDING

School mackerel are normally found over broken reef grounds within a few kilometres of shore. They do the bulk of their feeding between mid-water and the surface, preying on small fish and squid.

As their name implies, these fish often form large, dense schools, though bigger ones may travel singly or in small groups.

FISHING TECHNIQUES

School and spotted mackerel respond to most of the techniques which take Spanish mackerel and are often landed incidentally by anglers in pursuit of that species.

Using slightly smaller baits and lures will usually result in more catches.

In northern New South Wales — where spotted mackerel are sometimes prolific in autumn — drifted baits of gang-hooked pilchards, garfish, mullet or small tailor are favourites. They work well further north, too.

Tackle for spotted and school mackerel can range from a handline to a medium-weight casting or spinning outfit. Four to 8 kg breaking strain line will easily handle the very biggest run of school mackerel.

EATING QUALITIES

The school and spotted mackerels are delicious table fish, held in high regard wherever they are caught.

*A good-sized spotted mackerel taken off
Townsville in north Queensland.*

MACKEREL, SHARK

Grammatorcynus bicarinatus

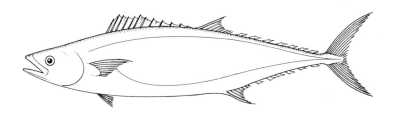

COMMON NAMES

The shark mackerel or 'sharky' is also known as the scaly mackerel, salmon mackerel and large-scaled tuna.

DESCRIPTION

The 'sharky' or 'scaly' is a mackerel-like fish whose position on the taxonomic tree is partway between the true *Scombridae* mackerels, such as the Spanish mackerel, and the various tunas. Shark mackerel are easily identified by their unusual double lateral lines.

Typical colouration is dark green to grey-green on the back, yellowish-green on the flanks, and pale on the belly, often overlaid with dark spots, blotches and vague bars.

SIZE

Most shark mackerel taken by anglers weigh between 3 and 7 kg, with the odd specimen approaching 10 kg.

DISTRIBUTION

A fish of northern, tropical seas, the shark mackerel occasionally rides the warm summer and autumn currents as far south as northern New South Wales and Perth.

It prefers habitats similar to those of the Spanish and spotted or school mackerels, although it is a little less nomadic. This fish is seasonally abundant along the ocean rocks in northern West Australia, and is very popular with land-based anglers.

HABITS AND FEEDING

The shark mackerel is both a schooling and a solitary predator, hunting small pelagic and reef fish along coral drop-offs and around islands, bomboras and headlands.

FISHING TECHNIQUES

All the techniques described for catching Spanish and school mackerel will catch shark mackerel. Lures, particularly trolled minnows and rapidly-retrieved jigs or 'lead slugs' are particularly effective.

Because of the shark mackerel's smaller size, lighter tackle than that used to catch Spanish mackerel may be used. Some superb 'sharkies' have been taken on fly and ultra-light spin tackle

EATING QUALITIES

Despite the strong, shark-like odour it gives off while being cleaned, shark mackerel flesh is white and tasty, though a little inferior to that of the Spanish mackerel.

Shark mackerel are easily distinguished by their double lateral line system. Most exhibit spots on the belly and lower flanks.

MACKEREL, SLIMY

Scomber australicus

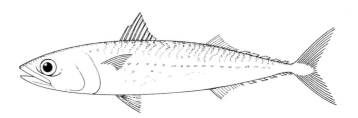

COMMON NAMES

Called blue mackerel in southern states and slimy mackerel or 'slimy' in the east, this fish is also known as the common or Pacific mackerel.

It belongs to a worldwide family of small, but commercially important, pelagics.

DESCRIPTION

The slimy mackerel is a small, tuna-like fish of the family *Scombridae* characterised by a nearly cylindrical body, narrow tail wrist, finlets and deeply-veed tail.

Colouration is dark bluish-silver to blue green when alive, turning silver-green after death. The base colour is overlaid with very dark blue or green wavy lines, dots and dashes. The belly is bright silver to silvery-white.

The fins are lighter, except for the tail, which is dusky, sometimes with a tinge of yellow.

Fish from offshore waters are more blue than green.

SIZE

Most slimy mackerel caught by anglers measure 20 to 35 cm and weigh from 0.2 to 0.7 kg, although schools of 0.5 to 1 kg fish sometimes move in to inshore areas and rare specimens may top 1.5 kg and even approach 2 kg.

DISTRIBUTION

Slimy mackerel are found right around the southern half of the continent, in bays, harbours and large estuaries, and also far offshore in deep water near the continental shelf.

The juveniles and young adults generally frequent inshore grounds, while the large adults form dense schools over reefs in 40 to 200 metres of water.

Reasonably clean water between 5 and 15 metres in depth with a broken bottom of sand, rock and kelp, make ideal inshore conditions for them. Krill, anchovy or other tiny baitfish attract them.

HABITS AND FEEDING

Slimy mackerel are a schooling species. They form vast, dense shoals in deep, offshore waters, and smaller ones inshore and in estuarine waters. Individual fish are rarely found far from the school.

They feed on plankton, small baitfish such as anchovy, sprat, whitebait and young pilchards, krill (oceanic shrimp or 'whale food'), small squid and small organisms such as pelagic crabs.

FISHING TECHIQUES

The hard-fighting little fish is usually taken on lightly-weighted or unweighted baits of fish flesh strip, or peeled prawn on a small hook. Long–shanked hooks make extraction easier.

Slimy mackerel are a popular bait species. Those from inshore waters are greener in overall appearance than the very blue examples from the open ocean.

They respond well to a berley trail of soaked bread and fish scraps mixed with a little tuna oil. Once 'berleyed up', mackerel will bite ferociously and can be taken on small lures, white–painted barrel sinkers and even alfoil-wrapped hooks.

Commercial multi-jig bait rigs from Asia are ideal for catching slimy mackerel. Any light tackle may be employed. Many jetty and boat anglers prefer a handline of 2 to 4 kg breaking strain nylon. A single-handed rod, light threadline reel and 3 kg line can be even better as it allows baits to be cast further out and slowly retrieved — a technique which can be particularly productive.

EATING QUALITIES

Although dark–fleshed and oily, the slimy mackerel has a good flavour and makes an excellent smoked fish.

Most are used as bait and are superb when used alive for large predators such as kingfish and tuna. They can be rather hard to keep in live bait containers as they need aeration and space. Mackerel also make fine dead baits, either whole or cut into strips.

MACKEREL, SPANISH

Scomberomorus commerson

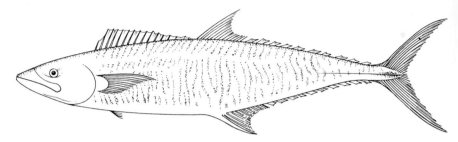

COMMON NAMES

The narrow-barred Spanish mackerel is commonly known as Spanish mackerel or 'Spaniard', 'narrow-bar' or 'macko'. In some parts of the world the species is known as 'tanguigue'; in Fiji the fish is called 'walu'.

A very closely related fish, the broad-barred Spanish or grey mackerel *(S. semifasciatum)*, often confused with the narrow-barred Spanish, is less common. It is smaller, a little deeper in the body, and has higher, more rounded second dorsal and anal fins.

DESCRIPTION

An elongate fish with a pointed nose and a row of sharp teeth in each jaw. The tail is deeply forked and there are a number of small finlets behind the second dorsal and the anal fins.

The colouration is variable; usually green to dark greeny-blue on the back, and silver on the flanks, with shimmers of purple and violet when fresh. The flanks are overlaid with dark, wavy vertical bars of grey, dark green or purple. The number of bars increases with the size of the fish.

The colour fades to steely-grey or blue after death, although the bars may still be evident.

SIZE

Spanish mackerel commonly weigh from 2 to 15 kg and tend to school in groups of similar-sized fish. Mackerel over 20 kg make prized catches. Isolated specimens from 40 to 50 kg are occasionally reported, and the growth potential of the species may be close to 60 kg.

DISTRIBUTION

The Spanish mackerel is a tropical Indo-Pacific species. Although mainly found in tropical seas, they range as far south as Port Macquarie on the east coast and Rottnest Island in Western Australia.

It is mainly an open ocean and inshore fish found over and around reefs inside the continental shelf. It prefers relatively clean, blue or green water with a temperature of between 21⁰C and 29⁰C.

Juveniles and even adults occasionally enter bays, harbours and estuaries.

Large mackerel frequent channels, passages and run-throughs among the deeper coral reefs. They also school near islands, cays and around deeper rock headlands, long breakwalls and jetties.

Larger ones form small schools and patrol reef edges and drop-offs. The very biggest fish may become solitary and dominate a reef-pass or island corner, much in the manner of a large barracuda.

Normal sized ones form moderately large schools and undertake seasonal migrations, south through the tropics in winter and into more temperate waters in summer. However, there also appear to be year-round 'resident' mackerel present in northern waters.

Left: A much larger than average Spanish mackerel weighing in excess of 25 kg.
Below: Spanish mackerel in the 4 to 12 kg range are more common in most areas.

Left: A 15 kg Spanish mackerel or 'Spaniard' taken on medium weight trolling tackle. The Spanish mackerel's teeth are razor sharp and capable of inflicting serious injuries on the unwary.
Right: Gaffing with pilchard baits off north Queensland. The stripes or bars of the 'Spaniard' are particularly distinct while the fish is alive.

HABITS AND FEEDING

The Spanish mackerel is an active, pelagic predator and is attracted by concentrations of baitfish such as gar, mullet, small tuna and 'banana fish' or fusiliers. It will also take squid. Juvenile 'Spaniards' living close to shore may also prey on prawns and other crustacea.

FISHING TECHNIQUES

The fast-running and exciting Spanish mackerel fall to trolled or drifted live baits, whole dead fish and fish strips. They will also take squid.

Baits of dead garfish, mullet, tailor or wolf herring, rigged to 'swim' in a natural manner when trolled behind a boat at 3 to 6 knots, are particularly effective.

Lures such as Konahead-style skirted trolling heads, feather jigs, spoons and minnows — both bibbed and bibless — also account for excellent catches of Spanish mackerel. From the shore, cast and re- trieved metal lures, minnows or pilchards and garfish on ganged hooks all work well.

'Spaniards' have a habit of slashing and mutilating live or large dead baits without hooking up. Big, sharp hooks, ganged flights, trebles and 'stingers' rigged in the bait all help to secure a hold in the toothy jaws.

Land-based specialist anglers, particu- larly on the west coast, often use air or gas- filled balloons to carry their rigged baits

well out into the currents and deep, blue water where the mackerel are more prolific.

They often use deep-spooled sidecast reels, or large overheads filled with up to a kilometre of 12 to 20 kg line and matched to a heavy actioned 3 or 3.5 metre rod, when ballooning or drifting rigged baits from rocks, beaches and piers.

Shore–based anglers may spin for mackerel with lures or rigged baits using a 2.8 to 3.5 metre casting rod, large thread- line or medium overhead reel and 8 to 15 kg breaking strain line.

Tackle for catching Spanish mackerel runs the full gamut from sash cord or nylon rope trolling lines to single-handed bait- caster or spin outfits.

A preferred outfit for trolling is a medium overhead reel and 2 metre fast tapered rod with line in the 8 to 15 kg breaking strain range.

The same rig can be used to cast baits or lures from a boat or shore location fronted with deep water, although some anglers choose a big threadline (spinning) reel for this purpose.

EATING QUALITIES

The popular Spanish mackerel is a delicious, white — fleshed table fish. Specimens over about 10 kg are regarded as a ciguatera toxin poisoning risk in certain areas. Always seek local advice before eating large mackerel.

MANGROVE JACK

Lutjanus argentimaculatus

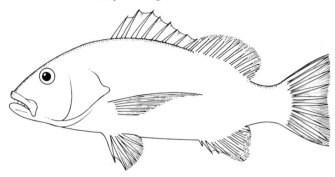

COMMON NAMES

The mangrove jack or 'jack' is also called red bream or red chopper in some areas and, less commonly, dog bream or red perch.

Mangrove jack are occasionally confused with two similar and closely related fish: the often poisonous red bass *(L. bohar)* and the fingermark bream *(L. johnii)*.

DESCRIPTION

This deep-bodied, medium-sized member of the family *Lutjanidae* is characterised by large eyes, powerful jaws and strong, canine teeth.

The mangrove jack varies from olive-green through grey to a rusty or ochre-red. The base colour is usually overlaid with lighter vertical stripes, but these are not always evident. Another variation is a dark centre to each scale.

Juvenile 'jacks' are particularly striking. The vertical bands are pronounced and they have fine, electric-blue lines around their eyes and a flush of crimson and yellow in their white-tipped ventral fins.

Mangrove jack lack the dark blotch on each flank below the second dorsal fin which characterises the fingermark bream.

The mangrove jack can easily be distinguished from the closely-allied red bass. The red bass has deep olfactory pits or grooves ahead of its eyes and an overall reddish-hue which is usually much brighter

than that of the jacks. Red bass tend to remain offshore, while only the largest jacks move out to the reefs.

SIZE

Most jacks caught on hook and line weigh from 0.4 to 2 kg, although 2.5 to 4 kg fish are reasonably abundant in more remote areas. Exceptional fish weighing up to 12 kg mainly come from offshore reefs.

DISTRIBUTION

Mangrove jacks are found from about the Hawkesbury River just north of Sydney, right around the tropical north of the country to Shark Bay in Western Australia, but are far from common at the extreme southern end of their range.

'Jacks' are common in Niugini and Irian Jaya. Identical or very closely related species are found in South East Asia, the Pacific Islands and Central America.

Mangrove jacks range from the freshwater, mountain feeder-streams of large rivers, down through the tidal reaches and out to headlands and reefs.

Large adult 'jacks' may move several kilometres offshore to take up residence on reefs or wrecks.

HABITS AND FEEDING

They feed mainly on small fish, prawns, crabs, shrimp and octopi.

An active and aggressive predator

Left: A lovely lure-caught mangrove jack.
Below: Two anglers fishing a stretch of prime
'jack' water in the Northern Territory.

capable of taking surprisingly large prey, 'jacks' seek a holding point close to the main channel where the current is likely to bring food to them.

Whatever their size and location, 'jacks' are rarely found far from cover, be it a sunken tree, jumble of rocks, or wall of mangrove roots.

FISHING TECHNIQUES

The mangrove jack is one of the most popular and sought after tropical estuarine species.

Most are taken on live or dead baits fished close to cover, or on lures — especially minnow-style wobblers — cast and retrieved from a boat or river bank. A few are taken on trolled lures, if the boat can be kept close to the bankside or snags.

They are powerful, no-holds-barred battlers that will dive back into the snags and cut a line through if given the slightest chance. Their strike is sudden and hard, often taking the angler by surprise.

Perhaps the most effective tactic of all is the use of a small, live mullet or herring cast close to cover, and either suspended by a float or lightly weighted, depending on the structure of the riverbed.

EATING QUALITIES

The mangrove jack is a delicious, sweet-fleshed fish but very large specimens tend to be dry. If there is any doubt about distinguishing mangrove jacks from red bass (such as with large, reef-caught fish) the fish should **not** be consumed, as the red bass is a regular carrier of the toxin ciguatera, which can cause illness and death.

MARLIN, BLACK

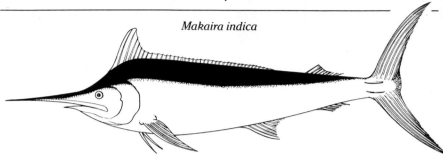

Makaira indica

COMMON NAMES

The black marlin is sometimes confused with other marlin, particularly the blue. This is most likely when the fish is young, before the pectoral fins become rigid.

In the past, juvenile black marlin were often thought to be a separate species. The so-called 'd'Ombrain's marlin' is an example of this incorrect identification in Australasian waters.

DESCRIPTION

The 'black' is a heavy–shouldered, solidly-built marlin with a relatively short, stout bill and low dorsal fin. The fish is characterised by its fixed, aerofoil-shaped pectorals, though these fins are not necessarily fixed in fish under about 50 kg in weight.

Typical black marlin colouration is gunmetal - blue to black on the back, changing suddenly to silver-blue on the flanks and silvery-white on the belly. There can be pale lavender vertical stripes on the flanks, though these fade soon after death. A coppery flush on the gill plates and behind the pectoral fins is common on large, live fish. The eyes are pale blue around a black pupil.

The fins are dark, though in juveniles the dorsal may be spotted and blotched with powder-blue to azure.

SIZE

Australasian black marlin run from tiny juveniles weighing less than 10 kg to world record fish in excess of 500 kg.

The area just outside the Great Barrier Reef, between Townsville and Lizard Island in far north Queensland, is renowned as the spawning site of some of the world's biggest black marlin. Here, in September, October and November each year, hundreds of fish in the 150 to 500 kg-plus range gather. Further south, off southern Queensland and New South Wales, the fish mainly weigh from 25 to 120 kg. In northern Western Australia somewhat larger ones from 80 to 200 kg are taken, while in New Zealand the relatively few blacks caught often weigh more than 200 kg.

DISTRIBUTION

Black marlin are a wide-ranging fish of the Pacific and Indian Oceans, turning up in tropical, sub-tropical, temperate and, on rare occasions, cool waters.

They prefer the open ocean but often travel quite close to the coast of Australia which has a narrow continental shelf. Many small black marlin have been landed by rock fishermen in southern New South Wales.

In Australasian waters, black marlin are rarely seen south of Mallacoota in Victoria, Albany in Western Australia, or Auckland in New Zealand.

The fish prefers water temperatures in the 20^0 to 30^0C range.

HABITS AND FEEDING

Black marlin tend to travel and hunt in the surface and mid-water layers, 'surfing' or 'sailing' downwind and downcurrent, riding the waves and current with minimal

Left: Black marlin are characterised by their relatively heavy build, stout bill, low dorsal fin and rigid, aerofoil-shaped pectoral fins. However, it must be noted that these pectoral or side fins do not lock into place completely until the fish reaches a weight of 30 to 40 kg.

Below: a jumping black marlin. The bait — a whole striped tuna or skipjack — can be seen swinging on the trace behind the marlin's body.

effort and covering many thousands of kilometres. Marlin tagged off Cairns in north Queensland have been recovered around Fiji, Tahiti and New Zealand.

Ideal conditions for black marlin are relatively deep water not too far from a continental shelf drop-off, warm, blue currents and a good supply of small tuna, flying fish, sauris, scad and squid.

Small black marlin occasionally swim in packs or loose schools; outside the spawning season adult fish are mostly loners.

FISHING TECHNIQUES

Because of their large size and strength, black marlin demand quality tackle kept in good repair.

Trolling with lures, trolling with baits either live or dead, and fishing at anchor or from a drifting boat with baits, live or dead,

Black marlin are exciting adversaries, whether taken from a large vessel or a small runabout.

account for over 90% of the black marlin taken in our waters.

The best lures are Konahead-style skirted heads that run freely on the trace. A lure of this pattern with a flat or slightly angled head, called a 'pusher', trolled at between 7 and 12 knots behind a moving boat, is a proven method of attracting marlin.

Suitable live and dead baits range from 15 centimetre yellowtail or mullet, through 3 kg striped tuna to whole 15 kg Spanish mackerel, depending on the location, the strength of tackle, and the ambitions of the angler.

As a rule of thumb, marlin can swallow prey weighing approximately 10% of their body weight, so big fish will easily take large offerings.

Rigging baits for trolling — especially dead baits, which are pulled fairly quickly — is an acquired skill. Many fine marlin have been taken on baits of live tuna, bonito, salmon or kingfish hooked through the top jaw and trolled at walking pace near a current line or patch of bait.

In lure fishing, the strike is instantaneous, as the drag is left set and the hook either punches home or misses in the instant of the strike. However, if taken on a bait, marlin should be allowed to turn and run with the bait against minimal resistance for anything between one and 30 seconds before being 'hit'

EATING QUALITIES

Black marlin of all sizes are fine eating fish, though high mercury content of the flesh of larger fish precludes them from the commercial market.

The meat is white and firm, if a little dry, dryness increasing with the size of the fish.

Black marlin is well suited to being smoked and it retains its quality well when frozen.

MARLIN, BLUE

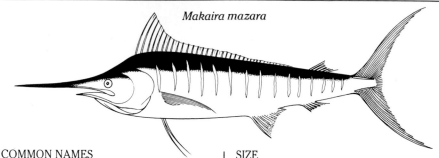

Makaira mazara

COMMON NAMES

The Indo Pacific blue marlin is also known as the Pacific blue marlin or simply, marlin. Anglers nickname it 'beakie' or 'beak'.

Until recent years the scientific name was *Makaira nigricans*, but this has now been changed to *M. mazara*.

Blue marlin are similar in appearance to black marlin, but may be distinguished in several ways.

DESCRIPTION

The blue marlin is a little less heavily built than the black and longer for a given weight.

The 'blue's' bill or spear is longer than that of the 'black' but shorter than the striped marlin's. The blue marlin's dorsal fin is higher than that of the 'black', but not as high as that of the striped marlin.

Finally, the blue marlin's pectoral fins are not rigid; and fold back easily.

Blue marlin are not as common in our waters as 'blacks', but are of a relatively high average weight. Juvenile blue marlin are practically unknown in Australasian waters.

Blue marlin colouration is variable, ranging from electric-blue to dark blue on the back, silver to silvery-white on the belly, sometimes with a coppery flush along the flanks. Blue marlin almost always display distinct vertical bars of lavender or powder-blue on the flanks, but these fade after death, unlike those of the striped marlin.

The blue marlin's eye has a bright blue iris around a relatively large, black pupil.

SIZE

Indo Pacific blue marlin grow as large as black marlin and possibly larger. Rare giants of 700 kg and more have been recorded and it seems likely that the maximum growth potential of this fish is close to 1000 kg!

In Australasian waters, most blue marlin taken on rod and reel weigh in at between 100 and 350 kg, but the occasional 400 kg-plus specimen is hooked.

DISTRIBUTION

The Indo-Pacfic blue marlin ranges widely through the tropical, sub-tropical, temperate and — on rare occasions — cool waters of the Pacific and Indian oceans. A near-identical fish found in the Atlantic is designated 'Atlantic blue marlin' for record-keeping purposes.

In Australasian waters, blue marlin can turn up almost anywhere in warm, blue currents, but is most common along the east coast between the grounds wide of Moreton Bay and the north east continental shelf of Tasmania, and off the west coast from Exmouth to a little south of Rottnest Island. Some fine specimens are also taken off New Zealand's north east coast, particularly out from the Bay of Islands.

In our waters these fish rarely come into water shallower than 100 metres and are more common in the 150 to 300 metre depth band along the continental shelf.

HABITS AND FEEDING

The blue marlin is a nomadic predator which feeds mainly between the surface

Blue marlin have relatively high dorsal fins, large anal fins and flat, flexible pectorals or side fins. Their bills are longer and more slender than those of black marlin.

and mid water, hunting fish of all sizes from tiny, semi-planktonic species to large tuna and dolphin fish. It will also take squid when these are available and has even been reported as feeding on penguins!

Adult blue marlin are commonly found in pairs.

FISHING TECHNIQUES

Because of their size and fighting ability blue marlin demand the use of strong tackle.

Trolling with lures or baits (either live or dead), and fishing at anchor or from a drifting boat with baits, alive or dead, account for over 90% of the blue marlin taken in Australasian waters.

The best lures are Konahead-style skirted heads or pushers, which run freely on the trace, above one or two large, sharp hooks.

Live and dead baits range from 15 centimetre yellowtail or mullet, through 3 kg striped tuna to whole 10 or 12 kg yellowfin tuna, depending on the fishing location and the strength of tackle being used.

As with black marlin, 'blues' can swallow prey weighing approximately 10% of their own body weight. Blue marlin in Hawaii have been landed with freshly eaten 30 to 50 kg tuna in their gullets.

Many fine blue marlin have been taken on live tuna, bonito, salmon or kingfish, although in our waters more 'blues' seem to be hooked on lures than on baits.

EATING QUALITIES

Blue marlin are rated as highly as 'blacks' when prepared for the table, though high mercury and other heavy metal concentrations in the flesh preclude the fish from the commercial market in most Australian states.

Blue marlin meat is well suited to being smoked.

MARLIN, STRIPED

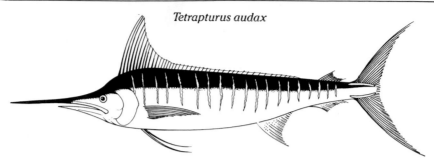

Tetrapturus audax

COMMON NAMES

The striped marlin or 'stripey', along with the other two Australasian marlin species described in this book, is also known colloquially as 'beakie' or 'beak'.

Striped marlin are readily confused with blue marlin, though they may be positively identified on a number of points, as described below.

DESCRIPTION

The striped marlin is the most lightly built and streamlined of all the marlin found in our waters. It is characterised by its long, fine bill, flat, flexible pectoral fins and very high dorsal fin. The dorsal is higher than the body depth through the fish's shoulder.

Live or fresh-dead striped marlin are bright blue to gunmetal-blue or mauve on the back, silvery-blue on the flanks, and silvery-white on the belly. A dozen to 14 clearly defined vertical bars of bright powder-blue are clearly evident on the flanks. These bars darken then fade after death, but are still visible several hours later.

SIZE

The striped marlin is the 'baby' of the three marlin species found in our waters, although it is capable of reaching 200 kg in weight on rare occasions, especially in New Zealand waters, the home of the world's biggest 'stripeys'.

In Australian waters, striped marlin mainly weigh between 50 and 120 kg, with the prolific grounds off Brisbane's Moreton Bay producing the odd 150 kg fish.

DISTRIBUTION

Striped marlin are found throughout the sub-tropical, temperate and cool waters of the Pacific and Indian Oceans, and occasionally in tropical latitudes.

Striped marlin prefer clean, green or blue water and temperatures of 18⁰ to 25⁰C, although they will tolerate cooler conditions than will the other two marlin species described.

In Australasian waters, striped marlin are most prolific around the North Island of New Zealand, off the east coast of Australia from southern Queensland to Tasmania and off the west coast from Exmouth to Albany. They seem to be more prolific in the east than the west.

Striped marlin were probably once the most prolific billfish in our waters, but intensive fishing by Asian long-lining and drift-netting fleets has dramatically reduced the stocks of these beautiful fish.

HABITS AND FEEDING

'Stripeys' are nomadic predators which hunt mainly in the surface layers of the ocean, though they descend to considerable depths in search of food, particularly squid.

Striped marlin occasionally form 'packs' of between three or four and 50 adults, though such aggregations are much less common than they were 20 or 30 years ago.

Left: The characteristically tall dorsal fin of this striped marlin has been split by the line or trace during the fight. Note that the stripes are still evident well after capture.
Below: This 60 kg striped marlin is being 'swum' by the bill prior to live release. Striped marlin have the longest and most slender bills or 'spears' of all the marlin in our waters, as well as the highest dorsal fins.

Striped marlin feed on a wide range of small to medium size fish and squid. In New Zealand they prey heavily on schools of kahawai (Australian salmon) and trevally.

FISHING TECHNIQUES

All the techniques described for taking black and blue marlin in Australasian waters will take 'stripeys', through an increased emphasis on trolling with small to medium–sized live and dead baits and lures is advisable.

Some very large striped marlin are taken on drifted live and dead baits, even those rigged on relatively heavy wire traces for shark fishing.

As with all marlin and sailfish, the 'stripey's' hard, bony mouth and sandpapery bill demand the use of very sharp hooks and scuff-resistant traces of heavy nylon or wire.

EATING QUALITIES

The flesh is considerably darker and more strongly flavoured than that of either the black or the blue marlin, although it is quite palatable. The Japanese rate the 'stripey' most highly of all the marlin.

Striped marlin flesh is well suited to being smoked.

MORWONG, SILVER

Nemadactylus douglasii

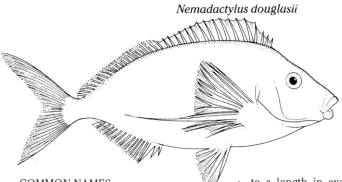

COMMON NAMES

The silver morwong is commonly known as the blue morwong, although this name can cause confusion with a larger, brilliant-blue morwong of southern waters, the queen snapper *(N. valenciennesi)*.

Other names are rubberlip morwong, 'mowie' and sea bream. The latter one is mainly used by fish shops and restaurants.

A closely related but smaller fish, the jackass morwong *(N. macropterus)*, is a very common trawl-catch in southern waters and is taken regularly by anglers fishing deep water.

DESCRIPTION

The silver or rubberlip morwong is a deep-bodied fish with a smaller mouth and large, fleshy lips. As with all the morwongs, several rays in each pectoral or side fin extend into long 'fingers'.

The fish's colour ranges from smoky-blue through grey to silver or silvery-blue, though this species is never as brightly hued as the strikingly-blue queen snapper *(N. valenciennesi)*.

The smaller jackass morwong *(N. macropterus)* is similar in colour to the silver morwong, but has a distinct black or dark grey bar or saddle over the back of the head, descending to the upper end of the gill slit on each side.

SIZE

The silver or rubberlip morwong grows to a length in excess of 80 cm and may weigh more than 6 kg, although any specimen over 4 kg is exceptional. The typical size range of line caught 'mowies' is 0.9 to 2.5 kg, although in Tasmania many smaller morwong in the 0.4 to 1 kg range are taken.

The jackass morwong, a much smaller fish, averages 0.4 to 0.9 kg in weight and rarely tops 1.5 kg.

DISTRIBUTION

The silver 'mowie' is a fish of temperate and cool southern seas, ranging from about southern Queensland to eastern Victoria and north-eastern Tasmania.

Rubberlip morwong prefer deep reefs and gravel beds, but are often found in shallower water than the jackass morwong.

Most 'mowies' are caught over broken rock, gravel and sand or mud, and are frequently taken in conjunction with snapper.

HABITS AND FEEDING

Morwong are schooling fish. The jackass, in particular, forms vast schools, silver mowies do so a little less often. The two species often travel together.

Silver morwong feed on prawns, worms, molluscs and larger forms of plankton and other small invertebrates. They may also graze on vegetation.

FISHING TECHNIQUES

The jackass and silver morwong are

Silver morwong have rubbery lips and an elongate, fleshy ray in the lower part of each pectoral or side fin.

the stand-bys of many deepsea anglers and the mainstay of the 'head boat' charter industry.

In deepwater, morwong are taken on heavily weighted handlines or deck winch lines rigged with several hooks and baited with fish-flesh, prawns or squid pieces.

Deep water morwong are willing victims and little finesse is needed to hook them. The skill lies in finding their habitat, a 'mowie ground' of gravel or broken reef bed in 30 to 200 metres of water, adjacent to undersea pinnacles or distinct drop-offs. Other fish taken on the same grounds include nannygai, snapper, red rock cod, sergeant baker and tiger flathead.

A handline of 15 to 30 kg breaking strain nylon, or a deck winch or short rod and reel outfit spooled with lines of similar strengths are the favoured tackle.

These fish may be taken while boats are at anchor, but catches are usually much greater when they are drifting.

EATING QUALITIES

The silver or rubberlip morwong is a palatable and popular table fish, though inferior to snapper and flathead. It is a little less tasty than the smaller jackass morwong and the larger queen snapper.

Morwong should be filleted and skinned prior to cooking to help remove the slight iodine taint sometimes evident.

MULLET, SAND

Myxus elongatus

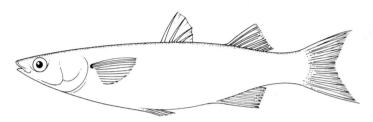

COMMON NAMES

The sand mullet is commonly known as the 'lano' or 'tellegalene' mullet in some areas; juveniles of the species — in common with all other mullet — are often called 'poddy mullet' or 'poddies'.

A closely related species with similar habits, the yellow-eye mullet or pilch *(Aldrichetta forsteri)* is found in southern waters of Australia where it is a common catch among beach fishermen.

DESCRIPTION

The sand mullet is a streamlined, attractive mullet with a more pointed head than most of its relations. It is caught on baited hooks more often than most other mullet, excluding the yellow-eye.

Typical sand mullet colouration is greenish on the back and bright silver to silvery-white on the flanks and belly. A small, dark blotch is evident at the base of the pectoral fins.

The lower fins are transparent or pale, sometimes with the faintest tinge of yellow. The tail is darker, and occasionally has a black, trailing edge.

SIZE

Most sand mullet caught on baited hooks measure between 18 and 30 cm in length and weigh less than 0.6 kg, although a very occasional specimen exceeds 0.8 kg.

DISTRIBUTION

The sand mullet is an estuarine and inshore fish of the southern half of the continent, ranging from southern Queensland to southern Western Australia. The related yellow-eye mullet's range is confined to more southerly waters, and a similar or identical species is found in New Zealand.

HABITS AND FEEDING

Sand mullet are a schooling fish which generally swim and feed near the surface, or over shallow water with a sandy bottom.

They are omnivorous, feeding on algae and weed as well as tiny crustacea, marine worms and small pieces of refuse or decaying animal and vegetable matter.

FISHING TECHNIQUES

Many mullet species are difficult to catch, but both the sand andyellow-eyecan be taken on baited hooks on light tackle, and small hooks baited with bread, dough, peeled prawn, worm pieces or maggots.

Yellow-eye mullet are more willing 'biters' and will take flesh baits and pieces of pilchard or whitebait.

Ideal tackle for sand mullet consists of a very light rod, 1.8 to 3 metres in length, matched to the smallest threadline, sidecast or centrepin reel filled with 1 to 3 kg breaking strain line.

Most of the successful rigs for this species incorporate a light float, such as a quill or small bobby cork, though the fish can be taken on unweighted or very lightly weighted lines and respond extremely well to a berley trail of soaked bread.

Left: This typical sand mullet or 'lano' was taken on a light fly fishing outfit and artificial fly.

Below: Sand mullet frequent sandy shallows and flats in estuaries, bays, harbours and inlets.

EATING QUALITIES

Sand mullet are arguably the tastiest of the entire mullet clan, their flesh com-paring favourably with that of the sand whiting — a species with which they share many habits and dietary preferences.

MULLET, SEA

Mugil cephalus

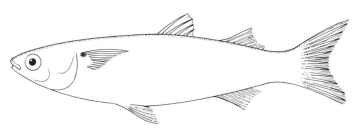

COMMON NAMES

The sea mullet is more commonly known as the bully mullet or 'bully'. Other names for this wide ranging species include hardgut mullet and river mullet.

Juveniles are frequently referred to as 'poddy mullet' or 'poddies'.

DESCRIPTION

The sea mullet is the giant of the mullet clan, although rivalled by the tropical diamond-scaled mullet for maximum growth potential.

The sea mullet is a fat, cylindrical fish characterised by a thick, gelatinous covering over the eyes, known as an 'adipose' eyelid.

The colouration of the bully mullet varies with habitat, and is dark on the back and grey through the flanks in freshwater, but changes to green on the back with bright-silver flanks at sea.

SIZE

Bully mullet commonly weigh from 0.2 to 1 kg, although those taken commercially in beach-netting operations often weigh between 1.5 and 2.5 kg apiece, with exceptional giants approaching 5 kg.

DISTRIBUTION

Found right around Australia, but more common along the stretch of coast between central Queensland and southern New South Wales, sea or bully mullet are a schooling fish at all sizes, especially when migrating.

Sea mullet are found in estuaries, harbours, bays, along beaches, and a short distance out to sea.

They range from high in the freshwater reaches of a stream, often above rapids, to the warm, blue currents of the inshore reefs, and at times visit every environmental niche between these extremes.

The species undertakes extensive migrations, and moves from one river system to another.

In northern New South Wales and southern Queensland, the sea mullet migrations in autumn and winter trigger concentration and feeding sprees by larger predators such as mulloway, mackerel, tuna, cobia and tailor.

HABITS AND FEEDING

Sea mullet are largely vegetarian, feeding on algae, decaying mangrove leaves and tiny diatoms. They will also eat zooplankton, water fleas, sand hoppers and marine worms.

Bully mullet often feed on food scraps and the waste from fruit processing plants, or factories processing dairy products.

FISHING TECHNIQUES

Bully mullet are notoriously difficult to catch on a line and baited hook.

Large sea mullet are sometimes 'jagged' or intentionally foul-hooked with big treble hooks, especially when found in massed schools, though this technique is illegal in most states.

In isolated instances, sea mullet

Left: Youngsters love catching mullet, especially relatively large sea mullet or 'bullies' like these.

Below: Sea mullet are heavily built, with large scales and big eyes which are partially covered by a transparent, fleshy covering known as an adipose eyelid. This specimen weighed about one kilo.

feeding around the waste outflow pipes of canneries or food processing plants will bite on delicately-presented baits which look similar to the effluent flowing from the pipe. This may include such bizarre offerings as sweet corn niblets, beetroot slices or diced pineapple!

Once hooked, all sea mullet provide sport far in excess of what might be expected considering their size.

Tackle should be similar to that described for sand mullet, though with stronger lines if very large 'bullies' are likely.

EATING QUALITIES

Sea mullet rate as fair to good table fish, depending on their diet and the way they are handled after capture.

They must be cleaned promptly and thoroughly and, ideally, filleted and skinned.

The flesh is superbly suited to being smoked, and its high oil or fat content make it a fine berley and bait.

MULLOWAY

Argyrosomus hololepidotus

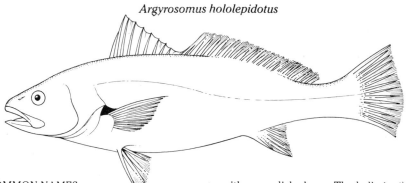

COMMON NAMES

The mulloway has a range of common names, their usage largely dictated by geography.

In New South Wales and Queensland this fish is almost exclusively known as jewfish, 'jew' or 'jewie'.

In Victoria and South Australia the official name of mulloway is widely accepted, although in South Australia the fish is sometimes called butterfish or 'buttery'.

In Western Australia, this species is called mulloway, kingfish, river king or silver king.

On the eastern seaboard, juvenile mulloway up to about 3 kg are often nick-named 'soapies', while fish from 3 to 8 kg are commonly called 'schoolies'.

Close relatives of the mulloway include the smaller teraglin *(Atractoscion aequidens)* of eastern offshore waters and the black or spotted jewfish *(Prontonibea diacanthus)* of our tropical north.

DESCRIPTION

A large, long-bodied, predatory fish of the ocean, estuaries and tidal rivers, mulloway are characterised by a large mouth, heavy scales and a convex, spade-like tail.

Colouration varies considerably with size and location, from dark bronze or brassy-green on the back to blue-green or even purple. The flanks are lighter, overlaid with a purplish sheen. The belly is silvery-white. Sometimes the fish have a distinct reddish tinge. Juveniles may be silvery all over.

The fins are mainly dark and there is a well-defined black patch just above the base of the pectoral fins.

When alive or fresh-dead, mulloway have a string of bright spots along the lateral line, not unlike the portholes of a ship. These and their rose-red eyes glow under artificial light.

Another characteristic is a distinct, kerosene-like smell when they are freshly landed.

SIZE

'Soapies' are small fish in the 0.4 to 2.5 kg weight bracket, 'schoolies' run up to about 8 kg, and adult fish range between 8 and 35 kg, with rare giants to 45 kg and very occasionally beyond. Maximum growth potential is probably in the order of 60 kg.

DISTRIBUTION

The mulloway belongs to a worldwide family of croakers, grunter and drum. A nearly identical fish is found in South Africa; the popular red drum or channel bass of the United States' eastern seaboard has much in common with our mulloway.

In Australia, mulloway are found southwards from about Rockhampton in Queensland, around the southern half of

Left: Mulloway are very handsome fish. In the eastern states they are far more commonly known as jewfish or 'jewies'. However, in Western Australia, where this 11 kg specimen was taken, they are mostly called mulloway or river kingfish.

Below: A beautiful 30 kg-plus mulloway from South Australian waters. The species is very popular in this state.

Left: A very silvery mulloway from Perth's Swan River.
Below: The author with a pair of black jewfish (Prontonibea diacanthus) from Darwin Harbour, in the Northern Territory.

Right: A haul of eight mulloway from 9 to 27 kg.

the continent to at least Carnarvon in northern Western Australia. They are practically unknown in Tasmania and have not been recorded in New Zealand.

While mulloway can tolerate water that is almost completely fresh, they are rarely found so far upstream. Their usual haunts lie between the upper tidal limits of coastal rivers and inshore reefs a few kilometres off the coast.

Estuaries, harbours, bays, beaches, breakwalls, rock headlands and reefs, gravel beds or mud holes up to 40 metres or so deep are their favourite haunts.

HABITS AND FEEDING

These fish are opportunistic predators and prefer to let the current and waves bring food to them.

Although largely nocturnal, mulloway will feed in daylight hours, especially if the water is muddy or the sky overcast.

They feed mainly on small to medium-size live fish, especially mullet, yellowtail, tailor, bream, pike, slimy mackerel, salmon and luderick. They prey on sand crabs and octopi, and are particularly partial to squid.

Mulloway of all sizes will form schools, packing very closely together and lying almost motionless in a gutter, reef hole or wreck. They undertake relatively extensive migrations in these close-knit schools.

On the other hand, large mulloway will forsake the company of their own kind to hunt alone along an ocean beach or estuary channel.

FISHING TECHNIQUES

Small mulloway mainly succumb to baits of prawns, worms, yabbies or fish

pieces intended for bream or flathead. They will also take small live bait.

Larger fish are best sought with live baits such as mullet, yellowtail, slimy mackerel, pike, tailor or sweep, or dead baits of whole or cut fish. Tailor, luderick, pilchards and pike fillets are favourites in some areas. Squid is also a very good bait, especially if used alive or very fresh.

Despite their generous mouths, mulloway often fumble a bait or run with it for some distance before spitting it out. Using big, sharp hooks and being willing to strike while the fish is running give the best results.

Times of heavy rain and discoloured run-off are excellent for mulloway fishing. When floodwaters cause a distinct colour change in the water at a river mouth mulloway can be caught on lures. White, or red and white lead-head feathers, strong-actioned minnows and so-called 'chair-leg' poppers are the stock in trade of the 'jewie' spinning specialists.

Soft plastic-tailed jigs have recently made something of a breakthrough in successful mulloway fishing.

EATING QUALITIES

The mulloway or jewfish is unusual in that the flesh quality of small fish is inferior to that of adults. Jewfish, over about 5 or 6 kg, are excellent table fare, despite their fairly strong smell. Below 3 kg the flesh is soft and rather flavourless, hence the name 'soapy'.

MURRAY COD

Maccullochella peeli

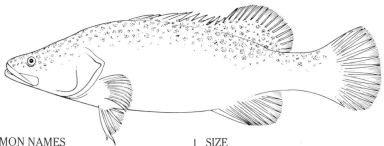

COMMON NAMES

This famous Australian freshwater fish is nearly always known as Murray cod or 'cod'. However, it is unrelated to the true cod family of the northern hemisphere and is a member of the perch family which contains the golden perch and the Australian bass.

Murray cod are occasionally confused with their much less common brethren, the trout cod *(M. macquariensis)* and with the several endangered (and in some cases extinct) east coast cod species of the Clarence, Richmond, Brisbane and Mary River systems.

DESCRIPTION

Australia's largest and most noteworthy freshwater fish, the Murray cod is big, robust and barrel-shaped with a cavernous mouth and small eyes set well forward on the head.

Colouration varies considerably depending on the environment and particularly on water clarity. However, most are olive-green to yellow-green on the back, becoming yellowish on the flanks and creamy-yellow or white on the belly. The back is overlaid with darker green or brown mottlings and reticulations, which often extend well down the flanks. The eyes are brown.

The second dorsal and tail or caudal fins usually have white margins and sometimes such a margin is also found on the ventral fins. The white margins are particularly striking on fish from clear, fast-flowing streams.

SIZE

The giant of our outback rivers, and among the three or four largest freshwater species in the world, the Murray cod has the potential to reach 100 kg-plus, and probably once did. Today, a 45 kg fish is large indeed. Mostly they weigh from 1 to 9 kg, with a few 10 to 40 kg specimens still taken each year.

DISTRIBUTION

Native to the Australian outback, Murray cod were once found throughout the entire Murray/Darling system with the exception of the alpine and sub-alpine headwaters.

This range has been reduced by dam and weir construction, pollution and over-fishing, but fortunately cod are still present through most of their traditional range and even appear to be staging a modest comeback in some areas.

Cod have also been introduced into many dams and some eastern flowing or coastal drainage systems.

A group of sub-species, the endangered 'east coast cod', exists, or once existed, in the Clarence, Richmond, Brisbane and Mary Rivers of northern New South Wales and southern Queensland.

Murray cod are found in habitats ranging from shallow, fast-running streams with gravel beds, to deep, turbid, slow-flowing western rivers. They thrive in dams, especially where forage species such as bony bream, redfin or goldfish are found.

Even in quick-flowing streams, cod

Left: A Murray code (top) and the much rarer trout cod. Note the slightly larger eye and overshot top jaw of the trout cod.
Below: Some of our best cod fishing occurs in large, outback dams and impoundments — especially those with plenty of drowned trees and other cover.

tend to seek out holes, slicks and back-eddies. They like deep water, cover and ready access to food.

HABITS AND FEEDING

Murray cod are predatory hunters feeding mainly on smaller fish, yabbies, shrimps and frogs. Large fish will also take waterfowl, snakes, lizards and even mice and kangaroo rats.

Cod normally lie close to or within the cover provided by fallen trees, rock bars, weed beds and undercut banks, relying on a sudden burst of speed and that cave-like mouth to surprise and secure their prey.

Small cod occasionally form loose schools, while larger ones tend to be more solitary.

The fish pair off or form small groups for spawning in late winter or spring. Spawning is activated by rising water temperatures, particularly if these are accompanied by rising water levels.

Spawning takes place in hollow logs, on drowned tree stumps and between large boulders, with the adult cod often standing guard over the nest site and actively defending it for some days or weeks after the eggs are laid.

FISHING TECHNIQUES

Traditionally, cod were taken on heavy set-lines baited with yabbies, whole fish, rabbit pieces or galah (parrot) breasts.

Today, anglers have come to appreciate the sporting qualities of these fine fish and

Outback rivers like the Darling continue to produce some fine cod, despite over-fishing and habitat destruction.

they are more often sought on medium or even lightweight tackle baited with live yabbies, bardi grubs, shrimp or small, live fish.

Murray cod respond actively to lures, especially if visibility through the water exceeds 30 cm.

Deep-diving plugs, metal spoons and bladed spinners all work well. A slow, steady retrieve or walking-pace troll is best.

Popular tackle is built around a 1.7 to 2.2 metre hollow glass, graphite or composite rod mated to a medium thread-line (spinning), baitcaster or sidecast reel and lines of 5 to 10 kg breaking strain.

In deference to their increasing scarcity, many sportfishermen release most of their catch, keeping only the occasional fish between 2 and 8 kg.

EATING QUALITIES
Murray cod are regarded as one of our best outback table fish. The flavour of smaller fish is excellent, especially from fast flowing, clear-water streams. They tend to be oily or fatty at weights over about 15 kg.

NANNYGAI

Trachichthodes affinis

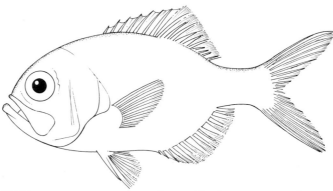

COMMON NAMES

The nannygai, 'gai' or 'nanny' is sometimes nicknamed 'goat' or 'nanny goat' by anglers, and is almost always marketed commercially as redfish.

Several related species occur aroung the Australian coastline, with the swallowtail nannygai *(Centroberyx lineatus)* of South Australian waters being one of the most significant.

DESCRIPTION

The nannygai is a small, deep-bodied and laterally compressed species characterised by over-size eyes, large, rough scales, a cavernous mouth and overall colouration of bright red to reddish-orange, grading to silvery-white on the belly. The eyes are red around a large, black pupil.

SIZE

Most nannygai taken by anglers measure between 15 and 30 cm and weigh less than 0.8 kg. However, in deeper water 1 kg specimens are far from uncommon and rare examples may approach or even exceed 1.5 kg.

DISTRIBUTION

The nannygai is a cool and temperate-water fish mainly found on offshore reefs and grounds in the 40 to 200 metre depth zone.

The largest nannygai generally come from the 100 to 200 metre zone, although occasional ones are landed by anglers on rock ledges fronting deep water.

Nannygai prefer a broken reef or gravel bottom, but are sometimes found over sand and mud.

HABITS AND FEEDING

Nannygai form medium to very large schools over reef pinnacles and rubble grounds.

These fish are opportunistic and varied feeders and take smaller live fish, prawns, crabs, squid and octopi, as well as scraps and offal of all types.

FISHING TECHNIQUES

Nannygai are mainly an incidental catch taken when anglers are fishing deep reefs for snapper and morwong, or drifting broken ground for these same species and flathead.

Nannygai will take most cut baits as well as prawns, squid and the like. They are easily caught on multi-hook baitcatching jig rigs.

Most nannygai are taken on handlines or short boat rods and centrepin or sidecast reels. Their large mouths will easily accommodate sizeable hooks and baits intended for much larger and more desirable targets.

As well as being a tasty and popular table fish, nannygai also make superb live baits for large yellowfin tuna and yellowtail kingfish.

EATING QUALITIES

Nannygai are fine table fish with sweet, slightly moist white flesh. There is a good deal of wastage due to the size of the head, but as large bags of nannygai are common, Nannygai should be filleted and skinned for best results.

This species also makes a superb live bait for big yellowfin tuna and yellowtail kingfish.

PARROT FISH, BLUE-THROATED

Pseudolabrus tetricus

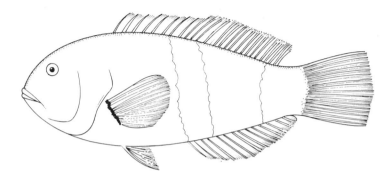

COMMON NAMES

The blue–throated or blue–throat parrot fish is a member of the family *Labridae* and is more correctly known as the blue-throated wrasse.

Other common names for this southern inshore fish are 'blue head' and 'kelpie', while in Tasmania the species is sometimes marketed as 'winter bream'.

A similar and closely related fish, the crimson-banded wrasse or crimson-banded parrot fish *(P. gymnogenis)* is found further north along the east coast. However, it is smaller and of less interest to anglers.

DESCRIPTION

The blue-throated parrot fish is robustly built with large scales, slightly-rubbery lips and peg-like teeth.

The colouring varies considerably between the drab juveniles and females and the more brightly-hued adult male.

Juveniles are mottled-red and brown with a whitish tail. Females vary from green to reddish-brown with a reasonably distinct white band around the body a little more than half-way back towards the tail. There is often a less distinctly defined dark band just ahead of the white one.

Adult males are brownish-red with a distinct white band around the middle of the body, another band around the tail wrist and a blue to blueish-white chin and throat area.

SIZE

The blue-throated parrot fish grows to about 60 cm and 3.5 kg in weight although fish over 2.5 kg are uncommon.

In some areas juveniles and females up to about 0.8 kg are prolific; exposed reefs and deeper locations will often harbour quantities of mature males in the 1 to 2.2 kg range.

DISTRIBUTION

The blue-throat wrasse likes the cold and cool southern waters, ranging from the far south coast of New South Wales to Victoria, Tasmania and South Australia, westwards to about Nuyts Archipelago or Ceduna in the Great Australian Bight.

Large ones are more common around offshore islands such as Flinders, Kangaroo, the Joseph Banks Group and the Neptunes.

The fish ranges from lower estuarine and harbour areas to offshore reefs, always favouring locations with healthy kelp or sea grass beds.

HABITS AND FEEDING

The blue throat feeds mainly on

Left: Gaffing aboard a 2 kg blue-throated parrotfish or wrasse taken on light tackle at the Neptune Islands, south of Port Lincoln, South Australia.
Below: An adult male blue-throat, showing the species' characteristic colouration and blue chin area. Females of this species are more drably coloured, as is often the case with fish from the family Labridae.

crustacea and shellfish, but will also take worms, octopi, small squid and small fish.

Juveniles and females form small schools; males are rather territorial. In areas with dense populations of the species, territories may be very small and close together, giving the effect of a loose school.

FISHING TECHNIQUES

Parrot fish mainly succumb to baits of crab, prawn, worm, cunjevoi, scallop or abalone gut, squid pieces or, more rarely, cut fish flesh.

Male blue–throats will sometimes strike at small lures or jigs worked close to the seabed.

EATING QUALITIES

The blue-throat parrot fish has rather soft, bland flesh which flakes easily. Some people enjoy it though many find it mushy and tasteless.

PEARL PERCH

Glaucosoma scapulare

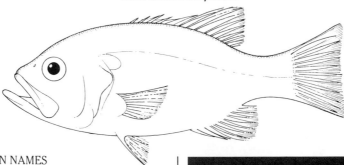

COMMON NAMES

The pearl perch or 'pearly' has no other common names and no relatives on the east coast of Australia. Its only relative in Australian waters is the highly–prized Westralian jewfish *(G. hebraicum)*.

DESCRIPTION

A large–eyed, deep–bodied and laterally-compressed fish with moderately large scales and a large mouth.

Typical colouration is brassy to silver-grey on the back and lighter on the flanks and belly.

SIZE

Pearl perch taken by anglers commonly weigh between 0.8 and 2 kg, with exceptional specimens up to 3 kg and even a little heavier.

DISTRIBUTION

The pearl perch is exclusive to deep reefs and gravel patches off the New South Wales north coast and southern Queensland. The species is rarely encountered in water shallower than about 60 metres.

HABITS AND FEEDING

Pearl perch prey on small reef fish, deepwater crabs, prawns and other crustacea, octopi and squid.

They are a schooling fish, often found in relatively large shoals over deep gutters, reef pinnacles and the gravel beds and drop-offs adjacent to reefs.

FISHING TECHNIQUES

The highly–prized and much sought-after pearl perch is almost exclusively taken on heavily weighted lines with baits of squid, prawn and cut fish flesh.

It bites best at dawn, dusk and through the night.

A depth sounder is invaluable in pinpointing potential fish-holding territory, and will often reveal the presence of the fish themselves if they are schooling densely.

EATING QUALITIES

The pearl perch is an exceptionally fine table fish held in high regard wherever it is taken. Its name is often included on short lists of our very best eating species.

Left: The pearl perch is regarded by seafood fanciers as one of our most delicious saltwater species.
Below: Pearl perch are taken on offshore grounds along a relatively short stretch of coast in northern New South Wales and southern Queensland.
Opposite: Pearl perch have very large, dark eyes and a large mouth.

PERCH, GOLDEN

Macquaria ambigua

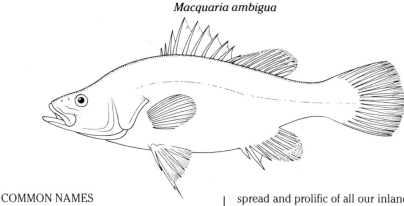

COMMON NAMES

It is widely known throughout inland New South Wales and Queensland as 'yellowbelly'; in South Australia and parts of Victoria, as callop, and at the markets, occasionally, as Murray perch. However, the name 'golden perch' is gaining increasing acceptance.

DESCRIPTION

A large perch with a convex or outward-curving tail margin and strongly scooped 'forehead'.

Colouration ranges from a handsome, dark coppery-bronze with green reflections in clear water, though to yellowish-white in muddy locations. It is faintly barred or irregularly speckled. The belly is often creamy-yellow.

Fins range from dusky through yellowish-red to near white, depending on body colour.

SIZE

Most 'goldens' taken by anglers weigh from 0.2 to 3 kg, though in some areas 4 kg specimens are far from uncommon. Fish over 6 kg are prized everywhere, and though 9 kg-plus is exceptional, the species has been reported at weights as great as 23 kg!

DISTRIBUTION

The golden perch is the most wide-spread and prolific of all our inland natives, and is found in four states and both territories.

It natural range encompasses all of the Murray/Darling system, excluding the highest alpine headwaters, the Dawson/Fitzroy drainage of central Queensland, Lake Eyre and the Coopers Creek system, as well as some coastal rivers in northern New South Wales and Queensland.

Golden perch have been introduced successfully into many dams and pondages from Cairns to Perth. They prefer slow-flowing, slightly turbid water with snags or rock cover and need a water temperature in excess of 22°C to spawn, but will survive short periods in water as cold as 4° and as hot as 38°C!

HABITS AND FEEDING

This opportunistic hunter and scavenger lives mainly on small fish, shrimp, yabbies, frogs, insects and their larvae, worms, grubs and terrestrial creatures which fall into or swim through inland rivers, dams, lakes and ponds.

Small 'goldens' form quite large schools, while fish over 2 kg or so hunt in packs of three to a dozen. Larger aggregaions occur during the pre-spawn build-up in spring, when the fish often 'suspend' in mid-water close to shore.

Goldens are the most migratory of our inland natives, and, given the floods and

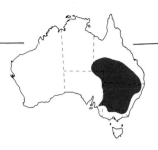

Golden perch — also known as 'yellowbelly' and 'callop' — are widespread throughout the inland waterways of New South Wales, Queensland, South Australia and Victoria. They vary considerably in colour from location to location and even between individuals in the same body of water. However, their scooped forehead, relatively large mouth and convex or outwardly curving tail allow for easy identification.

freshes needed to negotiate the many weirs and dams now found on our major rivers, it is conceivable that during its life a fish could move from Murray Bridge in South Australia to Goondiwindi in Queensland — a distance of many thousands of kilometres.

FISHING TECHNIQUES

Golden perch caught by outback anglers are mainly taken on natural baits such as yabbies, shrimps, earthworms, wood or bardi grubs, and small live fish fished on or near the riverbed close to snag cover or rocky drop-offs.

A willing lure-striker, golden perch will take a variety of diving plugs, spoons, spinners, soft-tailed jigs and even flies.

Big fish will hit very large lures intended for Murray cod.

Similar tackle to that used for Murray cod is ideal for golden perch fishing.

EATING QUALITIES

It is rated by many pundits as the tastiest of our inland natives; fish weighing less than 2 kg are generally superior in table quality to their larger kin.

Fish from clean, slightly cool water taste better than those from hot, muddy waterholes.

PERCH, MACQUARIE

Macquarie australasica

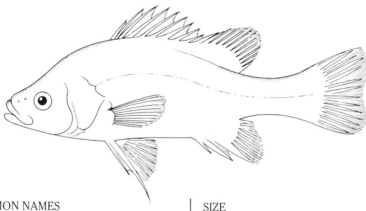

COMMON NAMES

The Macquarie perch or 'Macquarie' is also known as the mountain perch, white-eyed perch, bream or black bream.

Macquarie perch can be distinguished from other inland native species by their small, slightly overshot mouth and humped 'shoulder'. The fish with the closest resemblance in the same waters is the silver perch *(Bidyanus bidyanus)*, but it has a slightly concave or forked tail, as opposed to the Macquarie's convex or outwardly curving tail.

DESCRIPTION

The 'Macquarie' is a medium–sized perch with a moderately large eye, prominent 'shoulder' area, scooped forehead and convex or outwardly curving tail.

A lightly coloured area around the pupil of the eyes of adults is typical.

Colouration ranges from almost coal black through smoky-grey to greenish-brown on the back, paler on the flanks and creamy or creamy-yellow on the belly. This species is the darkest coloured of the perches. Juveniles may be mottled with a dark over light patterning.

The fins are dark, sometimes with a purplish tinge, though the pelvics are lighter.

SIZE

These days the average 'Macquarie' caught on rod and reel weighs from 0.2 to 0.8 kg, although in Victoria's Dartmouth Dam, 1 to 1.2 kg fish are far from uncommon, and 2 kg specimens not unknown.

This relatively short-lived perch may weigh more than 3.5 kg if optimum conditions prevail.

DISTRIBUTION

The Macquarie perch frequents the higher Murray/Darling system, well into sub-alpine regions. It is also found in the Shoalhaven, Nepean and Woronora Rivers of coastal New South Wales, and in the Mitta Mitta and Snowy River systems of Victoria, as well as in dams in both states.

Macquarie perch have been successfully introduced to Melbourne's Yarra River.

'Macquaries' prefer slightly faster, clearer and cooler water than does the golden perch. They are particularly fond of gravel–bottomed streams with plenty of boulder and snag cover and spawn at water temperatures above 16⁰C.

HABITS AND FEEDING

Macquarie perch travel in small schools, singly, or in pairs.

Left: Macquarie perch in an aquarium. Note the small head and mouth, scooped forehead and distinct white or silver area around the pupil of the adult fish. Below: A lovely, dark-hued Macquarie perch of about a kilo from Victoria's Lake Dartmouth

They feed near the bottom close to shore. In lakes and dams, they rarely stray away from the bank or submerged cover.

'Macquaries' eat insect larvae such as dragonfly nymphs or mudeyes, as well as shrimps, small yabbies and — less frequently — small forage fish like galaxids and smelt.

Spawning takes place during spring in shallow, flowing water much the same as that chosen by trout. Very large spawning 'runs' or aggregations once occurred, but are only a memory today.

FISHING TECHNIQUES

Techniques are the same as those described for the golden perch, but with more emphasis on smaller baits and lures.

This perch will take insect and insect larvae baits, such as grasshoppers and mudeyes, and artificial flies intended for trout.

The best tackle to use is a single-handed spin or baitcaster outfit and 2 to 4 kg breaking strain line.

EATING QUALITIES

The Macquarie perch is a very good to excellent table fish, with a taste and texture not unlike, but superior to, that of the bass.

Their population is dwindling so wary anglers opt to release the majority taken, especially during the spawning run in spring and late summer.

PERCH, SILVER

Bidyanus bidyanus

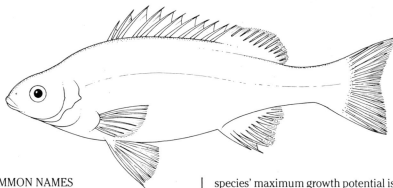

COMMON NAMES

The silver perch is known as the bidyan, grunter, perch, black bream, bream and terapon.

This small–mouthed outback perch with its relatively tiny scales and slightly concave or forked tail is quite distinctive and unlikely to be confused with any other freshwater fish, native or exotic. The possible exception is the smaller spangled perch or 'bobby cod' *(Leiopotherapon unicolor)*, though that fish has a stouter body, larger mouth and is usually mottled.

DESCRIPTION

The silver perch actually belongs to the *Teraponidae* or 'grunter' family, not that of the perch.

'Silvers' are characterised by their slightly concave or inwardly curving tail margin, relatively small mouth, small scales, small eyes and straight 'forehead' profile, which contrasts with the scooped 'foreheads' of golden and Macquarie perch.

Silver perch colouration varies from nearly jet–black through smoky-grey to olive-green, gold or silver. Most are lighter on the belly, and juveniles may be mottled or faintly barred.

SIZE

The majority of 'silvers' taken by anglers weigh between 0.2 and 1.8 kg, with a very rare trophy up to 3 kg or more. The species' maximum growth potential is close to 8 kg, but they are practically never seen at such a size.

DISTRIBUTION

The silver perch is a native Australian freshwater fish found through most of the Murray/Darling system, including sub-alpine regions, and also in the Coopers Creek drainage system.

'Silvers' have been introduced into many dams, lakes and some eastern flowing streams. A very similar species occurs in the Fitzroy/Dawson and some other Queensland coastal systems.

'Silvers' prefer running water with a sand, mud or gravel bottom.

Prolific schools of silver perch are sometimes found downstream of dams, weirs and barrages.

HABITS AND FEEDING

Silver perch of all sizes are a schooling species, and as with most fish, small specimens tend to form larger aggregations than adults. Exceptionally large 'silvers' may become solitary.

Despite their small mouth and diminutive size, silver perch can be extremely aggressive and territorial. As a result they are not a popular aquarium fish.

'Silvers' feed on shrimp, small yabbies, freshwater plankton, insects and insect larvae, worms, grubs and vegetation.

Left: A very large silver perch carrying a fisheries' department gill cover tag.
Below: Silver perch habitat in outback New South Wales.

FISHING TECHNIQUES

When silver perch are specifically targeted, anglers tend to use lighter tackle, smaller hooks and a little more finesse than is commonly employed in catching the larger outback natives.

Silver perch spend much of their time feeding on algae and freshwater plankton, but will readily take baits of worm, shrimp, insects or peeled yabby tail. Small spoons, spinners and diving plugs also attract them.

These territorial and aggressive little fish will chase and hit big lures intended for cod or golden perch.

Tackle is much as for other inland sportfish, though if 'silvers' are being specifically targeted, single-handed outfits and lines as light as 2 kg breaking strain which allow these marvellous scrappers to show their liveliness and strength, can be used.

EATING QUALITIES

The silver perch, with its fine bones, is often rated as the least appealing of the outback natives when it comes to the culinary department. Fish from turbid waters often have a weedy or muddy flavour, though those from clean water cook up quite well.

PIKE, LONG-FINNED

Dinolestes lewini

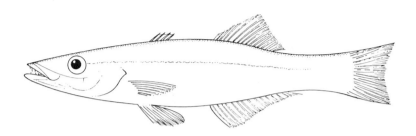

COMMON NAMES

The long-finned, longfin or yellowfin pike is also known simply as pike or, in parts of western Victoria, as 'lythe'.

This fish is unrelated to the snook or shortfin pike *(Sphyraena novaehollandiae)* and bears only a superficial physical resemblance to it.

DESCRIPTION

The long–finned pike is a small, elongated fish with big eyes and a large mouth with long, sharp teeth near the front of the jaws. Its second dorsal and anal fins have much longer bases than those of the snook or short-finned pike.

Colouration is olive-green to greenish-yellow on the back, silvery to silver-yellow on the flanks, and silver on the belly. The tail third of the body is flushed with yellow.

The fins are yellowish, particularly the tail, which is bright yellow.

When freshly landed, pike have a strong, distinctive odour.

SIZE

Pike are mainly taken at weights of 0.3 to 0.9 kg, although the species occasionally tops 1 kg and may rarely exceed 1.5 kg.

DISTRIBUTION

A fish of temperate, cool and cold southern seas, the pike is rarely found far offshore, unless around   or reefs.

Pike prefer shallow reef areas with good weed growth, and do not often range beyond the 40 metre depth mark.

HABITS AND FEEDING

Pike are lightweight predators feeding on small fish, prawns, squid and offal or scraps.

They are almost always found in small to medium schools hovering close to the seabed, and are most active during the night and at dawn and dusk.

FISHING TECHNIQUES

Pike are rarely fished for specifically outside western Victoria and Tasmania, and are usually an incidental catch taken by anglers targeting tailor, salmon, barracouta, snapper and trevally.

Pike take strip baits, whole or cut pilchards, garfish, prawns and squid. They also strike at small, silvery spoons and lures or small minnows, and will occasionally attack small live baits being used to attract kingfish, mulloway or John dory.

EATING QUALITIES

If cleaned promptly and eaten within 24 hours, pike are very palatable, but they are rarely eaten outside Victoria and Tasmania.

Pike make superb live or cut bait for large kingfish, mulloway and snapper.

Although not held
in high regard by many
anglers, pike are quite reasonable table fish if
cleaned promptly and eaten fresh.

QUEENFISH

Chorinemus lysan

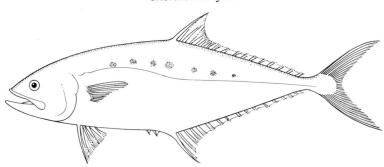

COMMON NAMES

The queenfish or 'queenie' is popularly known in the Northern Territory and other parts of tropical Australia as the 'skinny fish' or 'skinny'. In other parts of the world this species or closely related fish are called leatherskin or whitefish.

Several species of queenfish are found in our waters, although *C. lysan* is by far the largest and most important. A much smaller, less deeply-bodied queenfish *(C. tala)* sometimes forms large schools in northern waters and makes a good skip or swimming bait for marlin and other gamefish. Sometimes called tala queenfish, this species rarely tops 1.2 kg in weight.

DESCRIPTION

The common queenfish *(C. lysan)* is a long, fairly deep and extremely laterally-compressed saltwater and estuarine tropical fish of the tropics.

Its typical colouration is dark green along the top of the back, metallic-silver to silvery-white on the flanks and belly, sometimes with a yellowish tinge.

A series of oval-shaped dark blotches forms a broken line down the flanks.

SIZE

Most 'queenies' caught weigh from 1 to 7 kg, with occasional specimens up to 10 or 12 kg and very rare giants of 15 kg or slightly more.

DISTRIBUTION

This tropical fish is rarely found in large numbers far south of the Tropic of Capricorn, although stragglers are sometimes taken in Hervey Bay, southern Queensland and turn up in reasonable numbers in and around Shark Bay, Western Australia.

HABITS AND FEEDING

Queenfish range from the upper tidal reaches of tropical rivers, down through the mangrove estuaries to inshore bays and harbours, islands, shallow reefs and, occasionally, out to the reef complexes and cays near the edge of the continental shelf. They roam singly or in schools.

They prefer warm to hot green or slightly discoloured water, with plenty of current or tidal movement and hunt from mid-water to the surface over the sand or mud bottom inshore.

Sand spits, back eddies, rock bars, wharves and river mouths are all likely places to prospect for the fast-swimming, hard-hitting queenfish.

They prey on small fish such as mullet, garfish, herring, anchovy, mudskippers and whiting. They will also take prawns and squid.

FISHING TECHNIQUES

This exciting sportfish falls for live baits, dead baits, fish strips and pilchards or

Left: A big, beautiful queenfish taken from the shore at East Point, Darwin.
Below: Queenfish respond to a range of angling techniques. This small specimen took a bucktail jig fished on lightweight threadline tackle. A fast-swimming predator, queenfish can often be excited by a high speed, erratic retrieve.

gar on ganged hooks, as well as lures.

The emphasis should be on movement and speed which will excite the queenfish. Fast trolled or rapidly–retrieved sliced chrome lures, poppers, spoons, minnows and saltwater flies are all excellent choices.

A wire or heavy monofilament nylon trace is advisable when pursuing queenfish, as their hard, sharp-edged jaws can easily damage light nylon fishing line.

EATING QUALITIES

Although often denigrated in the tropics because of the availability of more 'glamorous' table fish, 'queenies' have firm, white meat with an excellent flavour, though tending towards dryness. Smaller specimens are not generally popular because of the very thin fillets and excessive wastage. Queenfish should be bled and kept on ice after capture.

RAINBOW RUNNER

Elegatis bipinnulata

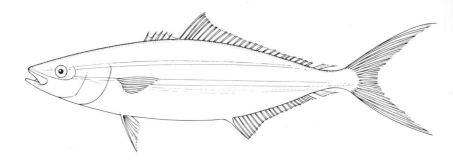

COMMON NAMES

The rainbow runner or 'runner' belongs to the same large family as the trevallies, amberjack and kingfish *(Carangidae),* and bears a close resemblance in body shape to the yellowtail kingfish *(Seriola lalandi).* However, the 'runner's'colouration and an isolated finlet behind the second dorsal and the anal fins distinguish it from the kingfish.

DESCRIPTION

The rainbow runner has much the same shape as the kingfish but with a slighty more elongated and cylindrical body, a more pointed head profile, a smaller mouth and separate finlets between the second dorsal fin and tail and the anal fin and tail.

When alive or freshly dead, the rainbow runner is strikingly coloured. The back is green to deep blue, the flanks silvery-white, overlaid with two to four longitudinal bands or stripes of alternating yellow and electric-blue along each side, close to the midline. The large crescent-shaped, forked tail is yellow.

SIZE

In some parts of the world rainbow runners heavier than 10 kg have been recorded, however, weights over 7 kg are exceptional and most caught in Australa-

sian waters weigh between 1.5 and 6 kg.

DISTRIBUTION

The rainbow runner is a native of the Indo-Pacific tropical and sub-tropical seas, but makes occasional forays into more temperate waters.

Runners are rarely encountered south of Narooma or Bermagui in New South Wales or Rottnest Island off the west coast. They make very occasional visits to New Zealand's north coast. Very similar fish are found in the Atlantic Ocean.

They prefer the deep, warm and clear-blue water of the open ocean, but are sometimes found in shallower areas around reef complexes, atolls and islands.

HABITS AND FEEDING

'Runners' are schooling fish in all but the very largest size.

They feed on small fish, squid, large planktonic organisms, krill and pelagic crab larvae. Most of their feeding is done between the surface and mid-water.

FISHING TECHNIQUES

Most of the rainbow runners landed in Australasian waters are incidental captures taken while anglers are trolling small to medium-size lures for tuna, mackerel and other small to mid-range pelagics.

Runners respond well to unweighted

Rainbow runners are shaped very much like yellowtail kingfish, though their body is more cylindrical and their tail significantly larger. Fresh out of the water, these handsome fish display a series of longitudinal blue and yellowish gold stripes down each flank.

or lightly weighted fish flesh strip baits and whole pilchards free-drifted in a berley trail. They will also attack small live baits.

Although mainly an offshore target, runners have been landed from deep-fronted rock ledges, particularly around Jervis Bay in southern New South Wales.

EATING QUALITIES

The rainbow runner is a fine table fish, tasting not unlike a small kingfish, although the meat is a little darker. They are good smoked.

Small runners, alive or dead, make superb bait for large gamefish and sharks.

REDFIN

Perca fluviatilis

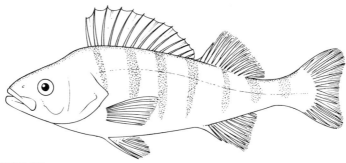

COMMON NAMES

This introduced freshwater fish is commonly known in Australia as the redfin, redfin perch or 'reddie', but is more correctly titled European perch or English perch. In its native waters in western and central Europe the fish is simply called 'perch'.

DESCRIPTION

A relatively deep-bodied fish, with a smallish head and scooped 'forehead', the redfin is characterised by its very high, spiky first dorsal fin. The tail is small.

The redfin's colouration is olive-green on the back, creamy on the belly with six or more dark green to khaki bands running down each flank.

The fins, particularly the pectorals, ventral and anal, are bright red.

SIZE

In the years immediately following introduction to a waterway, 0.5 to 2 kg fish are common, but over-population stunts the average length to 15 to 20 cm and weight to less than 0.3 kg. Rare examples exceed 3 kg and the species has been recorded to 9 kg-plus, which is much larger than the largest perch found in their native Britain.

DISTRIBUTION

Native to Europe, the introduced redfin is now widespread through much of the Murray/Darling system as well as in many other inland rivers, lakes, dams, ponds and swamps through New South Wales, Victoria, South Australia, Tasmania and southern Western Australia. Redfin are also present in some New Zealand waters.

This fish prefers warm, slow-moving water with plenty of cover, weed growth and a good population of small fish. It does well in dams, lakes and pondages below alpine levels.

HABITS AND FEEDING

This introduced, freshwater predator from Europe has become widely established here in rivers, lakes and dams, often to the detriment of native species or more desirable imports.

It is an extremely active predator and will take small fish almost half as big as itself, as well as yabbies, shrimp, insects and insect larvae.

Redfin are a schooling fish in all but the very largest sizes. Schools tend to contain fish of identical size, possibly because of the redfin's cannibalistic nature.

FISHING TECHNIQUES

Redfin are mainly taken on worms, shrimps, yabbies, live minnows, gudgeons and small forage species such as goldfish.

They are susceptible to a wide range of lures, particularly spinners, spoons and wet flies.

Left: The redfin or European perch has scarlet to orange fins, a small, lobed tail, large mouth and dark-barred green back. When extended, the dorsal fin is very high and spiny.
Below: Redfin water in western Victoria.

One of the most productive techniques is to drop a weighted lure, jig or specially-designed bobber to the bottom, near cover such as drowned timber, and to jig this offering up and down using short, erratic jerks of the rod tip.

All redfin caught should be killed, as they are regarded as a noxious pest in our waters. On no account should live redfin be transported from one area to another.

EATING QUALITIES

A very tasty, if slightly dry, eating fish. It requires skinning, as the scales are almost impossible to remove in the conventional manner.

SAILFISH

Istiophorus platypterus

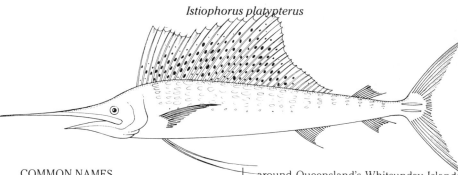

COMMON NAMES

The Indo-Pacific sailfish is also known as the 'sail', 'spear–chucker' or 'spearfish'. The two latter names may cause confusion with the related, but rare, shortbill spearfish *Tetapturus angustirostris*.

Sailfish may occasionally be confused with small marlin, but their distinctive sail-like dorsal fin and light build are distinguishing features.

DESCRIPTION

The sailfish is a large but lightly-built pelagic gamefish of tropical and sub-tropical waters, characterised by having a top jaw which extends into a long, slender bill, and an extremely high and ornate dorsal fin.

Colouration is usually electric-blue to blue-green, darker on the back and overlaid with broken vertical bars and dashes of lavender or powder-blue. Some fish have a golden or coppery flush to the gill covers and flanks when alive.

The sail-like dorsal fin is dark, steely-blue with many blue/black or purple spots and broken dashes.

SIZE

Sailfish grow to almost 4 metres in length and weights of close to 100 kg, but are much more common at half that length and weights of 15 to 45 kg.

The biggest ones found in our waters have come from northern Western Australia, between Exmouth and Dampier; around Queensland's Whitsunday Islands, and near Lord Howe Island.

DISTRIBUTION

Indo-Pacific sailfish are found throughout the tropical and sub-tropical areas of the Indian and Pacific Oceans. A related but smaller sailfish also occurs in the Atlantic.

Sailfish are surface wanderers of the warm currents of the inshore and continental shelf.

They prefer depths of 20 to 80 metres, temperatures in the 24^0 to 30^0C range and relatively clean blue or green water but are sometimes found close to muddy colour change lines.

HABITS AND FEEDING

Sailfish are free-swimming pelagic wanderers, although tagging studies indicate that isolated stocks or populations may remain in the same general area throughout their adult lives. They travel in loose schools, in pairs or singly.

Sailfish do most of their hunting and feeding over relatively flat sand or mud bottoms adjacent to reef areas. They feed mostly on small to medium baitfish and squid.

Abundant bait of pilchards, garfish, mullet or even brown toadfish will attract them to an area.

FISHING TECHNIQUES

Sailfish caught by anglers in Australia are mainly taken on trolled, rigged baits of

With its extremely high, sail-like dorsal fin, slender body and long, fine bill or 'spear', the sailfish is unique, and could hardly be confused with any other species once viewed clearly.

garfish or mullet, pulled behind a boat travelling at 5 to 8 knots, or small to medium live baits drifted, or cast close to feeding 'pods' of fish.

In northern Western Australia a growing number of sailfish are being taken on live baits from the ocean rocks.

Sailfish chase and strike at fast-trolled lures such as jet-heads and straight-running skirted heads pulled at 10 to 18 knots. However, many strikes on these 'artificials' fail to connect because of the 'sail's' long bill and hard mouth.

Sailfish often 'bill' a bait, or hit it with their spear, then run some distance with it held tightly in their mouth. Such finnicky feeders can be very difficult to hook.

Popular tackle for sailfish is built around a 1.8 to 2.2 metre rod matched to a large threadline or light to medium overhead reel filled with 4 to 15 kg breaking strain line. Some fine 'sails' have been taken by competent operators on saltwater fly fishing tackle.

EATING QUALITIES

The sailfish is quite palatable despite its dark, somewhat sinewy flesh which is ideally suited to being smoked.

In Australia, the vast majority of sailfish taken on rod and reel are tagged and released. They are pursued only for the superb sport they provide on light tackle.

SALMON, AUSTRALIAN

Arripis trutta

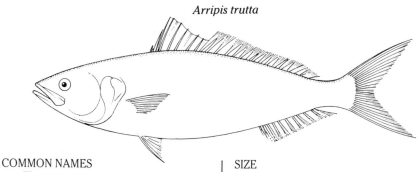

COMMON NAMES

The Australian salmon is nicknamed 'sambo' by some anglers, and known in its juvenile stages as salmon trout or bay trout, particularly in Victoria, Tasmania and South Australia. Very large examples are sometimes called 'black backs'.

In New Zealand this abundant species is called kahawai, while oversize specimens are known as 'ahuriri'.

This fish is unrelated to the true salmons of the northern hemisphere, which are characterised by their fleshy adipose fin, located between the single dorsal and tail fins (as found on trout). The only close relative of the Australian salmon is the tommy ruff or herring *(A. georgianus)* of southern waters.

There are eastern and western sub-species of salmon, though they exhibit no external differences.

DESCRIPTION

A medium-sized, elongate marine fish with a nearly cylindrical body and large, forked tail. Salmon are almost always bluish-green to black on the upper back, silver to greenish-silver or purplish-silver on the flanks, and silvery-white on the belly. The back is patterned with darker green spots and dashes, which are much clearer in juveniles. There are often gold spots on the flanks. The eye is yellowish around the pupil.

The fins are light-coloured, except that the dusky tail often has a dark trailing edge. The pectorals may be tinged with yellow.

SIZE

Most Australian salmon taken by anglers weigh between 0.2 and 3.5 kg. The eastern sub-species may occasionally reach 5 kg, while the western fish has been reported at weights of up to 10 kg. The strain found in New Zealand may grow even larger.

DISTRIBUTION

A migratory, pelagic or semi-pelagic species of our cool and temperate waters, salmon are found right along our southern seaboard, up the east coast as far as about Port Macquarie and sometimes north along the west coast to Geraldton. The fish is also prolific around the New Zealand coastline.

The salmon is a near-shore species found in larger estuaries, bays, harbours, along beaches and rocky shorelines and also out on deeper reefs, particularly in the south.

They are rarely found over water deeper than 30 to 40 metres unless undertaking migration and prefer cool to temperate water with abundant baitfish in the form of pilchards, garfish, anchovy or krill.

They frequently hunt in areas of strong wave or current action with a covering of 'white water'.

HABITS AND FEEDING

An active, schooling predator, the salmon feeds on small baitfish, large planktonic organisms, small squid, prawns and crustacea.

Left: A fine Australian salmon or 'kahawai' of around 3 kg taken on light, single-handed baitcaster tackle and a metal casting lure.

Below: Australian salmon have a mottled back, silvery white flanks and yellowish eyes around a dark pupil. Very large specimens develop a much darker back, while juveniles have mottled flanks, gold spots and short, broken bars, giving them an appearance not unlike that of the tommy ruff.

Left: The author wades ashore with a solid kahawai taken on a New Zealand beach.
Above: Reaching for a salmon taken on light tackle from a rocky point.

Juvenile salmon — the so-called bay trout or salmon trout — rely heavily on marine worms and small crustacea such as sandhoppers for their diet.

FISHING TECHNIQUES

Salmon are commonly taken on baits of cut fish flesh, whole pilchards and garfish on ganged hooks, bottle squid or squid pieces, prawns, beachworms and pipis. They will also occasionally take crabs, cunji or even bread, particularly in a berley trail. Larger specimens will take live yellowtail or mullet.

They prefer lightly-weighted or moving baits rather than those anchored to the bottom.

Salmon are also avid lure takers. They succumb to cast and retrieved, or trolled metal slices, lead 'slugs', spoons, spinners, jigs, minnows, plugs, poppers and flies.

Because of their habit of jumping and shaking their heads when hooked, many salmon hooked on lures are lost.

The usual beach and rock fishing tackle for salmon is built around a 2.5 to 4 metre rod, large threadline, medium overhead or sidecast reel filled with 5 to 12 kg breaking strain line.

In areas where salmon are unpopular table fare this fine sporting fish should be carefully released to fight again.

EATING QUALITIES

The Australian salmon provides reasonable table fare. It is a dark-fleshed, strongly flavoured fish suitable for smoking, baking or being made into fish cakes. It is popular in Tasmania, Victoria and parts of South Australia and Western Australia, but not highly regarded as a table fish in New South Wales.

SALMON, CHINOOK

Oncorhyncus tshawytscha

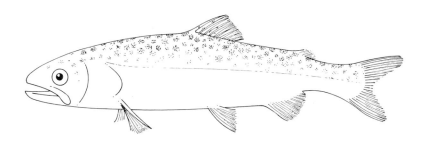

COMMON NAMES

The chinook salmon, a native species of countries bordering the North Pacific from Japan in the west to the United States in the east, is also known as the quinnat salmon, Pacific salmon, king salmon, spring salmon, silver salmon and tyee.

The chinook is one of the six Northern Hemisphere salmonoides to be introduced into Australasian waters with partial success.

DESCRIPTION

The chinook is a big, robust salmon with large jaws and relatively small eyes. The small, silvery scales are easily dislodged by rough handling.

The colouring of fresh or sea-run fish is green, blue or purplish-blue on the back, bright silver on the flanks and silvery-white on the belly. The flanks are peppered with small black spots.

As the fish approach spawning their bodies darken and their jaws begin to grow; those of the male fish become grotesquely hooked. By the time they spawn the fish may be almost jet black.

SIZE

In their native waters, chinook salmon have been recorded weighing in excess of 50 kg. The maximum size in other areas is closer to 35 kg.

Land-locked chinook in Australia rarely exceed 8 or 9 kg and are more common at less than half that weight. However, the New Zealand sea-run fish grow much larger, with occasional specimens topping 20 kg and even approaching 25 kg. The more typical sea-runner on New Zealand's South Island weighs in at between 4 and 12 kg.

DISTRIBUTION

Chinooks are native to the coastal streams and seas around northern Japan, China, Korea, Pacific USSR, Alaska, Canada and the north western states of continental USA.

In Australasia they are limited to a few land-locked lakes and ponds in Victoria (most notably Lakes Purrumbete and Bullen Merri in the west of the state), and to certain rivers on the east coast of New Zealand's South Island. These latter fish represent the only viable population of sea-run chinooks ever established outside their native, northern waters.

HABITS AND FEEDING

Chinook salmon have a life-cycle of between three and seven years. In their natural state they run to sea from the river of their birth, returning to spawn and die three, four, five or six years later.

At sea, salmon form schools and hunt a

Chinook salmon are still called 'quinnats' in some parts of Australia and New Zealand. They are muscular, handsome members of the same broad group of fish which contains the brown and rainbow trout.

range of baitfish, krill, shrimp and squid.

Most salmon are taken by anglers during their late summer and autumn spawning run. At this time they largely cease feeding, but will still strike or bite instinctively at baits and lures.

FISHING TECHNIQUES

In Australia's land-locked put-and-take quinnat fisheries, most of the salmon are taken on trolled or cast lures or deeply fished baits of small live or dead fish such as whitebait, galaxids or even saltwater pilchards.

New Zealand's sea-run fish are taken on heavy spoons and sliced chrome or hexagonal bar lures which must be fished right on or very close to the river bed for best results. Flies fished on fast-sinking lines also take a few salmon.

Because they are big, powerful fish frequenting very fast flowing water, most New Zealand chinooks are taken on sturdy double-handed casting gear, medium to large threadlines or large baitcaster reels and lines of 6 to 12 kg breaking strain.

EATING QUALITIES

The chinook is a pink or red-fleshed salmon held in high regard by gourmets. It is perfectly suited to being smoked, canned and cured.

Fresh-run or sea-going fish are superior in taste and texture to those about to spawn.

SALMON, THREADFIN

Family: *Polynemidae*

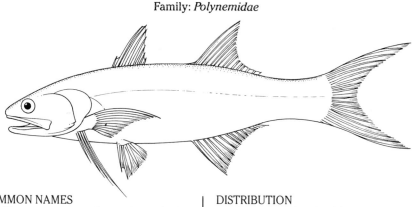

COMMON NAMES

There are several species of this tropical, inshore and estuarine fish found in Australian waters; the best known and most popular are the blue threadfin *(Polydactylus sheridani)* and the larger gold threadfin or king salmon *(Eleutheronema tetradactylum)*.

Other names for these fish include Sheridan's threadfin, Burnett salmon, Cooktown salmon and 'giant salmon'.

DESCRIPTION

This group of related fish are characterised by their overshot upper jaw, hard, bony head and long, filamentous rays ahead of the pectoral fin area.

Threadfin colouration varies from blue to bluish-grey or green on the back through to brassy-gold in some species. The flanks are usually silvery-white or grey, and the belly creamy.

Fins are mainly dusky, although the ventrals and anal may be strongly tinged with yellow.

SIZE

Average sizes of threadfin vary with species and location. The more commonly caught blue threadfin *(P. sheridani)* usually weighs from 1 to 4 kg, though the golden threadfin or king salmon *(E. tetradactylum)* may be from 5 to 10 or even 15 kg. Rare specimens could top 18 kg.

DISTRIBUTION

An inshore family of the tropical north, threadfin rarely range as far south as Hervey Bay in the east and Shark Bay in the west.

They are mainly found in northern estuaries, where they range upstream as far as the tidal limit and also in bays, inlets, harbours, and over coastal mud and sand-flats. They are rarely found far from shore or in deep water.

HABITS AND FEEDING

A loosely schooling group of fish, larger threadfin are also found singly or in pairs.

Their food intake varies according to species and location. Prawns, shrimp, crabs and small fish are common favourites which they seek in back eddies and water where a sudden colour change is clearly evident.

FISHING TECHNIQUES

Threadfin are taken both deliberately and incidentally by fishermen pursuing barramundi and other tropical sportfish.

They show a preference for live or very fresh baits of herring, mullet, prawn or crab but will also take cut fish-flesh, particularly a strip or slab of wolf herring or some other oily fish with a bright skin.

They sometimes strike at lures, particularly small artificials. The smaller

Left: A typical blue threadfin (Polydactylus sheridani) *from the Northern Territory.*
Below: Threadfin are encountered mostly in estuarine and inshore locations close to stands of mangrove trees. They are particularly fond of distinct colour changes and tidelines in the water.

blue threadfin is a more common lure-catch than the bigger golden threadfin.

Tackle for threadfin can be identical to that used on barramundi and mangrove jacks, though some salmon experts use a relatively heavy handline or a longer rod and a sidecast or threadline reel. A trace of some sort — ideally nylon, three or four times stronger than the main line — is useful for although salmon lack obvious

teeth, their hard jaws and grinding pads damage light line.

EATING QUALITIES

Most threadfin are superb table fish. In the north they are rated more highly than even the saltwater barramundi, though their flesh does not respond well to freezing or rough handling.

Threadfin should be cleaned promptly.

SAMSON FISH

Seriola hippos

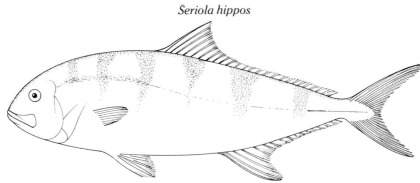

COMMON NAMES

The samson fish or samsonfish is also known as the 'sea kingfish', particularly in Western Australia, where it is reasonably prolific.

This species is often confused with the amberjack *(S. dumerilli)* and, more rarely, with the yellowtail kingfish, *(S. lalandi)*, its close relations.

DESCRIPTION

The samson fish is a medium to large, deep bodied predatory fish distinguished from the amberjack by the number of fin rays and gill rakers.

The samson has from 23 to 25 soft rays in its second dorsal fin, while the amberjack has between 29 and 35 fin rays.

The colouration of the samson fish is variable. Adults are normally blue-green to greeny-gold or bronze on the back, paler on the flanks, and yellowish-white on the belly. Younger fish are often reddish-bronze with fairly distinct vertical blotches and bars of very dark brown or black on the back and upper flanks. These bars fade with age.

The samson fish's teeth and mouth lining are often red-tinged, but this is not a diagnostic feature.

The fins are reddish-yellow or dusky.

SIZE

Samson fish grow to at least 50 kg in weight although specimens over 30 kg are exceptional. Juveniles in the 0.8 to 5 kg range are seasonally abundant in some areas.

DISTRIBUTION

The samson fish is an Australian species confined mainly to temperate and sub-tropical waters, but occasionally found in cooler southern seas.

Good populations are found off some southern Queensland ports and offshore from Nambucca Heads in northern New South Wales, but the fish are relatively uncommon elsewhere on the east coast though schools of juveniles sometimes frequent the Jervis Bay area of southern New South Wales during summer.

Samsons are far more frequently found in the west, where they range from the Recherche Archipelago to about Shark Bay.

The samson fish is more inshore and reef-oriented than the amberjack. It prefers the habitats of the yellowtail kingfish.

HABITS AND FEEDING

'Samsons' favour headlands, reef pinnacles, buoy lines and wharf pilings. In deeper water they do much of their feeding fairly close to the seabed.

Small fish form extensive schools, while large individuals swim in loose groups or singly.

Samson fish feed primarily on small to medium-sized fish and squid, occasionally taking crabs, prawns and octopi.

Left: An attractively marked juvenile samson fish.
Below: This adult samson fish of around 8 kg was taken off northern New South Wales.

FISHING TECHNIQUES

Methods and tackle used for taking samson fish are much the same as those described for yellowtail kingfish, with particular emphasis on deep-fished live and dead baits, squid and heavy jigs.

The samson is a strong, determined fighter and big ones demand quality tackle.

EATING QUALITIES

Small to medium-size samson fish make fine table fare. They have white, slightly dry meat, but larger fish tend to be too dry.

All samsons intended for the table should be killed promptly, bled, and kept on ice.

SARATOGA

Scleropages leichardti, Scleropages jardini

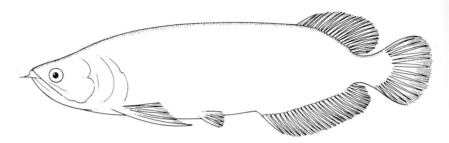

COMMON NAMES

Our two closely related saratoga species are sometimes distinguished by the names Northern saratoga *(S. jardini)* and Dawson River saratoga *(S. leichardti)*. Both are called 'toga' by some anglers.

These species were once known as spotted barramundi or Dawson River barramundi, though this practice is to be discouraged as it leads to confusion with the true barramundi *(Lates calcarifer)*.

DESCRIPTION

This striking, rather prehistoric-looking member of the small, ancient and international family of fresh and brackish water fish called *Osteoglossids* is characterised by an elongated, very laterally – compressed body, a large, upturned mouth, very big scales and small barbels or 'whiskers' under the lower lip.

The saratogas are greenish-grey to brown on the back and silvery-green or coppery-gold on the flanks. The belly is lighter. An orange spot on each scale is common. The saratoga's fins are similar to, or darker than, its body colour.

SIZE

Saratoga usually weigh from 0.5 to 3 kg, with prize specimens reaching more than 4 kg. The northern species is generally considered to grow larger than its southern cousin; both may very rarely

weigh nearly 8 kg. In Niugini the saratoga occasionally exceeds 10 or 11 kg.

DISTRIBUTION

There are two species in Australia, one found in the Dawson/Fitzroy system of central Queensland *(S. leichardti)* and the other, widely but discontinuously, through western Cape York, the Gulf country and the eastern Northern Territory *(S. jardini)*.

S. leichardti has been introduced into several other rivers as well as dams as far south as Brisbane and Noosa.

Both species prefer tropical rivers and creeks, particularly quiet, lily-covered back-waters and pandanus-lined waterholes, although the southern species is quite happy in the main stream.

The Dawson River fish will tolerate water temperatures as low as 10 °C, but the northern saratoga cannot survive if the temperature goes much below 15 °C.

HABITS AND FEEDING

Saratoga are mainly surface-feeders and stay close to cover. Lily pads, pandanus roots and the areas under flying-fox or fruit-bat colonies are prime holding points.

They prey on small fish, shrimp, fresh-water prawns and the like, but also rely heavily on frogs, lizards, snakes, insects and even small birds for food.

The saratoga are mouth-brooders. Their relatively few, large eggs are hatched

Left: The primitive saratoga, a unique native fish.

Below: A hooked saratoga explodes through the placid surface of a Top End billabong. They are superb sporting fish, and most are released alive to fight again.

in the mouth of the female, where the juveniles stay until ready to fend for themselves.

FISHING TECHNIQUES

Many saratoga are caught by anglers pursuing barramundi in tropical water-holes, lagoons and rivers. However, these days more and more sportfishermen are targeting these exciting and challenging fish.

'Barra' fishing tackle is ideal for saratoga, though lighter lines from 3 to 6 kg breaking-strain will handle most of them.

Baits of live or fresh-dead herring, frogs and large insects will all take saratoga, but this fine sporting fish responds more readily to lure-casting with spoons, spinners, plugs, smaller minnows and poppers. The saratogas are also superb flyrod targets.

Because of their slow growth rate, poor eating qualities and limited habitats, saratoga should be released unharmed.

EATING QUALITIES

The saratoga is an inferior table fish with soft, tasteless flesh and many fine bones. For this reason almost all saratoga taken are released alive.

173

– SHARKS, GUMMY & SCHOOL –

Mustelus antarcticus, Galeorhinus galeus

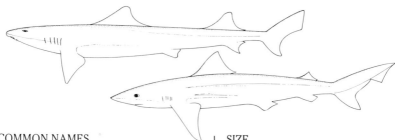

COMMON NAMES

The gummy shark or 'gummy' *(M. antarcticus)* is often confused with the similar-looking school shark *(G. galeus)*. Both belong to the family *Triakidae*.

Other names for the school shark include 'tope' and 'snapper shark', while the flesh of both species is marketed as 'flake', particularly in southern states.

DESCRIPTION

The gummy shark *(M. antarcticus)* is a long, relatively lightly built shark. The second dorsal fin is almost as large as the first, and both are slightly rounded at the top. There is a small tentacle or whisker adjacent to each of the nostrils.

The gummy shark's back is dusky grey to greenish-grey or greenish-brown, fading to white or cream on the belly. The back and upper flanks are sprinkled with small, light-coloured spots.

The school shark or 'tope' is more streamlined. The first dorsal fin is considerably larger than the second and the snout is more pointed, giving it a whaler-like appearance. There are no obvious tentacles or whiskers around the nostrils.

The school shark's back is grey to bronze, fading gradually to white or cream on the belly, and it has no light spots.

The most conclusive way of distinguishing these two edible sharks is by examining the teeth. The gummy has flat, grinding molars arranged like the cobbles in a footpath, while the 'schoolie' has sharp, whaler-like cutting teeth.

SIZE

The gummy shark grows to a maximum of about 1.6 metres in length and weights approaching 25 kg, although it is more common at half that size.

The school shark or 'tope' is larger, occasionally attaining 1.8 metres in length and weights of 30 to 35 kg.

DISTRIBUTION

Gummy sharks are found in the waters of central and southern New South Wales, Victoria, Tasmania, South Australia and around the West Australian coast to about Geraldton or Shark Bay.

'Gummies' prefer deep, offshore waters, but will range along beaches and rocky foreshores and occasionally enter large, deep estuaries, harbours and bays.

School sharks range through our temperate and cool to cold waters from southern Queensland to about Geraldton in Western Australia. They are also found in Tasmanian and New Zealand waters.

The 'tope's' habitat preferences are similar to those of the gummy shark, though they range inshore more often than 'gummies' in pursuit of food.

HABITS AND FEEDING

Gummy sharks are a loosely schooling species which feed mainly on shellfish, crustacea, worms and dead or decaying material.

'Tope' form schools, and prey on small fish, rays, crustacea, octopi, squid and carrion.

Left: A large school shark or 'tope' from South Australian waters.
Below: The gummy shark is more slender, with dorsal fins of near equal size. The back and flanks are often sprinkled with light spots.

Both the school shark and the 'gummy' are long living and relatively slow growing, particularly the 'gummy', which may live for 30 years without exceeding 1.6 metres.

FISHING TECHNIQUES

Both these sharks, particularly the 'gummy', are eagerly targeted by southern anglers. The majority are taken by surf-casting fishermen along ocean beaches and around the mouth of larger estuaries and bays, but many are landed by boat fishermen working offshore grounds, bays and harbour waters.

Besides those caught deliberately, many are taken, or at least hooked, by anglers targeting snapper, flathead and salmon.

Best baits for both types of shark are large slabs of fresh fish fillet or strip, whole pilchards or garfish, squid or octopi.

In their larger sizes both these sharks are strong and active fighters, and sturdy tackle is needed to cope with them. A wire trace is best when fishing for school sharks.

A berley trail of chopped fish pieces, bait scraps and crushed shellfish is particularly good for attracting both sharks.

EATING QUALITIES

Both these small sharks are highly rated table fish, especially in southern states, where 'flake' is the ubiquitous accompaniment to fried potato chips.

Both have firm, white meat and no bones. The flesh is particularly well-suited to frying or deep frying in batter.

To improve the flavour of the cooked flesh both 'tope' and gummy sharks should be killed and bled by severing the head.

175

— SHARKS, HAMMERHEAD —

Family: *Sphyrnidae*

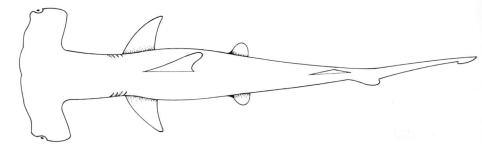

COMMON NAMES

This world-wide family of sharks with distinctive heads are represented by several species in Australasian waters; the most common are the smooth hammerhead *(Sphyrna zygaena)*, the scalloped hammerhead *(S. lewini)*, and the giant of the family, the great hammerhead *(S. mokarran)*.

These sharks are rarely known by any name other than hammerhead, hammer-headed or hammer sharks and are unlikely, to be confused with any other fish.

DESCRIPTION

The obvious distinguishing feature of the hammerheads is their curious T-shaped head, and eyes set at the end of the stalk or cross piece.

The different species of hammerhead are distinguished by the shape of the leading edge of the head. The great hammerhead has a characteristically high and sickle-shaped dorsal fin.

Colouration varies from brown through grey to blue-grey or gunmetal on the back, lighter on the flanks and creamy to white on the belly.

SIZE

The great hammerhead *(S. mokarran)* can attain a length of at least 4.2 metres and weight in excess of 450 kg, though such monsters are rare.

The other hammerheads are smaller, rarely longer than 3 metres or heavier than 200 kg, though they occasionally reach 3.5 metres and 260 kg.

DISTRIBUTION

The great and scalloped hammerheads are both tropical species which occasionally stray into sub-tropical waters. The scalloped hammerhead has been recorded in temperate seas as far south as Perth and Sydney.

The smooth hammerhead likes sub-tropical, temperate and cool waters, and is found around all southern states (only rarely around Tasmania), and in New Zealand waters.

All the hammerheads are open water pelagics which will sometimes enter bays, estuaries and harbours. The tropical species are more likely than the southern variant to be found close inshore over shallow water.

HABITS AND FEEDING

Juvenile hammerhead often school in large numbers, and sightings of these harmless, lightly built 1 to 1.8 metre sub-adult hammers often trigger the warnings of shark packs cruising off city beaches during summer months.

Large hammerhead sharks are likely to be solitary travellers, though even big fish occasionally form small groups.

The unusual configuration of the hammerhead's head is immediately recognisable. Distinguishing between the three most common species is a little more difficult, and is largely dependent on the shape of that strange head's leading edge.

Hammerheads prey on many types of small to medium fish and squid, and are active scavengers.

Large hammerheads, particulary the great hammerhead, pose a potential risk to humans and have been implicated in attacks overseas.

FISHING TECHNIQUES

All the methods described for medium to large sharks will take hammerheads. There should be particular emphasis on berleying and the use of live baits.

Hammerheads are keen-eyed, suspicious and harder to tempt than other large sharks. They are unlikely to bite on heavy, clumsy traces and roughly presented baits. It may be necessary to use unobtrusive single strand wire, small hooks and live baits.

Hammerheads will sometimes follow and strike at lures. They will also take trolled live and dead baits intended for marlin and other gamefish.

EATING QUALITIES

Smaller hammerheads, particularly the smooth hammerhead, make fine table fare, though the flesh of larger specimens may be a little coarse.

They should be knifed and bled within a few minutes of landing.

—— SHARKS, MAKO & BLUE ——

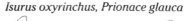

Isurus oxyrinchus, Prionace glauca

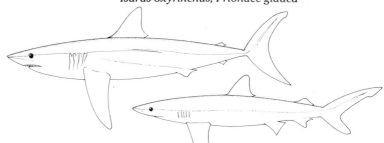

COMMON NAMES

Although only distantly related, these two sharks are dealt with together because they share so many habits and are so often taken together.

The mako short-fin mako *(I. oxyrinchus)* is related to the white pointer shark *(Carcharodon carcharias)*. It is called 'blue pointer' and 'blue dynamite'. Mako is pronounced 'may-ko' in Australia, but 'mar-ko' in New Zealand.

The similar-looking but more lightly built and longer-finned blue shark is called the 'blue whaler', 'oceanic blue' or 'blue'. It is a member of the whaler family *(Carcharhinidae)*, but is quite unlike any of the other whalers.

DESCRIPTION

The mako is a robust, heavily built, almost bullet-shaped shark with a pointed head, symmetrical tail and large, dark eyes.

Its colour varies from blue-green to bright, electric blue on the back to bluish-silver on the flanks and white on the belly. There is sometimes a blue, vertical herring-bone pattern on the flanks between the pectoral fins and the tail.

Blue sharks are much longer and more lightly-built for a given weight than makos, and are characterised by their long, floppy pectoral fins and non-symmetrical tail; the top lobe is noticeably longer than the bottom one.

Blue sharks are almost always bright blue on the back and white on the belly.

Their eyes are dark, and a little smaller than those of the mako.

SIZE

Makos are a large shark, growing to 4 metres in length and at least 450 kg in weight, but are rare at weights greater than 280 kg. Most makos encountered by anglers in Australasian waters range from 80 cm juveniles weighing 5 kg and less, to adults 2 to 3 metres long and weighing between 80 and 220 kg.

Blue sharks grow to the same maximum lengths as makos, but a 4 metre blue would weigh only half as much as a mako of the same length. Records for blues stand around the 200 kg mark, but they are rare at weights in excess of 140 kg.

DISTRIBUTION

Both these species are found world-wide, in tropical, sub-tropical, temperate, cool and even cold waters, though the blue is more common in tropical areas than the mako.

They are oceanic wanderers which rarely come close to shore or visit waters shallower than 60 metres.

Makos and blues have been recorded in every state of Australia, and are quite common in New Zealand waters.

HABITS AND FEEDING

They both hunt a wide range of small to medium-sized fish and will also scavenge. Squid play a large part in their diet.

Left: A fine mako of 128 kg taken by a young game fisherman off Bermagui, on the far south coast of New South Wales. Note the metallic blue and silver colouration, large, dark eyes and obvious teeth.

Below: A blue shark free-swimming beside a boat. Blues are immediately identifiable by virtue of their, long, floppy pectoral or side fins and lightweight build.

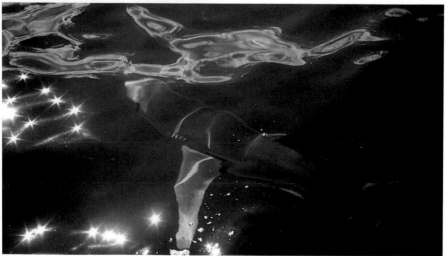

The blue shark is more likely to be found in schools and packs than the mako.

FISHING TECHNIQUES

All the methods described for catching medium to large sharks will take makos and blues, with particular emphasis on the use of berley, and baits of live or fresh-dead tuna and similar oily, blood-rich fish species.

Inexperienced crews or small boat fishermen should not try to tackle these fish. The mako is a notorious boat and tackle wrecker.

EATING QUALITIES

Both sharks are edible, though the mako tastes better. Small and medium-sized makos demand a good price at market.

Both sharks should be thoroughly bled and drained as soon as caught, particularly the blue, which may otherwise develop a strong ammonia taint.

SHARK, TIGER

Galeocerdo cuvieri

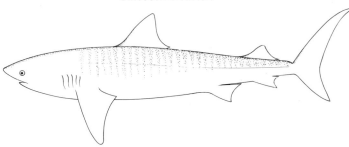

COMMON NAMES

The tiger shark or 'tiger' is a member of the same general group as the whalers but is distinct enough in appearance and habits to be dealt with separately.

DESCRIPTION

This big, heavily-built shark has a characteristically blunt head and large jaws filled with rows of slightly serrated teeth.

Adult colouring varies from light, almost bronzy-brown to a dirty mud-grey on the back. The flanks are always lighter and the belly is cream, off-white or white, sometimes with a vague yellowish or even reddish tinge.

Juvenile 'tigers' are barred with wavy and broken, vertical stripes of dark grey to brown or black over the back and upper flanks. This tiger pattern fades with age, but may still be evident on very large sharks.

SIZE

The 'tiger' is one of the largest of all sharks, very occasionally reaching lengths in excess of 4.5 metres and weights of close to 800 kg, though a rare giant could weigh as much as 1000 kg.

The more common weight in Australian waters ranges from 100 to 500 kg. Juveniles of less than 70 kg are uncommon outside tropical regions.

DISTRIBUTION

The 'tiger' is a tropical and sub-tropical shark which makes summertime forays into temperate and even cool waters.

In southern latitudes it stays in the open ocean and rarely comes close in shore. However, in the tropics it visits shallow lagoons, bays and even estuaries, especially under cover of darkness.

HABITS AND FEEDING

The tiger is big and potentially dangerous. People have been attacked in Australian waters, particularly around the tropical north of the continent.

Small tigers may group into schools, though large individuals are more likely to be solitary or to form pairs or trios. Heavy berleying has been known to concentrate as many as a dozen or more large 'tigers' into a small area.

Tiger sharks prey on stingrays, skate, smaller sharks, large crustacea, squid, octopi, dead animals and carrion of all kinds. They are probably capable of taking large, fast creatures such as tuna and dolphins.

FISHING TECHNIQUES

The angling methods used to take 'tigers' are similar to those described for all the other large sharks.

In southerly waters, where big 'tigers' are a popular target among the competition gamefishing fraternity, heavy berleying and the use of deeply-set baits of whole or cut dead tuna and similar fish is widely practiced. A whole 2 or 3 kg silver trevally, rigged on two large hooks and a heavy wire

Left: A game fisherman poses with a relatively small tiger shark which still has clearly defined stripes or bars.
Below: 'Tigers' are popular medium and heavy tackle opponents in some regions, providing a dour, if unspectacular, tussle.

trace, and set 20 or 30 metres beneath the surface in water 150 to 300 metres deep is a particularly successful approach.

Shark fishing should never be undertaken from small boats or with an inexperienced crew.

EATING QUALITIES

While the flesh of small tigers is quite palatable, particularly if the shark is bled and drained by severing the head, tail and fins as soon as it is landed, that of large ones is very coarse and rank.

SHARKS, WHALER

Family: *Carcharhinidae*

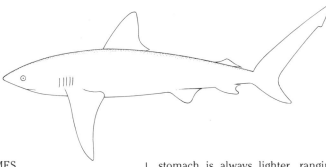

COMMON NAMES

This large family of sharks with a world-wide distribution includes such common Australasian species as the bronze whaler *(Carcharhinus brachyurus)*, black whaler *(C. obscurus)*, sandbar shark or northern whaler *(C. plumbeus)* and bull shark or river whaler *(C. leucas)*.

Several smaller tropical reef sharks also belong to the whaler family, as do the oceanic whitetip shark *(C. longimanus)* and the long-nosed grey, blacktip or inkytail shark *(C. brevipinna)*.

Australian fishermen refer to all these sharks as 'bronze whaler' or 'bronzy', though the name only belongs to one member of the family. The most commonly encountered, and the ones responsible for more attacks on humans in our waters than all other species combined, are the black or dusky whaler *(C. obscurus)* and the bull shark or river whaler *(C. leucas)*.

DESCRIPTION

The shape, size and colouration of the whalers varies considerably from species to species. However, most have stout, heavily built bodies, large, pointed first dorsal fins and considerably smaller second ones, tails with a top lobe almost twice as long as the lower one and small eyes with distinct, sometimes cat-like pupils.

Colours vary from dirty grey or brown to clean, metallic bronze or even blue or blue-grey on the back and flanks. The stomach is always lighter, ranging from creamy-grey through lemonish-cream to brilliant white.

SIZE

The largest of the whaler family represented in Australasian waters (excluding the tiger shark, which is dealt with separately) is the black or dusky whaler *(C. obscurus)*, which has been known to attain a length in excess of 3.5 metres and to weigh as much as 360 kg.

At the opposite extreme, some of the tropical reef whalers never exceed lengths of 1.6 metres and weights of 30 kg.

DISTRIBUTION

Whaler sharks of one kind or another are found in the waters of every Australian state and are also reasonably common around the North Island of New Zealand.

They generally prefer warm, tropical, sub-tropical and temperate waters, though species such as the bronze whaler and, to a lesser extent, the black or grey whaler, will sometimes venture into cool and cold southern waters.

Habitats range from the purely freshwater reaches far upstream in our coastal rivers to estuaries, bays, harbours, inshore area and deep, offshore waters.

HABITS AND FEEDING

All whalers decribed here are carnivorous predators and scavengers.

Left: A large whaler shark taken during a competition.

Below: One way of dispatching a pesky whaler!

They eat all manner of fish, rays, turtles, smaller sharks, squid, octopi, cuttlefish and carrion.

Although whalers hunt and feed as individuals, they frequently form loose 'packs' of three to 100 or so members.

FISHING TECHNIQUES

Whaler sharks are usually hooked unintentionally, and few large specimens are landed without the use of wire traces and heavy sport or gamefishing tackle. However, small whalers up to about 1.8 metres long and 55 kg in weight are taken from time to time by offshore fishermen using reasonably heavy lines or by land-based live bait anglers.

Fishermen specifically targeting large whalers and other big sharks employ a berley trail of blood, fish-oil and minced fishflesh to attract their quarry, then present large live, dead or cut baits of tuna or other species on robust tackle and heavy,

multistrand wire or light chain traces.

Shark fishing is not without its thrills, but the potential for injury should not be underrated. These are big, powerful creatures with immensely strong bodies and jaws filled with razor sharp teeth. They do not respond meekly to being hooked, fought and gaffed or lassoed!

Shark fishing should only be undertaken by experienced anglers in boats measuring 4.5 metres and more.

EATING QUALITIES

Small whalers, especially the juvenile bronze, black or grey, make fine table fare, with flesh not unlike that of gummy and school sharks. Larger whalers and species, such as the bull shark or river whaler tend to have rank, coarse flesh.

As with all sharks, the flavour of the cooked flesh is greatly improved if the head, tail and fins are removed soon after the fish is captured.

SHARK, WHITE

Carcharodon carcharias

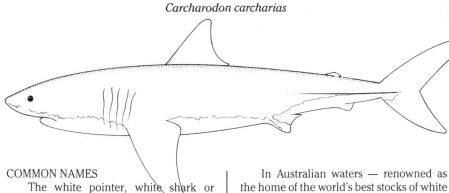

COMMON NAMES

The white pointer, white shark or 'great white' is nowadays — thanks mainly to Hollywood — also known by the romantic name of 'great white death'.

The closest relatives of the white pointer are the mako and the porbeagle.

DESCRIPTION

The white pointer is the largest of all the meat-eating sharks, and the third largest carnivore on earth after the sperm and killer whales. Its body shape is similar, though somewhat heavier, than that of the mako. It has a pointed, bullet nose, large dark eyes and a big, almost symmetrical tail.

White shark colouring varies from brown or even bronzy to grey or steel-grey on the back. It is never as blue as the mako.

The dark back colour gives way to dirty white along a distinct irregular line along the lower flanks. The belly is off-white, cream or white.

SIZE

Just how big white sharks grow is a matter of conjecture. Fossil remains indicate that it, or an almost identical shark, has reached lengths of 20 metres since the last Ice Age. However, the largest whites recorded by man have measured between 6 and 7 metres long and weighed about 5000 kg (5 tonnes). Any white over 5.2 metres and 1200 kg is exceptional today.

In Australian waters — renowned as the home of the world's best stocks of white pointers — whites in the 3 to 5 metre length range, weighing between 250 and 700 kg, are reasonably abundant, though not as prolific as they were 40 or 50 years ago.

Juvenile whites of less than 2.2 metres and lighter than 90 kg are almost never sighted, even in areas where the species is relatively abundant.

DISTRIBUTION

The great white is found in every ocean of the world. It prefers cool and temperate waters, but occasionally strays towards the tropics or the cold polar seas.

Around Australasia its major haunts are along our southern coastline from about Wilsons Promontory to Albany. It is quite rare in Tasmanian waters.

Whites travel up the east and the west coasts as far as Moreton Bay and Shark Bay, and have been recorded in New Zealand waters.

They vary their habitat according to the food available and may be found anywhere between the deep ocean far off the continental shelf and the inshore shallows of bays, beaches, harbours and larger estuaries.

HABITS AND FEEDING

Large whites seem somewhat territorial, although heavy berleying, a seal colony or a dead whale, will often attract sharks from far and wide, and bring as

NOTE: *White sharks are now totally protected in most Australian waters.*

Left: An underwater shot of a female white shark weighing in excess of 1000 kg.

Below: Seal colonies such as this one on South Neptune Island, South Australia, are prime feeding grounds for great whites.

many as a dozen large adults into a relatively small area.

Whites are opportunistic predators and scavengers. They eat rays, other sharks, fish, seals, dolphins, sick or injured whales and dead or decaying matter.

FISHING TECHNIQUES

A strong berley trail of blood, fish-oil and minced flesh, combined with the presentation of large, oily baits of tuna or similar fish on very strong wire or chain traces is the accepted method for catching white sharks. The tackle used is usually the heaviest available, with lines of 37 or 60 kg breaking strain. In shallow water, large whites have been taken on 24 and even 15 kg tackle.

Because of their enormous bulk and strength, whites are most dangerous, and it would be foolhardy in the extreme to attempt to raise and excite one from a boat under 6 metres in length!

EATING QUALITIES

White shark flesh is similar to that of the mako and is as highly rated. The meat from large specimens is reported to be palatable, but since these older sharks will have accumulated mercury and other potentially hazardous heavy metals and trace elements in their systems, repeated or large meals of their flesh are inadvisable. An increasing number of sport and game anglers are now choosing to release white pointers which are not record captures.

SNAPPER

Chrysophrys auratus

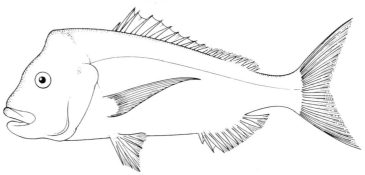

COMMON NAMES

Since it is one of Australasia's most popular and important species, it's hardly surprising that the snapper has earned an array of alternative and colloquial names.

Snapper, 'red', 'big red' and 'reddie' are the most common, although in much of Western Australia this fish is called 'pink snapper' in order to distinguish it from the unrelated spangled emperor or nor'west snapper *(Lethrinus nebulosus)*.

Snapper may also have different names at different sizes. There was once a strongly established system of size-gradation-by-name among east coast snapper anglers. The smallest fish were 'cockneys' or 'cockney bream', the next size up were 'red bream', the next, 'squire', the next, 'snapper' and the largest, 'old man snapper' — and woe betide any newcomer who wrongly called a 'squire' a 'snapper'! Thankfully, this archaic system is now largely a thing of the past.

Less formalised, but nonetheless popular, is the use of a nickname for smaller, 'pan-size' snapper. In Victoria and parts of New South Wales these fish, from legal length up to a kilo or so in weight, are called 'pinkies'. The same fish in South Australia are known as 'ruggers'.

Finally, it should be noted that snapper is still occasionally spelt incorrectly as 'schnapper' — usually by fish-shop owners and restaurateurs.

DESCRIPTION

The snapper is a deep-bodied fish with powerful jaws and peg-like teeth.

Large adults often exhibit a distinct hump on the head and even an enlarged 'nose' area, but this is by no means universal. In New Zealand waters, snapper almost never develop these humps and lumps, and in Victoria and South Australia, some very large specimens have practically no hump.

Colouration varies from one locality to another. Fish caught in deep water over hard reef tend to be a much brighter red than those taken on sand or mud.

Typical snapper colouration is red to pinkish-silver or coppery on the head and back, rosy-silver with blue reflections on the flanks, and silver or silvery-white on the belly. The flanks are heavily peppered with small, iridescent blue spots or highlights.

Fins are dusky red, and the anal fin is often edged with blue. The bottom lobe of the tail may be white along its lower edge.

The intensity of colouration is variable. Some snapper are dark, brick-red or ochre, others almost pillar-box red, and others the palest pastel-pink.

SIZE

To most anglers outside South Australia, a 9 kg 'red' is the catch of a lifetime. Most snapper taken on the east and south east coasts weigh from 0.4 to

Left: An adult snapper taken from the ocean rocks in New South Wales.

Below: The author with a 2 kg New Zealand snapper.

Above: This 5.5 kg 'reds' came from a reef off Bermagui, in southern New South Wales.
Left: Snapper are held in high regard, wherever they are caught.

5 kg, and even in Port Phillip Bay — a renowned hangout of big 'reds' — fish over 8 or 9 kg cause crowds to gather at the cleaning tables.

Many 8 kg-plus snapper are taken around New Zealand's North Island, though even here, 10 kg 'reds' are noteworthy.

The situation is somewhat different in parts of South Australia, especially in the Whyalla region, where snapper taken from inshore marks can **average** 9 kg or better! Here, fish must top 12 kg to make news.

The one location that could upstage Whyalla is Norfolk Island, far out in the Pacific. Here, snapper are by no means prolific, but those taken tend to be of gargantuan proportions, and 'reds' as heavy as 18 kg have been recorded.

DISTRIBUTION

A member of a worldwide family with close relatives in Japan, South Africa, North America and the Mediterranean, the snapper is found right around the southern half of the continent from Rockhampton in Queensland to Carnarvon in Western Australia, though it is practically unknown in Tasmanian waters.

In New Zealand the fish is found right around the North Island, and as far down the east coast of the South Island as Christchurch.

Snapper also occur around Norfolk Island and, sporadically, near Lord Howe Island.

Juveniles and occasional adults are taken in estuaries, while sub-adults and

South Australian 'reds' like this 12 kilo-plus Whyalla thumper are characterised by their pale colour and lack of a forehead hump.

fully grown fish range from the rocky foreshores out to deep reefs close to the continental shelf edge. They occasionally feed along ocean beaches, particularly in New Zealand.

The ideal habitat for snapper is open ocean reef or gravel-bottomed grounds 20 to 100 metres deep, close to structures such as pinnacles, headlands, islands and bomboras.

In southern waters, large spawning migrations occur in flat-bottomed sand and mud strata bays. These conditions account for the bulk of the spring and summer 'run' in Melbourne's Port Phillip and South Australia's big gulfs.

Along the eastern seaboard, snapper are frequently taken from rock ledges fronting deep water.

HABITS AND FEEDING

Snapper are an incredibly wide-ranging and opportunistic feeders.

Their diet varies considerably with location and size, but in most areas crustacea such as prawns and crabs, and molluscs like mussels and abalone, make up the bulk of the food intake. Additional nutrition comes from sea cucumbers, octopi, squid and small fish.

Snapper will also scavenge dead marine creatures and food scraps.

They have a slow growth rate, though this varies according to location. In most places a snapper is at least four or five years old before attaining the legal length, and trophy-fish in excess of 9 kg are often 20 to 25 years of age.

Though mainly a schooling fish, large snapper sometimes live singly or in small groups. The largest aggregations take place prior to spawning, usually in spring and early summer.

FISHING TECHNIQUES

Because of the diversity of environments in which they live and the size-range of the fish themselves, technique and tackle for snapper fishing vary immensely. For instance, a surf-caster on New Zealand's Ninety Mile Beach will have different needs to a party-boat customer, fishing the seabed in 100 metres of water off Coffs Harbour, or a small-boat angler, chasing finnicky winter 'reds' in the shallows of Geelong's Corio Bay.

However, despite the differences occasioned by geography, certain basic rules apply wherever snapper are found.

In water of less than 40 metres, the best results will be had by using unweighted or lightly weighted baits of cut fish flesh, particularly tuna and bonito, pilchards (whole or cut), garfish pieces, squid, octopus, prawn and crabs.

In deeper water, sinkers weighing between 100 grams and a kilo may be needed to take the bait or baits to the fish. Here prawns, squid and cut fish are the favoured options.

Rockhoppers and beachcasters mainly use 60 to 120 gram sinkers and baits of octopus, squid, pilchard or cut flesh, but at dawn, dusk and after heavy seas, good fish can be taken close to the rocks on unweighted 'floaters'.

Big snapper will succumb to live baits, and 'reds' of all sizes will occasionally strike lures, particularly jigs.

Tackle can range from a simple handline to a medium-weight threadline outfit and 6 to 10 kg line for shallow-water boat-work, to a stumpy boat rod, centrepin and 20 kg line for deep-reef drifting, or a 3 to 4 metre casting rod, big threadline, overhead or sidecast and 8 to 15 kg line for rock and surf casting.

EATING QUALITIES

Snapper are very highly rated as food. They have white, moist and slightly flaky flesh, occasionally tending towards dryness in very large specimens.

Fish in the 0.8 to 4 kg range are regarded as the best for the table, though they are delicious at all sizes. They freeze well and lose little of their flavour or texture if frozen soon after being caught.

SNOOK

Sphyraena novaehollandiae

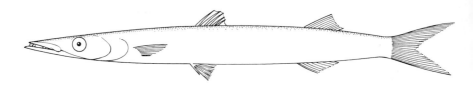

COMMON NAMES

This southern saltwater species, which is distantly related to the northern barracuda, is also known as the short-finned pike or shortfin sea pike, though snook is the most common name through much of its range.

There is occasional confusion between this fish and the unrelated long-finned pike *(Dinolestes lewini)*, which is found in the same waters as the snook, and further north.

It should also be noted that both Spanish mackerel and spotted or school mackerel are sometimes called 'snook' in northern New South Wales. These fish of the family *Scomberomorus* are unrelated to the true southern snook under discussion here.

DESCRIPTION

The snook is characterised by its elongated, almost cylindrical body, sharp teeth and widely separated, short-based dorsal fins.

The colouring is greenish to bluish-purple or brown on the back, silvery on the flanks, with two or three darker green or brown longitudinal stripes along each side.

The fins are light, the tail sometimes yellowish, but never as bright as that of the long-finned pike.

SIZE

Most snook taken by anglers weigh between 0.8 and 1.5 kg, although fish in excess of 3 kg are not unknown.

DISTRIBUTION

The snook ranges through our cooler coastal waters from the far south of New South Wales, through Victoria, Tasmania, South Australia and southern Western Australia.

It is an inshore predator of the seagrass beds and shallow reefs, although occasionally found close to the bottom over deeper reefs.

HABITS AND FEEDING

The snook preys on pilchards, whitebait, sprat, mullet, garfish and juvenile whiting which it ambushes in and around seagrass beds and over shallow reefs. It will also take squid and prawns.

Snook are a schooling fish which form large, fairly loose packs which frequent definite haunts. This means they can be fished on a regular basis.

FISHING TECHNIQUES

Most snook are taken on lightly-weighted or unweighted baits of whitebait, anchovy or pilchards on ganged hooks or single, long-shanked hooks. They also fall to fish flesh strips and pieces of squid.

Baits should be lightly weighted and kept moving. A gentle jigging motion will attract them.

Snook are lure-takers and fall to slow-trolled spoons, jigs, feathers and minnows, particularly on weighted lines or behind paravanes.

When a patch of snook is located, cast and retrieved lures work well.

Left: A large snook from South Australian waters. This specimen weighed over 2 kg.

Bottom Left: A snook (left) and a long-finned pike (right). Despite superficial similarities, the two are easily distinguishable by fin structure and shape.

Below: Snook are a favourite with many southern anglers.

EATING QUALITIES

The snook is a very good to excellent table fish, much prized in southern waters. The flesh is white, moist and sweet, though a little soft. Care should be taken not to bruise the meat, and snook should be cleaned promptly after capture.

SOOTY GRUNTER

Hephaestus fuliginosus

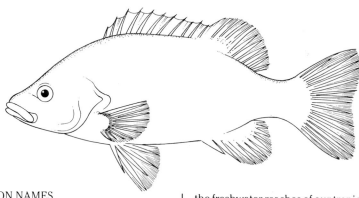

COMMON NAMES

The name sooty grunter covers several closely allied members of the family *Theraponidae*, which are also related to the silver perch and spangled perch of our outback rivers. The most common and widespread of the clan is *Hephaestus fuliginosus*.

Other common titles for this fish and its close relatives are black bream, khaki bream, 'blubberlips,' grunter and 'sooty'.

DESCRIPTION

This is a variable group of tropical freshwater fish and not all of them have yet come under scientific scrutiny. Most are small to medium-sized, deep-bodied fish with a squared-off or slightly-concave tail and a rubbery-lipped mouth.

Colouration is normally coal-black to smoky-grey, green, olive or khaki, often with off-white patches or blotches.

The fins are dark, as is the tail.

SIZE

Most sooty grunter encountered by fishermen weigh from 0.4 to 1.4 kg, but outstanding specimens sometimes top 2.2 kg and, on rare occasions, reach, or even exceed, 3 kg.

DISTRIBUTION

This wide-ranging family is found in the freshwater reaches of our tropical north, from central northern Queensland to the Kimberleys and Pilbarra in Western Australia.

Sooty grunter inhabit tropical freshwater streams, lakes and billabongs. They prefer relatively clean, flowing water with gravel or sandbeds, rock-jumbles and snags.

HABITS AND FEEDING

Sooty grunter are opportunistic feeders which will take shrimp, yabbies, freshwater prawns, small fish, insects and insect larvae, algae, aquatic weeds and even fruit which may fall into the stream.

'Sooties' form loose, competitive schools, but are also found alone or in small groups of two or three.

In lightly-fished waters, sooty grunter are inquisitive and aggressive, rushing out from cover to investigate every disturbance in their pool.

FISHING TECHNIQUES

Sooty grunter respond well to unweighted or lightly weighted baits of shrimp, earthworms, yabbies, prawns or insects.

They are enthusiastic lure-takers and will strike at a wide range of spoons,

*Left: A large sooty grunter taken on fly.
Below: Fishing in typical sooty grunter water:
a Northern Territory billabong.*

spinners, plugs, jigs, minnows and flies.

The ideal tackle for 'sooty' fishing is a light, single-handed outfit and 3 kg line similar to that used in the south for trout, bass or bream fishing.

EATING QUALITIES

Most 'sooties' provide good table fare, although their slightly 'weedy' flavour deters some people. Sportfishermen often release them alive.

SWEEP, SEA

Scorpis aequipinnis

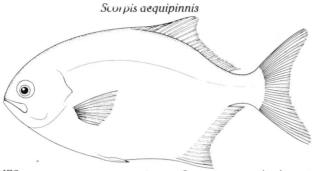

COMMON NAMES

The sea sweep is the largest and most sought after member of the *Scorpididae* family. Other sweep in the group include the smaller but prolific common or silver sweep *(S. lineolatus)* of the east coast, and the less abundant banded sweep *(S. georgianus)* of southern waters.

In western Victoria the sea sweep is sometimes called snapjack.

DESCRIPTION

The sea sweep is a deep bodied, thickset fish with a relatively small mouth and small scales.

The colouration of this cool water marine fish is usually slate grey to steely blue on the back and bluish grey to silvery grey on the flanks and belly.

There is an indistinct dark vertical band a third of the way back along the body on each flank. This band or saddle is wide at the top, tapering to a point behind the pectoral fin. A much less distinct band may also be evident under the base of the second dorsal fin. These bands are never as clearly defined as those of the banded sweep *(S. georgianus)*.

The fish have a small, yellow patch under the lower jaw. This can be quite bright.

The smaller and less sought after common or silver sweep of eastern waters has a more laterally compressed body, a smaller mouth, and is uniformly blue grey to slate on the back and flanks.

Sea sweep are the largest fish in the *Scorpididae* clan, and occasionally attain lengths of more than 60 cm and weights of 3.5 kg and more. However, fish half this length and weighing 0.8 to 1 kg are more common.

Banded sweep *(S. georgianus)* may sometimes reach weights around 2.2 kg, but are more common at less than a kilo, while silver sweep *(S. lineolatus)* mainly weigh from 0.1 to 0.8 kg, with exceptional specimens topping 1 kg.

DISTRIBUTION

The sea sweep is a fish of cool southern seas, and ranges the far south coast of New South Wales, and the coasts of Victoria, South Australia and southern Western Australia. It is also found around Tasmania.

The banded sweep is found around the coasts of far western Victoria, South Australia and Western Australia, north to about Shark Bay.

The common or silver sweep ranges along the east coast from about Moreton Bay to Wilsons Promontory.

HABITS AND FEEDING

Sea sweep are inshore fish which prefer turbulent water around rocky headlands, shallow reefs and islands. They sometimes enter large estuaries and bays.

All sweep are schooling fish which feed on the larger planktonic organisms, krill, shrimp, prawns, marine worms, small octopi and squid and dead or decaying

Left: An adult sea sweep (Scorpis aequipinnis) *from the waters of South Australia.*

Below: The silver or common sweep (S. lineolatus) *is a prolific but not particularly popular fish in New South Wales. It is generally smaller than the southern sea sweep.*

animals. Large sea sweep and banded sweep occasionally prey on small fish.

FISHING TECHNIQUES

Sea sweep are mainly taken on small, soft baits such as prawns, mussels, worms, pipis, cut fish flesh and squid pieces.

Light sinkers and smallish hooks on relatively fine lines are best. Many successful rigs incorporate a float which suspends the bait in mid-water.

Sweep respond actively to a berley trail of soaked bread, bran, boiled wheat, fish scraps and tuna oil.

Typical tackle for catching sea sweep from the ocean rocks is based around a 2.8 to 3.5 metre, light-tipped casting rod and a medium threadline or sidecast reel.

EATING QUALITIES

The sea sweep is the best table fish of all the sweep clan, the firm, white, moist flesh is superior in taste and texture to that of both the banded and common sweep.

SWEETLIP

Lethrinus chrystostomus

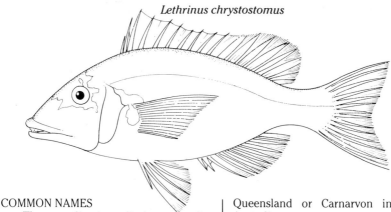

COMMON NAMES

The sweetlip, 'sweetlips' or sweetlip emperor is also known as the red throated sweetlip or 'lipper'.

This fish is related to the other emperors; the red emperor *(Lutjanus sebae)* and the spangled emperor *(Lethrinus nebulosus)*, described elsewhere in this book.

DESCRIPTION

The sweetlip is an attractive member of the *Lethrinid* clan with a steep forehead and a strong, rather pointed mouth.

Colouration varies considerably, but is most often golden to yellowish brown overlaid with darker vertical blotches and bars. The head is often red, especially around the 'throat' area and under the gills. The inside of the mouth is bright red.

The sweetlip's fins are also red, especially the dorsal, which can be very bright. There is a bright red blotch around the base of each pectoral fin.

SIZE

Most line-caught sweetlip weigh between 0.8 and 2.2 kg. Bigger specimens sometimes reach 3 kg but rarely atain more than 4.2 kg.

DISTRIBUTION

A fish of tropical reef waters, sweetlip rarely stray far south of Moreton Island in Queensland or Carnarvon in Western Australia.

They favour coral reef areas ranging from the inshore shallows to deep, continental shelf drop-offs.

Large sweetlips are generally found schooling over rough, broken ground on deeper reefs.

HABITS AND FEEDING

The sweetlip is a schooling emperor which feeds mainly on crustacea such as crabs and prawns, shellfish and soft molluscs, squid, octopi, cuttlefish, certain forms of coral and, less frequently, small fish.

FISHING TECHNIQUES

Sweetlip are very popular with tropical reef fisherman and are often landed in large numbers.

They are mainly taken on bottom-fished baits of cut fish-flesh but will eagerly devour crustacea and will seek out crabs, shellfish and prawns.

They are sometimes taken on lures, particularly in shallow areas around bomboras.

Most, however, are caught on handlines of 20 to 55 kg breaking strain, and rigs consisting of a heavy sinker and one or more strong hooks. Many reef anglers believe that painting the sinker red increases the number of fish caught.

EATING QUALITIES

This very tasty and sought–after member of the emperor clan is rated ahead of the spangled emperor, but a little inferior to the red emperor.

It is said to be connected with ciguatera poisoning, but appears to be a very minor offender in this regard.

Sweetlip or red-throated sweetlip are a common catch aboard tropical charter boats, where they are often called 'lippers'.

TAILOR

Pomatomus saltatrix

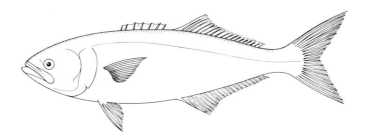

COMMON NAMES

This world-wide saltwater fish has different names in different countries. In the United States it is 'bluefish', in South Africa, it is called 'elf' and actively pursued from beach and rock. Here in Australia we call it 'tailor', (sometimes incorrectly spelt 'tailer') or use its popular nickname: 'chopper'.

In Victoria, tailor are sometimes called skipjack or 'skippies.'

DESCRIPTION

The tailor is a mid-sized predatory fish with an elongated body, forked tail and a relatively large mouth lined with fairly small but very sharp teeth.

Typical colouration is green to greenish-blue or grey on the back, silver on the flanks, and silvery-white on the belly. Fish caught well offshore tend to have steely-blue backs.

The fins are variable in colour but the tail is almost always dark, with a black trailing edge.

SIZE

The majority of tailor caught in Australia weigh from 0.2 to 2.2 kg. Smallish schools of big fish, in the 2 to 5 kg range, are regularly encountered in some areas.

Outsize tailor, which are often caught further offshore than their smaller brethren, may weigh as much as 6 or 8 kg.

The largest ones taken in Australia have topped the 10 or 11 kg mark, while in the United States specimens up to 18 kg in weight have been recorded.

DISTRIBUTION

In Australia, tailor are found in temperate and sub-tropical waters, being most prolific on the east coast between Eden and Fraser Island, and in the west from Albany to Carnarvon. They occur sporadically along the southern seaboard, are rare in Tasmania and unknown in New Zealand.

Tailor make use of a wide range of habitats, from the upper, almost freshwater, reaches of estuaries, through bays, harbours and inlets, to inshore grounds, shallow reefs, islands and on out to the edge of the continental shelf — perhaps even beyond, in the case of very large specimens.

Juveniles and small adult tailor are common in tidal rivers, estuaries, harbours and bays.

Larger fish tend to frequent inshore areas adjacent to rocky foreshores, headlands and beaches. They are particulary numerous in foamy 'wash' areas around exposed headlands, shallow reefs and bomboras.

HABITS AND FEEDING

Tailor are voracious predators which hunt in large packs or schools. They feed

Left: A very large tailor in excess of 7 kg from the waters of Shark Bay, Western Australia, which boasts some of the largest tailor or 'bluefish' in the world.

Below: A more typical 'chopper' of around a kilo in weight taken on a cast and retrieved lure.

mainly on small baitfish such as whitebait, anchovy, pilchards, herring and garfish, but will also attack larger prey like mullet, yellowtail, pike, slimy mackeral, juvenile salmon and even members of their own species.

Tailor feed by slashing and biting at the tail region of their prey in order to cripple it before returning for the kill. They are one of the few fish that will go on attacking long after their appetite is satisfied, and there are accounts of tailor regurgitating food in order to make room for more.

On the east coast there appears to be an almost year-long migration of tailor schools northward, starting around Eden in November or December and culminating at Fraser Island in August and September, or even October. It is not yet clear if a similar pattern occurs on the west coast.

Opposite: This Western Australian tailor of around 6 kg was taken on a large minnow-style lure cast and retrieved from the shore.
Left: Another big Western Australian tailor, this time taken on very light tackle.
Below: Tailor have extremely sharp teeth and can give the unwary angler a nasty bite.

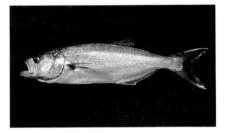

FISHING TECHNIQUES

Tailor are fished for in a variety of ways. One of the most productive techniques is to cast, and slowly retrieve, unweighted or very lightly weighted pilchards and garfish rigged on ganged hooks.

These gang-hooked rigs can also be used under bobby cork floats, or with heavier sinkers when casting distance is required — particularly on the beach.

Flesh strips and small live baits will also attract tailor.

They are one of the commonest lure-caught fish in our waters. They strike at cast or trolled chrome slices, spoons, lead slugs, minnows, jigs and flies.

A light wire trace is helpful although the fish rarely bites-off ganged hooks and large, hard-bodied lures.

The tackle needed will vary with location and individual tastes. One of the most popular land-based set-ups is a 3.5 to 4 metre casting rod and a large-spooled sidecast reel filled with 6 to 10 kg breaking-strain line. Big threadline reels replace the sidecasts in some areas.

For boat work or estuary and harbour tailor fishing, a shorter rod of 2 to 3 metres with a light, fast-actioned tip and a smaller sidecast, medium threadline, small overhead or baitcaster full of 4 to 8 kg line, is ideal.

EATING QUALITIES

Fresh tailor is delicious, although the soft, slightly-grey meat bruises very easily and does not respond well to freezing.

Tailor flesh is mildly flavoured, flaky and somewhat oily. It is ideally suited to smoking, particularly cold-smoking or curing.

All tailor destined for the table should be killed and bled as soon as they are landed, and cleaned within an hour or two. Avoid dropping the fish, stacking the fish on top of each other, and allowing *rigor mortis* to set in while the fish are bent or curled-up.

TARPON, INDO-PACIFIC

Megalops cyprinoides

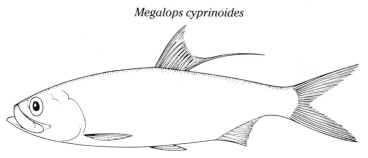

COMMON NAMES

The Indo-Pacific tarpon or ox-eye herring is related to the true tarpon of the Atlantic *(M. atlanticus),* but attains a much smaller maximum weight.

This fish could perhaps be confused with the giant herring *(Elops machnata),* though the giant herring is much longer and slimmer and lacks the trailing filament at the rear base of the dorsal fin which characterises the tarpon.

DESCRIPION

The ox-eye herring or tarpon is a small, lightly-built, large-scaled miniature of the much larger Atlantic tarpon.

Tarpon are characterised by their big eyes, over-size, upturned mouth, single dorsal fin with trailing filament, and big, silvery scales.

Colouration is mostly green to greenish-blue on the upper back, bright metallic–silver on the flanks, sometimes overlaid with purple or golden sheen. The fish are silver-white on the belly, and the tail is darker.

SIZE

Though mostly caught at weights ranging from 0.4 to 1.2 kg, very rare schools of 2 to 3.5 kg fish have been known. The fish is reputed to reach 8 kg, but no specimens of this size have been officially recorded.

The ox-eye's giant Atlantic cousin regularly tops 50 kg and occasionally reaches 100 kg and 2 metres in length!

DISTRIBUTION

A wide-ranging fish of the Indian and Pacific oceans, the tarpon is mainly confined to tropical and sub-tropical waters, occasionally wandering as far south as Coffs Harbour and Shark Bay.

Their range is from isolated, lily-covered billabongs and waterholes far inland, down through tidal estuaries and out beyond the river mouths to near-shore flats and reef systems.

HABITS AND FEEDING

The tarpon is a schooling fish, often seen 'rolling' in large numbers on the surface in calm water.

Tarpon feed mainly on shrimp, prawns, small fish, plankton, insects and sometimes even aquatic vegetation.

FISHING TECHNIQUES

They are sometimes taken incidentally on lures cast for sooty grunter, saratoga or barramundi. They take small baits such as live or fresh-dead herring and anchovy, or even insects.

A real fun fish on ultra-light tackle, tarpon will readily strike at small spinners, spoons, jigs, plugs and flies. Ideal tackle is a single-handed spin or plug outfit and 2 or 3 kg breading strain line. They also lend themselves perfectly to fly fishing.

EATING QUALITIES

Unless needed for bait, tarpon should be released alive, as they make inferior table fare.

Left: An ox-eye herring or tarpon.

Below: Although rarely exceeding 2 kg, the Indo-Pacific tarpon provides superb sport on light line. Most are released alive due to their poor eating qualities.

TARWHINE

Rhabdosargus sarba

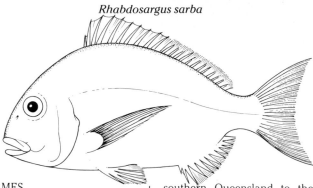

COMMON NAMES

This close relative of the three bream species described elsewhere in this book is known in some areas as silver bream, and is often confused with the other members of the family, particularly with the eastern black bream *(Ancanthopagrus australis)*.

DESCRIPTION

This bream-like fish is distinguishable from its relations by virtue of its more rounded head, slightly larger eye and — most noticeably — by the small gold spot or blotch on each scale.

The spots make the tarwhine's body look as though it is covered with horizontal gold stripes.

Apart from this gold patterning, the tarwhine is almost identical to the eastern black bream, and often has bright yellow pelvic fins, yellow anal fins, and a yellow-tinged tail.

A final distinguishing feature does not show up until the fish is cleaned; tarwhine have a black lining to the gut cavity.

SIZE

The average tarwhine is similar in size to the average bream; about 20 to 40 cm long and 0.3 to 1.2 kg. in weight. Maximum growth potential is probably close to 3 kg.

DISTRIBUTION

The tarwhine is an inshore fish of the east and west coasts, ranging from about southern Queensland to the Gippsland Lakes in the east and Albany to Carnarvon in the west.

Juvenile tarwhine are often found in large numbers in estuaries, but big ones are largely confined to the ocean surf beaches and rocky foreshores, and range out to deeper reefs.

HABITS AND FEEDING

The habits, schooling characteristics and feeding patterns of the tarwhine are almost identical to those of the eastern black bream, discussed elsewhere in this book.

FISHING TECHNIQUES

Tarwhine are rarely prolific enough to be specifically targeted, though they are reasonably common in the bags of surf fishermen working the south west corner of Western Australia.

For the most part, tarwhine respond to the same techniques as those described for the eastern black bream, and the same tackle may be used to catch them.

EATING QUALITIES

The tarwhine's rating as a table fish is much the same as that of the eastern black bream, though some people maintain that the tarwhine is inferior. The black gut cavity lining can be removed by scrubbing with a nylon-toothed brush or square of hessian when the fish is cleaned.

Left: This underwater shot shows bream and tarwhine together. The latter are readily identified by virtue of their rounded foreheads, and yellowish patterning.

Below: Tarwhine are very similar to bream, but have a more rounded head profile and longitudinal yellow or gold stripes.

TERAGLIN

Astractoscion eaquidens

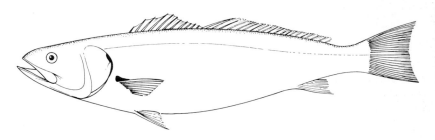

COMMON NAMES

The teraglin, 'trag' or 'trag-jew' is a very close relative of the mulloway or jewfish. *(Argyrosomus hololepidotus)* and is often confused with it.

DESCRIPTION

Though teraglin and mulloway look very much alike, the shape of the tail is different. The mulloway's tail is spade-like and outward curving, while that of the 'trag' is slightly concave or inwardly curving along the rear edge. The teraglin's scales are smaller than those of the mulloway.

'Trag' are usually bluish or brown on the back and silvery-grey or slightly brassy on the flanks. The tail is darker.

The inside of the teraglin's mouth is orange or yellow, and this colour sometimes shows on the fish's lips, even when the mouth is closed. The inside of the gill covers is also yellow.

SIZE

Exceptional teraglin may measure a metre in length and weigh close to 10 kg, although any 'trag' over 6 kg is a prize catch.

Most of these fish caught by anglers weigh from 0.8 kg to 3.5 kg.

DISTRIBUTION

The teraglin is confined to offshore waters along the east coast between about Moreton Island and Montague Island, and is more common in the northern part of its range than in the southern.

Teraglin prefer gravel or broken reef areas in waters 20 to 80 metres deep, and are rarely found close to shore unless a deep 'hole' or gutter is present.

HABITS AND FEEDING

Teraglin are schooling predators which feed on baitfish such as yellowtail, slimy mackerel, herring, pilchards and anchovy, as well as on prawns, crabs, octopi and squid.

They feed mainly between the seabed and mid-water, but will occasionally follow a food source towards the surface, especially at night.

Although largely a nocturnal feeder, 'trag' may also be active during daylight in deep water or during overcast conditions.

FISHING TECHNIQUES

Once prolific on many offshore grounds along the east coast, 'trag' populations have been in dramatic decline since the early 1970s, with only a partial recovery in the mid 1980s. It is not clear whether dwindling catches are a result of over-fishing or some cyclic pattern of distribution or abundance.

'Trag' are mostly taken on small live baits or large fillet or strip baits on relatively large hooks. They respond well to offerings of bottle squid and big prawns.

The typical tackle of the teraglin specialist is a number of handlines in the 15

Left: The teraglin is almost identical in body shape to the mulloway, but has a concave or inwardly curving tail margin, as opposed to the outwardly curved tail of the mulloway.

Below: Teraglin are taken on offshore grounds from southern Queensland to southern New South Wales.

to 30 kg breaking strain class. Very few 'trag' fishermen use rod and reels.

Once a school is located and induced to bite, big catches are the rule rather than the exception. However, losing or 'dropping' a hooked fish often scatters the school and brings an abrupt end to the session. This explains the use of heavy, no-nonsense lines.

As 'trag' begin to bite more avidly, the school may be drawn closer and closer to the boat until only 8 or 10 metres of line are needed to reach the fish.

'Trag' should be pulled to the boats smoothly and steadily when hooked as any slack in the line could easily result in a dropped fish and a scattered school.

EATING QUALITIES

The teraglin is a highly rated table fish, considered by many to be superior to its cousin, the mulloway.

TOMMY RUFF

Arripis georgianus

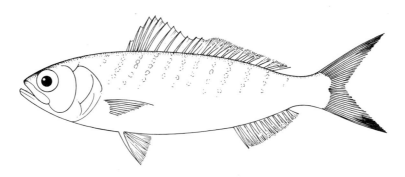

COMMON NAMES

In Western Australia and parts of South Australia, this small relative of the more widespread Australian salmon *(A. trutta)* is known as 'herring' or 'Australian herring' while in Victoria and eastern South Australia, tommy ruff (sometimes spelt 'tommy rough') or 'tommy', is a more popular title.

DESCRIPTION

The tommy ruff is very similar in body-shape to the salmon, but has noticeably larger eyes, and scales which are slightly rough to the touch.

Colouration is green on the back, greenish-silver to silver on the flanks, and silvery-white on the belly, with rows of gold spots along the flanks sometimes giving an overall yellow/gold hue when viewed from the side.

The tail of the tommy ruff is dusky-grey or yellowish with distinct black tips. These black tips are the main features distinguishing tommy ruff from juvenile salmon.

SIZE

Tommy ruff are mainly captured at weights of 0.2 to 0.4 kg and lengths ranging from 15 to 35 cm. These little fish rarely top 0.7 kg, although rare specimens weighing close to 1 kg may occur.

DISTRIBUTION

The tommy ruff is a cool-water fish largely confined to the inshore waters of western Victoria, South Australia and southern Western Australia. It is most common from Port Phillip Bay to a little north of Perth, but occasionally ranges north to southern New South Wales on the east coast and Shark Bay in the west.

The tommy ruff or herring is a shallow-water fish found in bays, estuaries and near-shore areas adjacent to reef or seagrass beds. The species is often prolific around jetties and breakwalls.

'Tommies' rarely range far offshore, although they do occur in large numbers around islands such as Kangaroo and the Neptunes in South Australia and the Recherché Archipelago and Rottnest in Western Australia.

HABITS AND FEEDING

They are a schooling fish which feed on small crustacea, plankton and very small baitfish.

Although sometimes fickle and shy in hard-fished waters, they usually respond avidly to a berley trail and feed actively and competitively, making big catches the norm rather than the exception.

FISHING TECHNIQUES

In Western Australia traditional herring

Tommy ruff are relatively small fish, rarely topping 0.4 kg in weight. Nonetheless, these lightweight cousins of the Australian salmon are very popular with southern anglers.

fishermen use a large wooden float called a 'blob', fitted with a fish-oil or berley dispenser, and baits of maggots on several small hooks set a metre or so below.

Tommy ruff take various marine worms, prawns and cut fish flesh. They will also strike readily on small lures, jigs and flies.

They respond well to a berley trail of bread, bran or pollard with a little fish-oil added.

Ideal tackle is based around a light, whippy casting rod measuring between 1.8 and 3 metres matched to a small or medium threadline (spinning) reel and 2 to 4 kg line. Sandgropers tend to use somewhat heavier tackle when casting their heavy, hardwood 'blobs'.

EATING QUALITIES

The tommy ruff if a tasty if slightly oily little fish that enjoys great popularity as a table species in South Australia and Western Australia. It is best grilled, but is also good smoked.

Tommy ruff should be bled and cleaned as soon as caught.

TREVALLY, GIANT

Caranx ignobilis

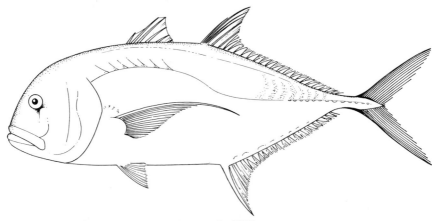

COMMON NAMES

The giant trevally or 'GT' is known by an extraordinary number of names. Once referred to, especially in larger sizes, as 'turrum', the fish then went through a period of being known as lowly trevally, before having its name changed to great trevally and — finally — to giant trevally! Many people still call this fish 'turrum', though that name more correctly belongs to the related gold-spotted trevally *(Carangoides fulvoguttatus)*.

Other names for the giant trevally include black trevally, 'bumper', 'blurter' and 'trevor'. In Hawaii this fish is called 'ulua'.

DESCRIPTION

The giant trevally is by far the largest and most robustly built of all the trevally clan. It is characterised by its steep 'forehead', heavy jaws, canine teeth and heavy scutes or sharp, modified scales on the tail wrist.

Giant trevally colouration is variable, ranging from almost black to blue green or purple grey on the back, lighter, often with silvery sheen on the flanks and silvery white on the belly. The flanks are also often overlaid with irregular black spots, blotches and vague broken bars.

SIZE

Giant trevally range in size from little 1 kg scrappers in northern estuaries, to reef and island-dwelling brutes measuring as much as 1.8 metres in length and weighing in excess of 50 kg. Exceptional specimens occasionally exceed 70 kg, especially in Hawaiian waters.

DISTRIBUTION

The giant trevally ranges widely through the Indian and Pacific Oceans and adjacent seas to the tropical north, though it sometimes wanders as far south as Sydney and Perth.

Juvenile and sub-adult trevally are common in mangrove-lined estuaries, tidal rivers and bays. Large specimens sometimes enter lower estuary reaches though they most commonly frequent inshore reef areas, coral drop-offs, bomboras, sand cays and islands, while very large fish frequent submarine cliff edges on the continental shelf edge.

HABITS AND FEEDING

Giant trevally like snags, bomboras, ledges, pinnacles, buoy lines, wharf pilings and drop-offs.

Small giant trevally form reasonably large schools, bigger fish travel in smaller

Left: A massive 29 kg giant trevally taken on a popper-style lure at Lizard Island, north Queensland.

Below: A beautiful specimen of a juvenile giant trevally or 'GT' showing well developed lateral line scutes (sharp, modified scales) towards the tail.

groups. The very largest are usually loners.

Giant trevally are opportunistic predators. They eat small to medium-sized fish — both pelagic and reef dwelling — prawns, crabs, squid and octopi.

FISHING TECHNIQUES

Giant trevally are a relatively common catch in tropical waters. They are often fished for deliberately by sportfishermen seeking a powerful and exciting adversary, but they are also taken as incidental catches. Bottom and mid-water fishing with cut fish flesh, live baits, whole dead baitfish, squid and the like is very effective, and the fish responds well to trolled, cast and retrieved or jigged lures, especially metal

spoons, minnows, plugs and poppers. For best results cast these close to the cover of coral bomboras or niggerheads, mangrove stands and wave-washed reef.

Tackle for giant trevally — which can range from a threadline casting outfit to a 15 kg game rig — needs to be in good repair to withstand the no-holds-barred fight.

EATING QUALITIES

Although denigrated by many in the north, the giant trevally is a very good to excellent table fish, particularly in sizes up to about 6 or 8 kg. Its flesh is firm, white and slightly dry, relatively bone free and deliciously flavoured. It is particularly well suited to curries, sauced dishes and the like.

TREVALLY, GOLDEN

Gnathanodon speciosus

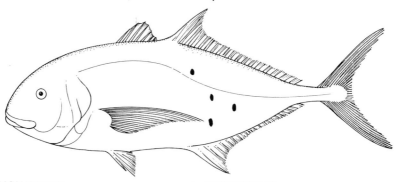

COMMON NAMES

The golden trevally is rarely known by any other name, although as with all the trevallies, large specimens are sometimes incorreclty called 'turrum', a name best applied to the gold-spot or gold-spotted trevally *(Carangoides fulvoguttatus)*.

DESCRIPTION

The 'golden' is a deep-bodied, reasonably heavily-built fish characterised by its extendable, toothless mouth and rubbery lips.

Golden trevally are usually greenish-grey and blue-grey on the back, silvery-gold on the flanks and lemon-yellow on the belly, overlaid with vague, dark vertical bands which are much more distinct on juveniles. Most adults have at least one fairly large black spot or patch on the lower rear half of the body.

The fins are dusky to yellowish. The anal fin is lemon-yellow to gold.

SIZE

Golden trevally grow to more than a metre in length and can weigh as much as 15 or 16 kg, but are rare at weights in excess of 10 kg.

Most of those caught weigh from 0.7 to 8 kg.

Very small, brightly coloured golden trevally are often seen 'escorting' sharks, turtles and groper.

DESCRIPTION

The golden trevally is a tropical species which occasionally strays into cooler southern waters. For the most part its distribution is similar to that of the giant trevally *(G. ignobilis)*, with a greater emphasis on sandy-bottomed areas and beaches.

HABITS AND FEEDING

The golden trevally feeds on or close to the seabed, specialising in crustacea and bottom-dwelling creatures, and is mainly found over sand, coral 'marl', gravel and mud. It will sometimes be encountered on hard-reef strata.

'Goldens' almost always form schools or at least small packs; large adults swim alone or in pairs.

FISHING TECHNIQUES

All the techniques described for giant trevally, the southern trevally and the silver and sand trevally will take 'goldens'.

'Goldens' are often caught by beach fishermen in tropical and sub-tropical areas, especially those using shellfish, prawns or small, whole fish as bait.

Reef fishermen and anglers drifting offshore gravel patches occasionally make incidental catches of them.

Tackle for golden trevally varies, depending on the environment and the size of the fish.

Golden trevally have fleshy, protrusible mouths with no obvious teeth and a barred, golden patterning that fades with age. Random dark spots are typical, but not diagnostic.

EATING QUALITIES

'Goldens' are regarded as the tastiest of all the trevallies, though their eating quality is rivalled by that of juvenile giant trevally.

'Goldens' should be bled and cleaned promptly for best results.

TREVALLY, SILVER

Pseudocaranx dentex

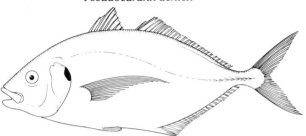

COMMON NAMES

The silver trevally is also known as white trevally, trevally, skipjack or 'skippy' — the last two names being most prevalent in Western Australia.

The trevally's popular nickname is 'blurter', a term which refers to the grunting noise make by freshly landed specimens as they grind together the crushing plates in the backs of their mouths.

A very close relative, the sand trevally *(P. wrighti),* is found in southern Western Australia where it is often caught along with silver trevally. The sand trevally is a much smaller fish, rarely exceeding 0.8 kg. Apart from the difference in size, *P. wrighti* is almost identical to *P. dentex* in appearance and behaviour.

DESCRIPTION

A deep-bodied, laterally-compressed fish with a relatively small mouth and rubbery lips.

Typical colouration is dark grey to blue/green on the back, silvery with blue and purple sheen on the flanks and silvery-white on the belly. A yellow, longitudinal stripe along the flanks is often evident in freshly-caught fish.

SIZE

The silver trevally averages between 0.4 and 2.5 kg; schools of 2 to 3.5 kg fish are occasionally encountered. Trevally over 6 kg are exceptional, although specimens in excess of 10 kg have been reported from Lord Howe Island.

DISTRIBUTION

The silver trevally is a fish of our temperate and cool southern waters, ranging from southern Queensland to about Geraldton in Western Australia. The fish is found in Tasmania and is prolific around the North Island of New Zealand.

The trevally's chosen habitat ranges from estuaries and bays to beaches, rocky foreshores, inshore reefs and offshore sand, mud and gravel patches.

HABITS AND FEEDING

The silver and sand trevallies do most of their feeding close to the bottom. They hunt worms, crustacea and small fish among the sand and seabed strata.

Divers have reported seeing schools of silver trevally nuzzling through sand and shell-grit, taking mouthfuls of it and blowing it into the water just clear of the seabed to reveal any small, edible organisms which might be living in the sediment.

Trevally schools will also feed enthusiastically on the surface when krill (a planktonic shrimp) or small baitfish are abundant.

FISHING TECHNIQUES

Silver and sand trevally are mainly taken on baits of cut fish flesh strips, small whole fish such as anchovies, whitebait and pilchards, or on baits of whole or cut squid, prawns, crab and cunji.

These baits are best used unweighted or very lightly weighted.

Left: A silver trevally of around a kilo from Gerringong, southern New South Wales.
Below: Landing a silver trevally from the rocks at Spirits Bay, on the northern tip of New Zealand.

Silver trevally are also reasonably regular lure-takers in some areas. They like metal spoons, chrome slices, lead slugs, small minnows, plugs and flies. Artifical lures should be used in mid-water or close to the seabed.

Silver and sand trevally respond well to a berley trail of soaked bread, minced fish and tuna oil.

Tackle may be similar to that used for bream, or if larger fish are anticipated, the same as that employed in shallow water snapper fishing or casting for tailor.

Many fine hauls of trevally are taken on handlines of 4 to 10 kg breaking strain, paticularly from wharves, jetties or boats.

EATING QUALITIES

The flavour of cooked silver trevally is fair to good, even very good in small, fresh specimens, though somewhat strong flavoured and dry in larger ones.

Big trevally are somtimes infested with worms.

TROUT, BROWN

Salmo trutta

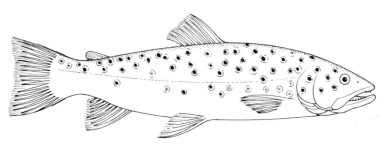

COMMON NAMES

The introduced European brown trout is normally referred to in Australia and New Zealand as brown trout, 'brown', 'brownie' or simply, trout. Sea-run stocks, which exist in parts of western Victoria, Tasmania and New Zealand, are called 'sea trout'.

In Europe, distinctions are made between separate population groups of this species. Thus we have Loch Leven trout, German brown trout and so on. In actual fact, they are all members of the same species: *Salmo trutta.*

DESCRIPTION

This European trout has a relatively large mouth and head and squared-off or slightly forked tail.

It is best distinguished from the rainbow trout by the fact that the rainbow's tail is liberally peppered with small, dark spots, while the brown's tail either lacks spots completely or has a small number of relatively large ones along its upper edge.

Brown trout colouration varies considerably between individuals, but is usually olive green to dark brown on the back and flanks and cream or creamy white on the belly. The base colour is overlaid with black and red spots, often with a lighter halo around each spot. There are large, widely spaced spots on the gill covers.

The edge of the adipose fin and leading edge of the pelvic fins may be flushed with red.

Sea-run brown trout and some lake-dwelling fish are silvery on the flanks and appear very similar to the related Atlantic salmon *(Salmo salar),* which is also present in some Australian waters. However, the salmon has a more forked tail, thinner tail wrist and smaller anal fin. The dark spots on the salmon also tend to take the form of a small 'x' rather than the round or oval marks found on the brown trout.

The only other 'trout' successfully introduced into Australian waters is the brook trout *(Salvelinus fontinalis),* which is actually a char, not a trout, despite its common name.

SIZE

The biggest 'browns' in the world have come from a reservoir in Utah, in the United States, and from Argentina. The largest weighed close to 20 kg.

In Australasia, any 'brown' over 6 kg is an exceptional catch, although during its peak in the 1970s, Tasmania's Lake Pedder produced many trophies in the 7 to 10 kg range. The largest brown trout yet recorded in Australia weighed almost 12 kg.

DISTRIBUTION

Once native to Britain and Europe, brown trout have been introduced all over the world. They are caught in the Hindu Kush of nothern India, the lakes and streams of Zimbabwe, the deep reservoirs of Argentina, the Greak Lakes of Canada

Left: An adult brown trout taken on fly tackle in Tasmania.
Below: Trout water; Lake Toolondo in north western Victoria.

and the United States, throughout New Zealand and in the cooler, southern portions of Australia.

Brown trout prefer cool rivers, creeks, lakes and dams, mainly in alpine and sub-alpine areas.

They like running, reasonably clean and well-oxygenated waterways, and do quite well in cooler lakes and impoundments.

In their native homelands, these fish only run to sea and ascend rivers at spawning time. Limited sea – run populations of 'browns' (sea trout) exist in western Victoria, Tasmania and New Zealand.

Brown trout distribution in mainland Australia is limited to the higher, cooler areas of New South Wales, Victoria, the Australian Captial Territory, South Australia and southern Western Australia. The species is widespread and prolific in Tasmania and on both islands of New Zealand.

Left: Preparing to clean a fine brown trout as the sun sets over a Victorian lake.

HABITS AND FEEDING

Brown trout feed on a wide variety of organisms, depending on their size and location.

Small, stream-dwelling fish rely mainly on insect larvae such as the nymphs and pupae of flies, and on shrimp, water bettles and terrestrial insects which land on or fall onto the surface of the water.

Larger fish, particularly those in lakes and dams, rely more heavily on shrimp, yabbies, small fish and freshwater plankton such as the copepod known as 'daphnia.'

Large ones tend to be solitary and territorial; small browns will school loosely at times.

Aggregations or 'runs' of adult 'browns' take place prior to spawning, which usually occurs in autumn and winter, although a few 'ripe' fish will be encountered throughout the year.

Spawning takes place in running streams with shallow gravel-beds, and very large, lake-dwelling trout will ascend relatively tiny brooks in order to spawn.

Although a few 'browns' die as a result of the stresses of spawning, most live to breed three, four or five times unless caught or killed by predators.

FISHING TECHNIQUES

Brown trout are usually taken on light tackle and fairly fine lines baited with earthworms, shrimps, insects and insect larvae — for example, live grasshoppers, frogs or small fish.

Baits should be float-suspended or very lightly weighted, rather than anchored to the bottom. Despite their reasonably large mouths, smallish hooks work best.

Trout also respond well to lures such as metal spoons and spinners, small minnows and tiny jigs. These may be cast and retrieved from the shoreline of a lake or river, or slowly trolled from a boat.

Popular lures include spinners such as Celtas, Mepps and Jensen Insects, spoons like the Wonder Wobbler and ABU Toby. Small minnows such as Rapalas and Nilsmasters. Flatfish, Tassie Devils and Baltic Minnows are extremely good for trolling.

Trout are ideally suited to fly fishing — a technqiue originated with this group of fish as its primary target.

Perhaps the most popular tackle for trout in Australia and New Zeland is a balanced outfit built around a light-actioned 1.8 to 2.5 metre hollow fibreglass, graphite, boron or composite rod, mated to a light threadline (spinning) or closed – face (spincasting) reel. Line strength should be from 1.8 to 4 kg — ideally around 2 or 3 kg. Such an outfit can be used for bait fishing, spinning, trolling and, if a couple of split shot or a partially water-filled bubble float are added to the rig to provide casting weight, even fly fishing.

For conventional fly fishing, a specially constructed fly rod of about 3 metres in length is mated to a simple, lightweight centrepin reel, holding a thick, heavy fly line. This line provides the weight to cast a tiny fly, which is attached to the end of the rig on a 2 to 4 metres leader of light nylon.

Flies are made in three basic types. The 'wet' fly is a sinking model designed to imitate a small fish, shrimp or insect nymph. The nymph is a slow-sinking artificial intended to imitate a hatching insect nymph. The 'dry', as its name implies, floats lightly on the surface and looks like a drowned insect or one alighting on the water to lay its eggs.

EATING QUALITIES

The brown trout provides good to very good table fare. It has pale pink to bright orange or even red flesh, depending on its diet, and is flavoursome, if a little dry. Trout flesh is ideally suited to being smoked.

TROUT, RAINBOW

Salmo gairdnerii

COMMON NAMES

This introduced sportfish, a native of western North America, is usually called rainbow trout or 'rainbow' in Australia. Sea-run populations in North America are known as 'steelhead'. Isolated sea-run stocks undoubtedly occur in New Zealand and a few Tasmanian streams.

DESCRIPTIONS

All *Salmonidae* fishes are charact-erised by their relatively elongate bodies, soft dorsal fin, fleshy adipose fin and the placement of the ventral fins well back on the belly.

The 'rainbow' has a slightly smaller head and mouth than the brown trout, and its tail is usually a little more forked.

As explained in the description of the brown trout, the 'rainbow's' tail is heavily peppered with small dark spots, while the 'brown' rarely shows any spots at all on its tail fin.

Colouration of most 'rainbows' is olive-green to deep steely-blue above, silverish on the flanks and silvery-white underneath. The back and flanks are overlaid with a peppering of dark spots. Most rainbow trout have a bright crimson or pink slash along both flanks.

As with all trout and salmon, these colours change and intensify during the spawning season (winter).

SIZE

In their native North American waters, 'rainbows' grow considerably larger than here in Australasia. Sea-run 'steelhead' in America, Canada and Alaska regularly top 8 kg and occasionally approach 15 kg.

In Australia, most rainbow trout caught by anglers weigh from 0.6 to 2 kg. This average is higher in New Zealand, especially in the Lake Taupo and Tongariro districts. Weights over 7 kg are exceptional.

DISTRIBUTION

A native of the Pacific watershed in North America, from southern California to Alaska, the rainbow trout has been successfully introduced to many parts of the world, but it remains less widespread than its European cousin, the brown trout.

In Australasia, rainbow trout extend over much of the same range as 'browns', although they are less able to survive the marginal conditions of some warmer, slow flowing lowland streams and lakes than the slightly more tolerant and hardy 'browns'.

Rainbow trout prefer swift-flowing, well-oxygenated, cold streams and rivers with plenty of boulders and broken whitewater. They also do reasonable well in alpine and sub-alpine lakes and dams.

HABITS AND FEEDING

Small rainbow trout will form loose schools; larger fish tend to be solitary outside the spawning season, which runs from about June to October in our waters.

'Rainbows' feed on much the same range of organisms as 'browns', with a little more emphasis on small fish, crustacea and freshwater plankton. They are generally a little less choosey and more diverse in their diet but can also become single-minded

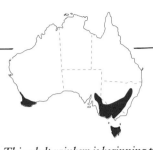

Left: This adult rainbow is beginning to develop spawning colouration.

Below: A lovely catch of rainbows up to about a kilo in weight. Note colour variations between individuals.

about a particular food source, just like their aristocratic European cousin.

FISHING TECHNIQUES

'Rainbows' respond to all the methods described for taking brown trout, and exactly the same tackle is employed. In fact, most Australasian anglers fishing for trout expect to take a mixed bag of 'rainbows' and 'browns' in most waters.

'Rainbows' are sometimes less sophisticated in their feeding than 'browns' and, as a result, can be easier to tempt with a baited hook, lure or fly.

Rainbow trout respond particularly actively to small, flashy lures, both cast and trolled. In lakes where they feed on small forage-fish such as whitebait, galaxids and smelt, live or dead baits of these fish, lures or relatively large streamer-style wet flies are particularly productive.

For more details on angling methods and gear see the section on fishing techniques under brown trout.

EATING QUALITES

Much as for the brown trout, though sometimes slightly inferior.

— TRUMPETER, TASMANIAN —

Latris linaeta

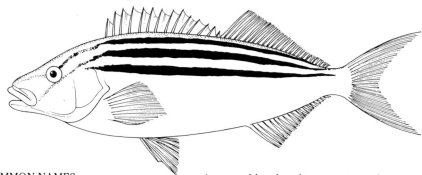

COMMON NAMES

The Tasmanian or 'Tassie' trumpeter is more commonly known simply as 'trumpeter' or 'striped trumpeter' in its home state. Elsewhere it is usually referred to by its full title.

The related silver or bastard trumpeter *(Latridopsis forsteri)* is a smaller species sometimes confused with the more sought-after Tasmanian trumpeter.

DESCRIPTION

The Tasmanian trumpeter is a medium to large, relatively deep-bodied fish with a long, sloping forehead and large, semi-protrusible mouth with fleshy lips.

The typical colouring is chocolate-brown on the back, lighter brown on the flanks and creamy below, with several longitudinal stripes of creamy – yellow running through the dark background colour on the upper flanks.

The fins are dusky, sometimes tinged with red or yellow.

SIZE

Tasmanian trumpeter commonly run from 1 to 8 kg, although 10 to 15 kg fish are far from rare on some deeper fishing grounds. Exceptional specimens may exceed 25 kg.

DISTRIBUTION

The Tasmanian trumpeter is a fish of our cold and cool temperate southern seas, ranging from Tasmania to the far south coast of New South Wales, though rarely found north of Montague Island off Narooma. It also ranges westward through the deeper waters of South Australia and southern Western Australia to near Albany.

Trumpeter prefer relatively deep, rocky reef and broken bottom strata.

In cooler, southerly locations they will move well inshore (particularly the juveniles), but further north they are rarely found inside the 120 metre or 60 fathom area.

HABITS AND FEEDING

The Tasmanian trumpeter is a forager and hunter, feeding primarily on crustacea, shellfish, squid and octopi, although large individuals will take small fish.

Juvenile trumpeter form schools, while adults are more common in loose groups.

FISHING TECHNIQUES

Most Tasmanian trumpeter are taken on bottom-fished baits of squid, prawn or cut fish flesh. They will also take small, whole fish and live baits and may occasionally succumb to jigs and lures. Not much is known about how they react to artificials.

In Tasmania, small trumpeter are often taken inshore or in estuarine waters, on relatively light tackle. However, larger fish

The delicious Tasmanian trumpeter is characteristically marked and grows much larger than the related silver or bastard trumpeter.

— both in Tasmania and further north — are usually fished for with heavy handlines, deck winches or short, stout rods and large capacity sidecast and centrepin reels filled with 15 to 25 kg breaking-strain line.

EATING QUALITIES

The Tasmanian trumpeter of all sizes is an exceptionally good table fish, and is often rated as the best of the cool-water reef species.

TUNA, DOGTOOTH

Gymnosarda unicolor

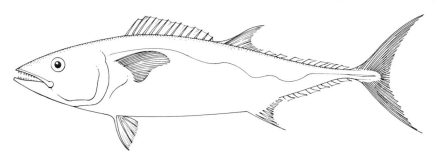

COMMON NAMES

The dogtooth, dog tooth or dog-toothed tuna is more rarely known as the white tuna, lizardmouth tuna or white tuna.

The closest relatives of the dogtooth are the bonitos *(Sarda australis* and *S. oreintalis)*, though neither of these fish grow anywhere near as large as the dogtooth, and both are characterised by distinct stripes along their back and flanks. Dogtooth tuna have no such stripes.

DESCRIPTION

The dogtooth tuna is a big, robust and almost cylindrical member of the bonito clan with heavy jaws and large, conical canine teeth.

This tuna's colouration is dark steely-blue to purple or green on the back and silver to silvery-white with a green or purple sheen below.

The second dorsal and anal fins have clearly defined white tips. The tail is dark, sometimes with a deep reddish or ochre tint.

SIZE

Dogtooth tuna commonly weigh from a little over 1 kg to 35 or 40 kg, with a reasonable number of Australian fish exceeding 55 kg. The maximum growth potential is well in excess of 100 kg.

DISTRIBUTION

Dogtooth tuna are found in tropical seas around the north of Australia and parts of Asia; occasionally as far north as Japan and Korea.

They like clean, deep-waters with temperatures in excess of 23^0 and deep drop-offs on the outside edges of outer reefs, deep water bomboras, pinnacles and reef passages.

They are rarely found over shallow water, especially when adult.

HABITS AND FEEDING

Small dogtooth will form schools, but large adults tend to be solitary or to hunt in small packs of two or three.

The dogtooth is a voracious predator which feeds on all types of fish, both pelagic and reef dwelling, as well as on squid, octopi, crabs, and the like.

FISHING TECHNIQUES

Dogtooth are rarely targeted specifically in Australian waters, but when they are fished for around deep reef edges of far north Queensland and the nor'west shelf, catches are often impressive.

They are mainly taken on lures and baits, particularly if they are trolled well below the surface. Downriggers or deep diving lures are ideal.

Live baits such as scad or small tuna, allowed to dive deeply or taken down by a weight, are often effective.

Boats trolling for marlin and other gamefish with rigged dead baits sometimes

Left: Dogtooth tuna have very distinct teeth, powerful jaws, large eyes and a prominent lateral line. This 15 kg specimen took a deep-fished live bait.

Below: The author with a 40 kg dogtooth from the waters north of Fiji.

hook big dogtooth when the boat has stopped and the baits have been allowed to sink.

Tackle for dogtooth should be robust and in good order. Most of the larger specimens are taken on big game tackle and lines of 24, 37 and 60 kg strain.

EATING QUALITIES

This tuna or bonito is a delicious table fish with pink flesh and a fine flavour, though very large specimens tend towards dryness.

All tuna and bonito should be bled promptly after capture.

TUNA, LONGTAIL

Thunnus tonggol

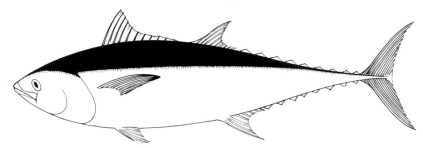

COMMON NAMES

Until recent years the longtail or long-tailed tuna was known almost exclusively in Australia as the northern bluefin tuna, and many anglers still know it by this name, despite the confusion this sometimes causes between this relatively small Indo-Pacific species and the giant northern bluefin of the Atlantic.

Other names for the species include northern blue, bluefin and oriental bonito (not be confused with one of the true bonitos, *Sarda orientalis*).

DESCRIPTION

The longtail or northern bluefin is a medium-sized tuna with a narrow, tapering tail section. It is more lightly built than many other tunas.

The longtail's colouration is blue-black on the back and silver to silvery-white on the belly. Live specimens have an irridescent blue band along each flank. The lower portion of the body is often marked with vague spots and blotches.

The fish's fins are dusky to dirty yellow. The finlets are dark-edged and the tail is dark.

SIZE

In the northern tropical part of their range, longtails taken on rod and reel mainly weigh from 4 to 12 kg. Further south, larger fish are more common, and along the New South Wales coast there are seasonal influxes of adult longtails in the 12 to 30 kg range; 40 kg giants are rare.

DISTRIBUTION

The longtail is an Indo-Pacific species confined to Australia, Niugini and parts of South East Asia.

Although mostly a tropical and sub-tropical species, it makes summer and autumn forays south in the warm ocean currents, to around Green Cape in the east and Cape Leeuwin in the west.

This tuna is rarely found more than a kilometre or two off the coast, especially in southern waters. The only exceptions occur around a few offshore islands within the continental shelf. Schools are migratory and fast-moving.

HABITS AND FEEDING

In the tropical north, small longtails form vast schools, much in the manner of mackerel tuna and skipjack. Further south, the fish is more likely to travel alone or in loose groups of 2 to 20.

Longtails feed on a range of small fish, squid, and occasionally large planktonic organisms such as krill.

They also scavenge trawler trash and fish scraps.

FISHING TECHNIQUES

In the tropics, the majority of small to medium – size longtails are taken by spinning or trolling with small, fish-shaped

Left: A very large longtail or northern bluefin tuna of almost 30 kg from Montague Island, New South Wales.
Below: Many fine longtails are taken from ocean ledges such as this one at Jervis Bay, New South Wales.

lures. Lead slugs, Stingsilda-style lures, feathers and flies are particularly effectively.

Most large longtails are taken by rock and wharf fishermen operating towards the southern limits of the fish's range.

Adult longtails take fast-trolled or rapidly retrieved lures such as those described above, as well as minnows and poppers. However, larger fish generally prefer live baits of yellowtail, mullet, slimy mackerel or garfish. They will also take fresh dead baits and — occasionally — pilchards and garfish on ganged hooks.

Tackle varies with location and the size of the fish. In the north, longtails are mostly pursued with double-handed casting outfits and 3 to 8 kg breaking strain line. Further south, live baiters and spin fishermen are more likely to opt for 10 to 20 kg line.

EATING QUALITIES

The longtail is not highly rated as a table fish. The meat is dark and rank, not unlike that of the mackeral tuna and skipjack or striped tuna.

However, if longtails are killed and bled promptly after capture and slabs of the flesh leached for an hour or two in a solution of salted water and vinegar, much of the blood is removed. After this treatment the meat is well suited to curries, casseroles and stews, and may also be baked or smoke-cured with good results.

TUNA, MACKEREL

Euthynus affinis

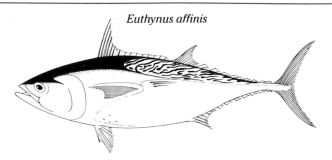

COMMON NAMES

The mackerel tuna or 'mack tuna' also carries the Polynesian title of kawakawa, by which name it is often listed in record charts.

This species is sometimes incorrectly called 'bonito,' especially in north Queensland.

A very similar fish in the Atlantic and Caribbean is known as the 'little tuna' or 'little tunny'.

DESCRIPTION

This small to medium-sized tuna is characterised by a patterning of wavy green lines on the upper back. Juveniles are very similar to frigate mackerel, but the mackerel tuna's first dorsal fin runs almost right back to the base of its second dorsal, while the frigate's is quite separate, with a much shorter base. The mackerel tuna has more prominent teeth.

Mackerel tuna are green to blue-green on the back, with some distinct wavy green lines, dots and dashes. The flanks and belly are silver. Most, but certainly not all, have one to nine, and sometimes even more, small black spots or blotches on the breast area below the pectoral fins.

SIZE

Mackerel tuna caught in Australian waters weigh from about 1 to 9 kg, with rare record-size fish around 12 kg. These fish are quite common in some areas at weights of 7 and 8 kg, yet 9 kg-plus examples are unusual.

DISTRIBUTION

This is a tuna of the tropical, sub-tropical and temperate Indian and Pacific Oceans.

Their environmental preferences are very similar to those of the longtail tuna, with greater emphasis on large bays, inlets, harbours, and the lower reaches of big estuary systems.

Mackerel tuna, especially big ones, are occasionally found well out to sea, particularly in tropical waters. They are also encountered around offshore islands, cays and reefs.

Mackerel tuna range south to at least Green Cape and Cape Leeuwin and, on rare occasions, turn up off the north coast of New Zealand.

HABITS AND FEEDING

The mackerel tuna is a schooling pelagic which feeds on schools of baitfish such as anchovy, pilchards, herring and whitebait, and on krill, larger forms of plankton and small squid. 'Mack tuna' will also feed on dead fish and scraps discarded during trawling operations.

Schools and small pods of this species will often mix with other tuna species, particularly striped tuna, juvenile yellowfin and longtails.

FISHING TECHNIQUES

While mackerel tuna are often found in vast, splashing schools, they can be frustratingly difficult to catch, especially while feeding on very small baitfish.

Mackerel tuna are plump bodied and yet streamlined, and are characterised by the pattern of navy green or blue markings on the back. One to 10 dark spots below each pectoral or side fin are common, but not diagnostic.

Kawakawa are mainly taken on fast-trolled or quickly–retrieved lures such as small skirted heads, plastic squids, feathers and lead slugs. However, they will also take live baits, fresh-dead baits, pilchards and sometimes even cut baits.

Tackle for catching kawakawa should be much along the lines of that used to take striped tuna, bonito, school mackerel and similar small to mid-range pelagics.

Casting for mackerel tuna while they are feeding with single–handed or light double-handed tackle and lines of 3 or 4 kg breaking strain can make for superb sport.

EATING QUALITIES

The dark, blood-saturated and somewhat sinewy meat is best suited to casseroles or to canning and smoke-curing. However, kawakawa may also be eaten raw, as sashimi, if bled promptly after capture and kept on ice for a few hours to firm.

— TUNA, SOUTHERN BLUEFIN —

Thunnus maccoyii

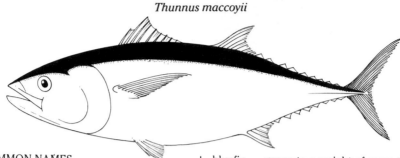

COMMON NAMES

Southern bluefin tuna are also called southern blues, bluefin and 'tunny'.

Southern bluefin are sometimes confused with other tuna, particularly yellowfin, bigeye and longtail or northern bluefin tuna. However, their stocky build, short pectoral, second dorsal and anal fins and yellowish caudal keels clearly distinguish them.

DESCRIPTION

The southern bluefin tuna is a medium to large tuna with a very heavily built, cylindrical body and short fins and is much shorter and more thickset than the longtail or northern bluefin tuna.

Southern bluefin are blue-black on the back and bluish-silver on the belly, often with broken vertical white bars on the flanks and belly, especially when young.

The fins are yellow, but never as bright as those of the yellowfin tuna. The finlets are edged with black. The caudal keels ahead of the tail are yellow.

SIZE

Southern bluefin tuna grow to almost 2 metres long and weights of more than 150 kg, although fish over 100 kg are unusual nowadays.

The fish in the inshore run of 'school' bluefin most commonly encountered by sport fishermen weigh from 6 to 25 or 30 kg.

The much rarer central Pacific bluefin — a near identical fish to the giant Atlantic bluefin — grows to a weight of more than 350 kg.

DISTRIBUTION

The southern bluefin is a cool and temperate-water fish of the southern Pacific, Indian and Southern Oceans. It is found in New Zealand waters and westwards to South Africa.

The southern bluefin ranges from inshore areas adjacent to rocky foreshores, out to islands and reef areas, and into mid-ocean well beyond the continental shelf.

This fish is rarely found in waters further north than Sydney or Newcastle on the New South Wales east coast but is quite prolific in waters further south and those off Victoria, Tasmania, the bottom half of the continent and the south-west of New Zealand.

Small bluefin are found well north along the West Australian coastline. It seems likely that this species breeds far out to sea off our north west coast.

HABITS AND FEEDING

The southern bluefin tuna is a schooling fish at all sizes; juveniles form much greater aggregations than adults.

Southern bluefin tuna feed on plankton, krill, small to medium baitfish and squid. Very large fish prey on small tuna and other pelagic species.

Bluefin grow fast, but do not mature sexually until they are seven to nine years old and weigh about 35 kg. Over-fishing has dramatically reduced their number.

Left: A school-size southern bluefin tuna from Victorian waters. Note the relatively short pectoral or side fins and dusky second dorsal and anal fins.

Below: This 10 kg southern bluefin was taken on fly tackle and was, for a time the world record in that tackle division. Discolouration of the fish's pupil has been caused by icing, although the yellow caudal keel just ahead of the tail is diagnostic of the species.

FISHING TECHNIQUES

Southern bluefin in Australasian waters are mainly taken on trolled lures, especially skirted, Konahead-style lures, feathers, jigs and flies. They will also take cast and retrieve chrome slices and fish-shaped lead slug lures.

Bluefin are more rarely taken on bait, though they are susceptible to live, dead and cut baits and whole squid, especially when these are used in conjunction with a berley trail of cut fish pieces.

The majority of southern blues taken by sportfishermen in our waters are caught on light to medium gamefishing tackle and lines of 4 to 15kg breaking strain; larger fish are better handled on 15, 24 or even 37 kg lines.

EATING QUALITIES

A dark-fleshed, somewhat blood-saturated tuna, highly rated by the Japanese for use in raw fish or sashimi dishes.

TUNA, STRIPED

Katsuwonus pelamis

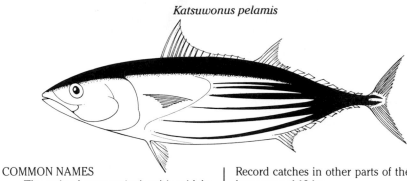

COMMON NAMES

The striped tuna or 'stripey' is widely known elsewhere in the world — including New Zealand — as skipjack or oceanic skipjack, a name that is gradually gaining acceptance here in Australia. In Hawaii the Polynesian name for this prolific lightweight pelagic is aku.

As with all the tunas, the name 'tunny' is sometimes applied to this species, though the usage is becoming less common.

Striped tuna or skipjack are often confused with bonito *(Sarda australis* and *S. orientalis),* though the 'stripey' lacks the obvious teeth of the bonito and has no stripes on its upper flanks and back.

DESCRIPTION

The striped tuna is small to medium-size fish with a very thickset, barrel-like body which tapers abruptly to the relatively small, upright tail. This fish is characterised by its belly stripes, which contrast with the upper back and flank stripes of the bonitos.

'Stripey' colouration is typically steel-blue to purple on the back, silvery-blue on the flanks and silvery-white on the belly. The belly area carries four to six longitudinal dark stripes which curve back up towards the lateral line before fading out.

SIZE

Most striped tuna caught by Australasian fishermen weigh from 1 to 5 kg, with a few bigger examples to 6 or 8 kg and the odd giant in excess of 10 kg.

Record catches in other parts of the world have topped 18 kg.

DISTRIBUTION

A world-wide species of tropical, sub-tropical, temperate and even cool waters, the striped tuna ranges from the entrances and lower reaches of larger estuaries, harbours and bays, out through inshore areas to the continental shelf and well beyond.

Striped tuna prefer relatively clean water with a temperature of 18° to 26° C, but will occasionally turn up in cooler or warmer seas.

The species forms vast schools, which could weigh hundreds of tonnes.

HABITS AND FEEDING

The schools frequently feed at or near the surface, often moving rapidly in pursuit of patches of small baitfish such as pilchards, anchovy, whitebait and sprat, as well as the planktonic shrimp known as krill or 'whale food'.

Larger skipjack will also eat squid and bigger prey such as flying fish, gar, yellowtail and slimy mackerel.

FISHING TECHNIQUES

Striped tuna are mainly pursued as bait for larger or more desirable targets, although they are brilliant sportfish in their own right, and provide one of the toughest tussles on a kilo-for-kilo basis of any pelagic in the sea.

Left: Striped tuna may be distinguished from the superficially similar bonito by virtue of the striped tuna's patterning of belly stripes and lack of obvious teeth.

Below: Striped tuna or skipjack are a basic link in the marine food chain and often exhibit injuries inflicted by predators, such as that near the tail wrist of this 3 kg specimen.

The vast majority of striped tuna taken by anglers fall to small lures trolled behind boats or cast and retrieved from boats or deep shorelines.

Small plastic squids, lead-head feathers, 'Christmas Tree' style tinsel lures, skirted heads, chrome slices and lead slug lures are the best choices. Small to medium saltwater flies, either cast or trolled, are also excellent.

Striped tuna will also take unweighted pilchards or small flesh-strip baits, especially when fished in conjunction with a berley trail.

Larger 'stripeys', those over about 3.5 kg, occasionally take small live baits.

EATING QUALITIES

Striped tuna are not often eaten in Australia and New Zealand because of their dark, blood-rich meat and strong flavour. However, if bled promptly and kept on ice they are quite palatable in casseroles, pies or when baked. They are also well suited to canning, smoking, salting and drying.

They are superb baitfish, and may be used alive for marlin, sharks and big tuna, dead for the same range of species, and cut into strips, cubes or slabs for practically any carnivorous saltwater fish.

TUNA, YELLOWFIN

Thunnus albacares

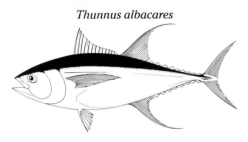

COMMON NAMES

The yellowfin tuna or yellowfin was once known as the Allison tuna or Allison 'tunny', though these names are rarely used today. However, it should be noted that in New Zealand all tuna are sometimes called 'tunny'.

Sport and game anglers sometimes nickname this species 'fin', while in Hawaii and parts of the Central Pacific it is known as 'ahi', which translates literally as 'ball of fire'.

Yellowfin, particularly juveniles, are occasionally confused with the much less common bigeye tuna as well as with albacore and bluefin tuna. However, in sizes beyond 40 to 45 kg the yellowfin's elongated, strap-like second dorsal and anal fins are quite distinctive.

DESCRIPTION

The yellowfin tuna is a big, barrel-bodied tuna with relatively large eyes and long fins. The pectoral fins reach back to a point roughly level with the start of the second dorsal fin.

When the fish is adult, the second dorsal and anal fins begin to grow and, when weights of 50 kg and more are attained have usually developed into long, strap-like 'sickles'.

The yellowfin's colouration is the most striking of all the tunas. Freshly caught or live specimens are blue to steel-black on the back, silver to silvery-gold on the flanks, and silvery-white on the belly. A band of bright gold or iridescent blue (sometimes both colours, one above the other) runs along the upper flank, separating the dark back from the lighter belly.

The stomach area sometimes carries oval, colourless patches and vague, broken vertical bars of white. These are more obvious in juveniles, though evident on some large fish, too.

The yellowfin's fins are — as its name implies — bright yellow. The finlets are canary-yellow with black margins. In very large fish the ends of the sickle fins may fade to white, though the bases are always yellow.

SIZE

Yellowfin tuna caught by Australasian anglers run from immature specimens of 2 to 4 kg, through 'school' fish of 5 to 20 kg and on up to bruisers of 60, 70 and 80 kg. Prize examples may top 100 kg in our waters, while Australasian all-tackle records stand around the 115 kg mark.

In some parts of the world, particularly around the islands far out off Mexico's Pacific coast, yellowfin to 200 kg are sometimes encountered by long-range charter boats and commercial long-liners.

DISTRIBUTION

The yellowfin is a world-wide fish of tropical, sub-tropical and temperate waters, occasionally ranging as far north as Spain and the southern shores of England, and as far south as New Zealand and Tasmania.

Yellowfin are a tuna of clean, warm currents and are rarely found close inshore unless there are deep drop-offs and warm currents along the coast. Such conditions

Yellowfin tuna vary considerably in colouration and fin structure between areas and individuals of different sizes.

Top Left: A juvenile yellowfin with clear vertical bars on belly and flanks.

Centre Left: A pair of 68 kg yellowfin from Fiji. Note elongated 'sickle' fins.

Bottom left: An adult yellowfin from southern New South Wales.

Below: Fresh from the water, yellowfin often exhibit a bright gold band down each flank.

Above: A beautiful, sickle-fined yellowfin or 'ahi' joins two marlin on the deck of an Hawaiian game boat.

Above: A 45 kg Lord Howe Island yellowfin .

prevail along parts of the New South Wales central and southern coasts in late summer and autumn, making this one of the few places in the world where yellowfin are taken from the shore.

Yellowfin prefer water temperatures of 17° to 27°C and rarely venture far into dirty, discoloured areas.

Found out to the continental shelf and well beyond, yellowfin feed both at the surface and well down the water column.

HABITS AND FEEDING

A top-line pelagic predator, the diet of the yellowfin tuna varies as the fish grows. Smaller specimens take baitfish such as pilchards, anchovy and whitebait, as well as small squid, large planktonic organisms, prawns, pelagic crab larvae and the like.

Bigger tuna prey on these too, and on larger fish up to and including striped tuna and juveniles of their own breed, as well as on big, oceanic squid.

Yellowfin will also scavenge, particularly on the 'trash lines' of reject or injured fish and prawns left by deepwater and inshore trawling operations.

Yellowfin form schools at all sizes, though the larger the fish, the fewer members a school is likely to contain. Fish over 25 kg sometimes travel alone.

FISHING TECHNIQUES

Yellowfin tuna are extremely popular with sport and game anglers, as well as with commercial fishermen who catch them for the lucrative Japanese sashimi or raw fish market.

Small yellowfin in the 2 to 12 kg range respond to the same techniques used for striped, mackerel and longtail tuna, particularly trolled or cast lures, small live baits and sometimes freely drifted pilchards or cut flesh-strips.

Larger yellowfin take small and medium live baits, up to and including live frigate mackerel, bonito and striped tuna weighing as much as 5 kg-plus. They will also take medium-sized Kona-style skirted head lures and diving minnows.

A favoured Australian technique for taking large yellowfin is to use unweighted flesh-strip baits or pilchards in conjunction with a berley trail of fish cubes.

Big yellowfin are extremely powerful and demand the best in tackle and gaffs. Most are taken on sturdy overhead reels, short, strong rods and lines of 15 to 37 kg breaking strain.

EATING QUALITIES

The yellowfin is rated only second tastiest to the albacore when cooked, and is up there with the highly prized bigeye when eaten raw in the Japanese style as sashimi or sushi.

All tuna destined for the table should be killed by a solid blow to the head immediately they are brought abroad and bled by severing one or more arteries.

The carcass should then be cooled as quickly as possible using ice or iced brine, and eaten fresh within 72 hours or snap frozen for future use.

WAHOO

Acanthocybium solandri

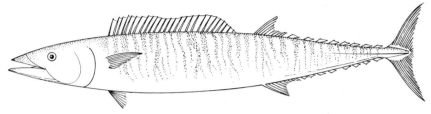

COMMON NAMES

This world-wide oceanic speedster is known in Hawaii as 'ono', in parts of North America as 'peto' and incorrectly in many areas as 'mackerel'.

Wahoo is the most widely accepted name in Australia.

DESCRIPTION

A very elongate, somewhat cylindrical fish with scissor-like jaws and very sharp teeth. It is similar in shape to the Spanish mackerel, but with a more cylindrical body, an almost upright tail and long first dorsal fin of roughly even height, unlike the mackerel's fin which is high at the front and low behind.

Colouration is steely blue-black to brilliant blue on the back, silver to silvery-blue on the flanks and silver underneath. Fresh specimens have slightly wavy vertical bars which may be either inconspicuous, or brightly tiger-patterned. The fish fades to a uniform gunmetal grey after death.

SIZE

Most wahoo caught by anglers weigh between 7 and 25 kg. Specimens under 6 kg are almost unknown.

Very large wahoo in excess of 40 kg are taken each year in Australian waters, and are almost common around Fiji, where the species tops 50 kg and on rare occasions approaches 65 kg.

DISTRIBUTION

The wahoo is found throughout the tropical, sub-tropical and warm temperate oceans of the world. In Australasia it is caught off Queensland, New South Wales and Western Australia. It may, very rarely, visit the Northland region of New Zealand.

The wahoo is an open-ocean pelagic species favouring clean, blue currents with a water temperature of 21° to 30 °C. It is rarely found close to the shore.

They like the areas adjacent to deep reef drop-offs, undersea mountains and reef pinnacles. Only large, isolated individuals appear to stray far beyond the continental shelf edge.

HABITS AND FEEDING

Wahoo are fierce predators with extremely efficient teeth. They drift slowly along in the broken shadows and refracted light near the ocean's surface until within range, then make a lightning-fast burst to intercept their prey, chopping it into several pieces in the twinkling of an eye.

Their prey includes skipjack or striped tuna, frigate mackerel, small dolphin fish, garfish, sauries and squid.

Although often solitary, wahoo will hunt in loose packs of two to a dozen fish, particularly in the tropics.

FISHING TECHNIQUES

Wahoo are mainly taken on fast-trolled lures such as Konahead-style skirted heads, feathers and diving minnows.

They are also fond of rigged skip and swimming baits such as mullet, garfish, scad and small tuna.

A wire trace is **essential** when fishing for wahoo, although many anglers are lucky

Wahoo are elongate, cylindrical and have a mouth full of wickedly sharp teeth that mesh like the blades of a pair of garden shears. Their overall appearance is vaguely similar to that of the Spanish mackerel, but the wahoo has a smaller, more upright tail and a dorsal fin of fairly even height.

enough to land large wahoo on monofilament nylon traces because of the fish's tail-biting mode of attack.

Wahoo are rarely targeted specifically in our waters. Instead, they are taken while fishing for tuna, marlin, sailfish, mackerel, kingfish and the like. However, they are nearly always a welcome catch because of their good looks, exciting bursts of speed when hooked, and superb table qualities.

EATING QUALITIES

On the table the wahoo is very good to excellent, with firm, white and sweet flesh that tastes not unlike that of the Spanish mackerel. Large slug-like parasites commonly found in the wahoo's gut do not affect the flesh in any way.

WAREHOU

Seriolella brama

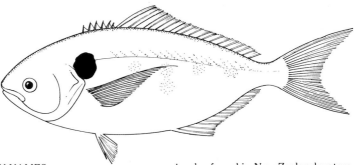

COMMON NAMES

The warehou is more commonly known through much of its range as snotty trevally, snotty trevalla, snotgall or trevalla. In parts of southern and eastern Victoria the fish is called sea bream', while in the west of that state local anglers often call the fish haddock or hake! Fish marketing authorities have promoted the names 'warrior' or 'blue warrior' for the species, but they are yet to gain widespread acceptance.

DESCRIPTION

The warehou is a small, deep-bodied, trevally-like fish. Its colouration is usually green to greenish-grey on the back, silvery-grey to silvery-green on the flanks, and silvery-white on the belly. Fresh specimens have a dark patch behind the head, above the pectoral fin, and sometimes a couple of vague vertical bars or patches on the flanks.

SIZE

Warehou commonly weigh from 0.4 to 1 kg, with occasional examples up to 1.8 kg and rare, record-size specimens of nearly 3 kg.

DISTRIBUTION

The warehou is a fish of our cold and cool southern seas, ranging from the far south coast of New South Wales through Victorian, Tasmanian, South Australian and southern Western Australian waters. It is also found in New Zealand waters.

It appears to be a deepwater fish which makes seasonal migrations into inshore reef areas, bays and estuaries, particularly during the cooler months.

HABITS AND FEEDING

Warehou are schooling fish, seasonally abundant in some areas. Schools commonly contain thousands, even tens of thousands of fish.

They feed on small baitfish such as anchovies, pilchards, sprat and whitebait, as well as larger forms of plankton, small crustacea and small squid.

FISHING TECHNIQUES

When a 'run' of warehou occurs, good hauls are taken on lightly weighted baits of prawn, lobster flesh or cut fish-strip.

The warehou will also take small lures, jigs and flies on occasions.

Tackle can be a light to medium rod and reel outfit, 3 to 6 kg breaking strain line and two or three hooks rigged on droppers above a sinker.

EATING QUALITIES

The warehou is a fine, if slightly soft-fleshed, table fish very popular in parts of Victoria and Tasmania.

The meat is easily bruised, and these fish should be bled and cleaned promptly. Warehou flesh does not respond particularly well to freezing.

Left: The warehou or snotty trevally is common in southern states at specific times of the year, when large schools enter harbours and bays.

Below: Warehou move into southern inshore waters during winter, and some big hauls are made from wharves and jetties such as this.

WHITING, KING GEORGE

Sillaginodes punctatus

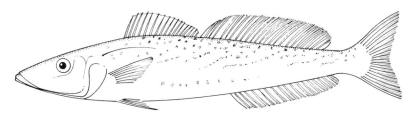

COMMON NAMES
This largest and most sought-after of all Australian whiting is known as the King George or spotted whiting, or — through much of its southern range — simply as 'whiting'. Occasionally, King George is abbreviated to the letters KG.

DESCRIPTION
A long, almost cylindrical whiting with a tapering tail-half and a small, slightly underslung mouth.

Typical colouration is light brown to dark brown on the back, silver or silvery-reddish-brown on the flanks, silvery-white on the belly and carrying many dark-brown or red-brown spots on the back and flanks.

SIZE
This is the largest of all Australian whiting, with specimens averaging 0.3 to 0.8 kg and occasionally topping 1 kg, especially in parts of South Australia and southern Western Australia. Exceptional King George whiting of 2 and even 3 kg have been recorded, mainly from offshore areas such as Kangaroo Island in South Australia.

DISTRIBUTION
King George whiting range through the inshore waters of our cooler southern coastline, from the far south coast of New South Wales to north of Fremantle and are also found in parts of northern Tasmania.

They prefer coastal sandy areas, gravel or mud patches and seagrass beds and are particularly fond of small sand patches among weed or reef in water less than 10 metres deep.

Larger individuals may sometimes be found in deeper water near a reef.

HABITS AND FEEDING
King George whiting form large, loose schools in prime feeding areas. They feed mostly on small marine organisms such as worms, shrimp, prawns, yabbies, small crabs and immature or soft-shelled molluscs.

Very large ones may occasionally prey on small fish, as well as octopi and even squid.

FISHING TECHNIQUES
The King George whiting responds best to fresh, natural baits such as marine worms, pink nippers or bass yabbies, cockles, clams, pipis and mussels.

Larger fish are often taken on squid pieces, and occasionally succumb to fish-flesh strips.

Much more rarely, a whiting will grab a small lure, jig or fly worked near the seabed.

Tackle should be light and sensitive. For boat fishing a handline will suffice, though many anglers prefer a light rod and reel. Two to 4 kg breaking strain line is ideal unless other fish such as snapper or gummy sharks are regularly encountered.

In general, sinkers should be kept as light as possible, but in certain areas — such as Victoria's Westernport Bay and some gulf waters in South Australia — comparatively heavy weights may be needed to overcome the tidal flow.

EATING QUALITIES

The King George whiting is a superb and highly rated food fish and among the best available in Australian waters.

A pair of large King George whiting weighing close to a kilo apiece. Note the dark colouration of these specimens — a variation common in larger King George whiting.

Below: King George whiting are popular surf fishing targets in the south and south west, though better catches are usually taken by small boat operators working shallow sand patches.

WHITING, SAND

Sillago ciliata

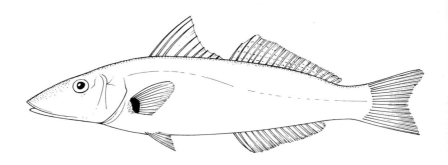

COMMON NAMES
Called sand whiting, silver whiting, yellow-finned whiting or summer whiting, this fish should not be confused with the small but prolific and popular winter or diver whiting *(Silago maculata)* of southern Queensland.

Oversize sand whiting are called 'blue nose whiting' in some areas.

DESCRIPTION
A small, elongate, silvery whiting lacking the spots of the King George whiting.

Typical colouration is goldish-yellow through light brown to greenish on the back, silvery-gold on the flanks and silvery-white on the belly.

The fins are yellowish, particularly the anal, ventrals and pectorals. The pectorals are sometimes edged with white.

Very large fish over 0.7 kg often have a blue tinge around the nose area, giving them the colloquial name of 'blue nose whiting'.

SIZE
The usual weight is from 0.2 to 0.7 kg, and very rarely over 0.8 kg. Record fish occasionally top 1.2 kg and even approach 1.5 kg.

DISTRIBUTION
The sand whiting tends to take over where the King George whiting leaves off, ranging north along the eastern seaboard from about Lakes Entrance in Victoria to the north coast of Queensland. A very similar fish *(S. schomburgkii)* occurs along a similar stretch of coastline in Western Australia.

The sand whiting is an inshore species of the estuaries, bays and ocean beaches, rarely found far from shore or in water deeper than 10 metres.

Sand whiting, as their name implies, do the bulk of their feeding over sand, mud or — more rarely — gravel.

HABITS AND FEEDING
A loosely schooling shallow-water forage fish, the sand whiting feeds mainly on marine worms, shrimp, small prawns, small crabs, yabbies and nippers, sandhoppers, sea lice and the like.

FISHING TECHNIQUES
Sand whiting are mainly taken on light tackle and small, long-shanked hooks baited with marine worms, yabbies or pink nippers, pipis (eugaris), clams, prawns or soldier crabs.

The sand whiting — also known as the summer or silver whiting — is an extremely popular angling species in southern Queensland and New South Wales. Most are taken on light tackle by surf and estuary anglers using baits of fresh marine worms, shrimp, prawns and small soldier crabs. Fishing for them is at its best from about October to April, though some are taken year 'round, particularly in the north.

Such bait should be weighted as lightly as possible and kept moving across the bottom, either by wave and current motion or by slowly retrieving line.

A short length of red plastic tube on the line above the hook will attract the fish.

Sand whiting sometimes take lures, particularly small spoons, plugs and jigs intended for flathead or bream.

Most beach-casters choose a light tipped 3 to 3.5 metre rod and shallow spooled sidecast or medium threadline (spinning) reel loaded with 3 to 5 kg line when specifically seeking whiting.

Estuary anglers prefer a 1.8 to 2.5 metre rod and threadline reel, although southern Queensland anglers will often opt for a 'Sloppy Joe' style of rig of 3.5 metre ultra-light rod and shallow-spooled sidecast. Two or 3 kg line is ideal for estuary whiting fishing.

EATING QUALITIES

A delicate, sweet-fleshed fish held in high esteem. Fine bones can be a problem in smaller sand whiting.

YELLOWTAIL

Trachurus novaezelandiae

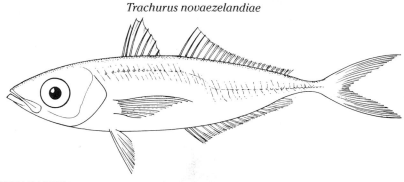

COMMON NAMES

The yellowtail or yellowtail scad has many regional names, including 'bung' and 'yakka' in New South Wales and 'chow' in South Australia. An almost identical fish — the koheru — is prolific in New Zealand.

Large yellowtail are easily confused with cowanyoung or jack mackerel *(T. declivis)*, Russel's mackerel scad *(Decapturus russelli)* and southern mackerel scad *(D. muroadsi)*. All belong to the same widespread and prolific family of scads, which are abundant in cool and temperate waters.

DESCRIPTION

A small, reasonably elongate member of the scad group of fishes with prominent scutes and sharp, plate-like scales on the lateral line ahead of the tail. Related and very similar species include the larger cowanyoung *(T. declivis)* Russel's mackerel scad *(Decapturus russelli)* and Southern mackerel scad *(D. muroadsi)*.

The colouration of the yellowtail or 'yakka' varies slightly between open ocean and estuarine or harbour - dwelling individuals, but is usually green to yellowish-brown on the back, silvery-green on the flanks and silvery-white on the belly.

The fins are yellowish, particularly the tail.

A large sea louse called a tongue biter or 'doctor' is often found in the mouth of yellowtail.

SIZE

Most yellowtail caught weigh from 0.1 to 0.6 kg, though occasional schools of larger fish are encountered. These may top 1 kg, but larger specimens usually turn out to be cowanyoung.

DISTRIBUTION

The yellowtail is a fish of our temperate and cool seas, although very similar and closely related members of the same family occur in tropical waters.

The yellowtail is mainly found in midwater over broken reef, kelp and sand patches in estuaries, harbours, bays and inshore reef areas between one and 20 metres deep.

It is common around wharves, jetties and some breakwalls, as well as in sandy holes along the ocean foreshores.

HABITS AND FEEDING

Yellowtail form dense schools of many hundreds or even thousands of individuals, although the size of these shoals cannot rival those of the cowanyoung or jack mackerel, patches of which sometimes extend over areas of several hectares in cold southern seas.

Yellowtail feed primarily on large planktonic organisms, krill, small prawns, marine worms, small crustacea and tiny fish. They will also scavenge dead fish and food scraps.

Top left:. An average-sized yellowtail, also known as a 'yakka', 'bung' or 'chow'.

Left: The cowanyoung (Trachurus declivis) is very closely related to the yellowtail. It lives in cool southern waters and grows to a greater size than the yellowtail.

Below: These rock fisherman at Jervis Bay in New South Wales are using a children's wading pool to keep yellowtail alive for bait.

FISHING TECHNIQUES

Yellowtail are mainly fished for as bait or by children. They will take lightly weighted or unweighted baits of cut fish flesh, prawn, squid, bread or mincemeat on small, long-shanked hooks.

They also strike at tiny lures, flies or multi-jig bait catching rigs.

A berley of soaked bread, bran or pollard with fish scraps and a little tuna oil works well.

Handlines or light rod and reel outfits are ideal for catching yellowtail, which often bite keenly on very light lines of 2 kg breaking-strain or less.

EATING QUALITIES

Yellowtail are not often eaten but are used as bait, either alive or dead. However, their flesh is quite palatable, if a little oily and strong flavoured. They taste quite good smoked.

ZEBRA FISH

Girella zebra

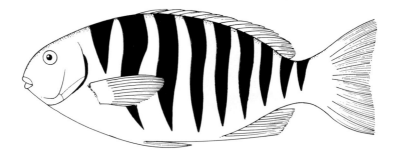

COMMON NAMES

The zebra fish has no other common names, although it is occasionally confused with two of its close relatives: the black drummer or eastern rock blackfish *(G. elevata)*, and the luderick or blackfish *(G. tricuspidata)*. However, the zebra's pug-like head and distinctive bars are diagnostic.

DESCRIPTION

The zebra is a small to medium-sized omnivorous member of the *Girella* family.

Colouration is typically purplish-brown with eight to 10 vertical bands of black. The bands are wider at the top, tapering towards the belly.

The zebra's fins are dusky to yellowish. The tail and pectorals are usually tinged with yellow.

SIZE

Zebra fish taken by anglers and spearfishermen commonly weigh from 0.4 to 1.4 kg and occasionally approach 3 kg. Maximum growth potential may be close to 4 kg.

DISTRIBUTION

The zebra fish inhabits inshore areas in cool to cold southern seas, rarely ranging as far north as Sydney or Geraldton. It is found right around the southern coastline and in northern Tasmanian waters.

They like rocky reef areas, kelp beds and cool wave-swept coastlines, and are found between the water's edge and a depth of about 15 metres.

HABITS AND FEEDING

Zebra fish form small schools as they cruise the turbulent, wave washed areas close to shore.

The species is largely vegetarian, eating mostly algaes, weed and kelp, and occasionally small crustacea and other marine invertebrates.

FISHING TECHNIQUES

The zebra fish is not a particularly common catch on hook and line and is mostly spear fished.

It will take baits of peeled prawns, cunjevoi, cut crab, abalone gut or the weed baits of the luderick specialist.

A berley trail of soaked bread and chopped weed will make a successful catch more likely.

EATING QUALITIES

The meat is firm, white and moist, though its flavour is variable and depends on what the fish has been eating.

Left: A zebra fish of about 0.8 kg taken on luderick tackle and a weed bait in Sydney's eastern suburbs — close to the northern limit of this fish's range.

Below: Zebra fish occupy the relatively shallow, wave-washed areas close to rocky shorelines.

TACKLE AND BAIT SELECTION CHART

The following set of charts lists all the species covered in this book.

It must be recognised that exceptions to these recommendations will occur in certain areas at certain times. For instance, a run of particularly small fish might call for smaller hooks and lighter lines than those suggested here, while strong fish living very

SPECIES	RECOMMENDED HOOK SIZES	RECOMMENDED LINE STRENGTH (kg breaking strain)
Albacore	2/0-7/0	6-15
Amberjack	4/0-9/0	8-24
Archer Fish	4-2/0	1-6
Barracouta	2/0-7/0	3-15
Barracuda	4/0-9/0	6-24
Bass, Australian	2-3/0	2-6
Bonito	2/0-5/0	3-15
Bream, Black	1-3/0	2-6
Bream, Pikey	1-2/0	2-6
Bream, Southern	4-2/0	2-6
Carp	8-1/0	1-4
Catfish, Eel-tailed	2-3/0	3-8
Catfish, Fork-tailed	1/0-5/0	4-8

close to cover might well demand the use of much heavier lines.

It should also be noted that practically every fish will fall for a lure or 'artificial' from time to time, though some must be regarded as extremely unlikely lure-takers. They are indicated by a blank space under the column heading 'Best Lure Patterns'.

BEST BAITS	BEST LURE PATTERNS
Small live fish, whole pilchards, fish strips and cubes.	Trolling heads, squids, feathers, small Konaheads, lead slugs and jigs.
Small to medium live fish, pilchards, gar, squid, fish strips and cubes.	Trolling minnows, squids, feathers, Konaheads, casting minnows, jigs, spoons and lead slugs.
Shrimps, prawns, yabbies, worms, fish strips and insects.	Small minnows and plugs, mini-jigs, spoons, spinners and flies.
Small live fish, whole pilchards and gar, fish strips and cubes, squid and prawns.	Trolling feathers, squids, spoons, lead slugs, minnows and jigs.
Small to medium live or dead fish, pilchards, gar, fish strips and cubes.	Trolling minnows, squids, feathers, spoons, casting minnows, lead slugs and jigs.
Live prawns, shrimps, yabbies, frogs, worms, grubs and insects.	Plugs, small minnows, spoons, spinners, mini-jigs, poppers and flies.
Small live and dead fish, whole pilchards and gar, fish strips and cubes.	Minnows, lead slugs, spoons, feathers, squids and metal slices.
Live and dead prawns, yabbies, crabs, worms, whitebait, sprat, fish pieces, gut, bread, cheese, pudding mix, steak and liver.	Small plugs and minnows, mini-jigs, spoons and flies.
AS ABOVE	AS ABOVE
AS ABOVE	AS ABOVE
Worms, maggots, grubs, bread, corn, dough, mussels, shrimp and small yabbies.	Small spinners, spoons, plugs, minnows and flies.
Worms, grubs, shrimp, yabbies and dough.	Small minnows, plugs, jigs, spinners and spoons.
Small fish, worms, frogs, shrimp, prawns, yabbies and cut fish flesh.	Minnows, plugs, spoons and spinners.

SPECIES	RECOMMENDED HOOK SIZES	RECOMMENDED LINE STRENGTH (kg breaking strain)
Cobia	2/0-9/0	6-24
Cod, Estuary	2/0-10/0	4-10 (estuary) 10-50 (offshore)
Coral Trout	2/0-8/0	6-24
Dart	4-2/0	2-6
Dolphin Fish	2/0-9/0	4-15
Drummer, Black	1-4/0	4-15
Emperor, Red	3/0-7/0	8-24
Emperor, Spangled	2/0-6/0	6-15
Fingermark	2/0-6/0	4-15
Flathead, Dusky	1/0-5/0 (long shank)	3-10
Flathead, Sand	1/0-4/0 (long shank)	4-15
Flounder	2-2/0	2-6
Garfish	12-6	1-4
Groper, Blue	2/0-6/0	8-35
Hairtail	2/0-6/0	4-10
Herring, Giant	1/0-5/0	3-10
Javelin Fish	1/0-4/0	3-8

BEST BAITS	BEST LURE PATTERNS
Small to medium live and dead fish, whole pilchards gar, squid, fish strips and cubes.	Minnows, trolling heads, squids, spoons, poppers, jigs and slugs.
Small to medium live and dead fish, crabs, prawns, fish strips and chunks or cubes.	Minnows, plugs, spoons and jigs.
Small live or dead fish, prawns, squid, octopi, fish strips and pieces.	Minnows, jigs, spoons, feathers and poppers.
Prawns, crabs, shrimp, squid pieces, worms, fish strips and pieces.	Spoons, slugs, mini-jigs and flies.
Small live fish, whole gar and pilchards, squid, fish strips, cubes and pieces.	Trolling heads, feathers, squids, minnows, spoons, slugs and jigs.
Crabs, prawns, shellfish, squid pieces, bread, cunjevoi and weed.	
Squid, whole small fish, crabs, shellfish, gar, herring, pilchards, fish strips and pieces.	Jigs, spoons and minnows.
AS ABOVE	AS ABOVE
AS ABOVE	Plugs, minnows, spoons and jigs.
Small live and dead fish, prawns, yabbies, worms, whitebait, fish strips and pieces.	Minnows, plugs, spoons and jigs.
AS ABOVE	AS ABOVE
AS ABOVE	Mini-jigs, spoons and small minnows or plugs.
Prawn pieces, shrimp, maggots, worms, squid pieces, fish strips and pieces, bread and dough.	Mini-jigs and flies.
Crabs, crab pieces, shellfish, squid, octopi and prawns.	
Small live and dead fish, pilchards, gar, fish strips or fillets and squid.	Spoons, plugs and minnows.
Small live or dead fish, gar, pilchards, prawns, yabbies, worms and fish strips.	Spoons, slugs, jigs, small minnows, plugs, poppers and flies.
Prawns, yabbies, worms, crabs, squid pieces, fish strips and pieces.	Mini-jigs, small plugs and spoons.

SPECIES	RECOMMENDED HOOK SIZES	RECOMMENDED LINE STRENGTH (kg breaking strain)
Jewfish, West Australian	4/0-9/0	8-30
Jobfish, Green	2/0-7/0	6-15
John Dory	3/0-7/0	3-15
Jungle Perch	2-2/0	2-4
Kingfish, Yellowtail	4/0-10/0	6-24
Leatherjackets	6-2 (long shank)	2-8
Long Tom	1-4/0	2-8
Luderick	10-4	1-6
Mackerel, School and Spotted	2/0-5/0	3-15
Mackerel, Shark	4/0-7/0	3-15
Mackerel, Slimy	10-4	1-6
Mackerel, Spanish	4/0-9/0	4-24
Mangrove Jack	2/0-5/0	4-15
Marlin, Black	6/0-14/0	8-60
Marlin, Blue	6/0-14/0	8-60
Marlin, Striped	6/0-12/0	8-37
Morwong, Silver	2/0-5/0	8-15

BEST BAITS	BEST LURE PATTERNS
Squid, octopi, cuttlefish, heavy jigs, small live or dead fish, pilchards, gar, fish fillets, strips and pieces.	
Small live baits, pilchards, gar, prawns, fish strips and fish pieces.	Minnows, plugs, spoons, slugs, feathers and jigs.
Small live baits, whole dead fish, pilchards, gar, fish strips and pieces.	Jigs.
Live prawns, shrimp, yabbies, grubs, worms and insects.	Spinners, spoons, mini-jigs, small plugs, small poppers and flies.
Small to medium live fish, whole dead fish, gar, pilchards, squid, octopi, cuttlefish, fish strips, fillets and pieces, prawns and yabbies.	Minnows, plugs, poppers, jigs, spoons, trolling heads, feathers, squids, lead slugs and flies.
Prawns, prawn pieces, squid pieces, shellfish, fish pieces and strips.	
Small live or whole fish, pilchards, gar, fish strips, prawns and yabbies.	Small minnows, plugs, spoons, jigs, slugs and flies.
Cabbage weed or sea lettuce, green weed, streamer weed, bread, worms, yabbies, prawn pieces.	
Small live or dead fish, pilchards, gar, fish strips and pieces.	Metal slugs, spoons, jigs, minnows, plugs, poppers, feathers, squids, small trolling heads and flies.
AS ABOVE	AS ABOVE
Fish strips and pieces, whitebait, prawns and prawn pieces and squid pieces.	Small metal slugs, slices, spoons, spinners, mini-jigs and flies.
Live or dead whole fish, gar, mullet, pilchards, herring, fish strips, fillets and pieces and squid.	Minnows, spoons, jigs, poppers, trolling heads, feathers, squids, metal slugs and flies.
Small live fish, small dead fish, fish fillets, strips and pieces, crabs, prawns, yabbies and squid.	Minnows, plugs, spoons, jigs, poppers and flies.
Medium to large live and dead fish, large strip baits and squid.	Trolling heads, Konaheads, large rubber or plastic squid, feathers and large flies.
AS ABOVE	AS ABOVE
AS ABOVE	AS ABOVE
Prawns, shellfish, squid and squid pieces, fish strips, cubes and pieces.	

SPECIES	RECOMMENDED HOOK SIZES	RECOMMENDED LINE STRENGTH (kg breaking strain)
Mullet, Sand	12-6	1-4
Mullet, Sea	10-6	2-6
Mulloway	4/0-9/0	6-24
Murray Cod	2/0-7/0	6-15
Nannygai	2/0-5/0	6-20
Parrotfish, Blue-Throated	1-3/0	4-10
Pearl Perch	2/0-5/0	8-20
Perch, Golden	1-4/0	3-10
Perch, Macquarie	4-2/0	2-8
Perch, Silver	4-1/0	2-8
Pike, Long-Finned	2-3/0	3-10
Queenfish	2/0-5/0	3-10
Rainbow Runner	2/0-5/0	3-10
Redfin	2-2/0	1-6
Sailfish	3/0-7/0	4-15
Salmon, Australian	1-5/0	4-10
Salmon, Chinook	4-2/0	3-15
Salmon, Threadfin	1-4/0	3-10

BEST BAITS	BEST LURE PATTERNS
Worms, bread, dough, cheese, shrimp, prawns and prawn pieces.	Mini-jigs, very small spoons and flies.
AS ABOVE	AS ABOVE
Small to medium live and dead fish, pilchards, gar, fish fillets, strips and pieces, squid, prawns and worms.	Minnows, metal slugs, slices, feathers, jigs and poppers.
Yabbies, shrimp, worms, grubs, large insects and small live fish.	Plugs, spoons, jigs and large spinners.
Fish strips and pieces, prawns, shellfish and squid pieces.	Small jigs, metal slugs and weighted flies.
Shellfish, crabs, prawns, squid pieces, octopi, fish strips and fish pieces.	Small jigs and metal slugs.
Prawns, squid and squid pieces, pilchards, fish strips and fish pieces.	Jigs.
Yabbies, shrimp, worms, grubs, insects and small live fish.	Plugs, spoons, spinners and jigs.
Small yabbies, shrimp, worms, grubs, insects and insect larvae.	Small plugs, spinners, spoons, mini-jigs and flies.
AS ABOVE	AS ABOVE
Pilchards, whitebait, herring, fish strips and fish pieces, prawns and squid.	Small minnows, metal slugs, spoons, jigs, slices and flies
Small live and dead fish, pilchards, gar, mullet, prawns, fish strips and pieces.	Minnows, plugs, poppers, metal slugs, slices, spoons, feathers, squids, jigs and flies.
Small live and dead fish, pilchards, gar, herring, small squid, squid pieces, fish strips and pieces.	Small trolling heads, feathers, squids, metal slugs, spoons, small jigs, flies, minnows and plugs.
Small live or dead fish, small yabbies, shrimp, worms, grubs and insects.	Jigs, bobbers, spoons, small metal slugs, plugs, small minnows and flies.
Small live and dead fish, mullet, gar, pilchards, herring and fish strips.	Trolling heads, small Konaheads, feathers, squids and minnows.
Small live or dead fish, pilchards, gar, whitebait, squid and squid pieces, prawns, fish strips and pieces.	Slices, spoons, metal slugs, minnows, plugs, feathers, squids, jigs, poppers and flies.
Small live and dead fish, pilchards, whitebait, shrimp, mudeyes and worms.	Minnows, slices, plugs, spoons, spinners, slugs and flies.
Small live and dead fish, pilchards, mullet, gar, squid, crabs, shellfish, fish strips and pieces.	Minnows, plugs, spoons, slices, small jigs, poppers and flies.

SPECIES	RECOMMENDED HOOK SIZES	RECOMMENDED LINE STRENGTH (kg breaking strain)
Samson Fish	4/0-9/0	8-24
Saratoga	1/0-4/0	2-8
Sharks, Gummy and School	3/0-6/0	6-15
Sharks, Hammerhead	5/0-14/0	8-37
Sharks, Mako and Blue	5/0-14/0	8-37
Shark, Tiger	8/0-16/0	15-60
Sharks, Whaler	4/0-14/0	8-37
Shark, White	10/0-20/0	24-60
Snapper	2/0-7/0	4-20
Snook	2/0-5/0	3-10
Sooty Grunter	2-2/0	2-8
Sweep, Sea	4-1/0	3-8
Sweetlip	3/0-7/0	8-30
Tailor	1/0-6/0	3-10
Tarpon	4-2/0	1-6
Tarwhine	1-3/0	2-6
Teraglin	3/0-8/0	8-20
Tommy Ruff	8-2	1-6

BEST BAITS	BEST LURE PATTERNS
Small to medium live and dead fish, pilchards, gar, squid, fish strips, cubes and pieces.	Minnows, jigs, trolling heads, squids, spoons and metal slugs.
Live prawns, shrimp, yabbies, worms, insects and small fish.	Minnows, plugs, spoons, spinners, poppers and flies.
Whole dead fish, fish fillets, strips and pieces, squid and shellfish.	
Medium to large live and dead fish, tuna, large fish pieces and squid.	Trolling heads and Konaheads.
AS ABOVE	AS ABOVE
AS ABOVE	
AS ABOVE	Minnows, trolling heads and Konaheads.
AS ABOVE	
Fish strips, pieces and cubes, pilchards, gar, prawns, shellfish, squid, squid pieces, cuttlefish, octopi and shellfish.	Jigs, spoons, minnows and weighted flies.
Pilchards, gar, whitebait, small mullet, fish strips, squid and prawns.	Minnows, spoons, slices, metal slugs and jigs.
Prawns, shrimp, small yabbies, worms, grubs and insects.	Small minnows, plugs, spoons, spinners, jigs, poppers and flies.
Prawns, squid pieces, worms, shellfish, bread, fish strips and pieces.	
Prawns, squid, shellfish, pilchards, herring, fish strips and pieces.	Jigs, spoons, metal slugs and minnows.
Small live or dead fish, pilchards, gar, prawns, squid, fish strips and pieces.	Metal slices, slugs, spoons, minnows, feathers, jigs and flies.
Small live or dead fish, herring, prawns, squid pieces, insects, worms and grubs.	Small minnows, plugs, spoons, spinners, mini-jigs, poppers and flies.
Prawns, yabbies, crabs, worms, whitebait, squid, shellfish, gut, bread, cheese and dough.	Small minnows, plugs, mini-jigs and flies.
Small live and dead fish, pilchards, gar, herring, fish fillets, strips and pieces and squid.	
Maggots, worms, prawns, prawn pieces, shrimp, squid pieces, fish strips and fish pieces.	Mini-jigs, small slices, spoons, spinners and flies.

SPECIES	RECOMMENDED HOOK SIZES	RECOMMENDED LINE STRENGTH (kg breaking strain)
Trevally, Giant	3/0-8/0	6-24
Trevally, Golden	2/0-6/0	4-15
Trevally, Silver	2-2/0	3-10
Trout, Brown	12-1	1-4
Trout, Rainbow	12-1	1-4
Trumpeter, Tasmanian	3/0-7/0	10-30
Tuna, Dogtooth	5/0-10/0	10-37
Tuna, Longtail	4/0-8/0	4-15
Tuna, Mackerel	3/0-6/0	4-10
Tuna, Southern Bluefin	3/0-10/0	6-37
Tuna, Striped	1/0-5/0	3-10
Tuna, Yellowfin	4/0-10/0	8-37
Wahoo	5/0-9/0	8-24
Warehou	4-1/0	3-8
Whiting, King George	4-1	2-6
Whiting, Sand	6-3 (long shank)	2-4
Yellowtail	12-4	1-4
Zebra Fish	4-1/0	4-10

BEST BAITS	BEST LURE PATTERNS
Small live and dead fish, pilchards, gar, mullet, herring, squid, prawns, yabbies, fish strips and pieces.	Minnows, plugs, poppers, jigs, slices, metal slugs, spoons, feathers, squids and trolling heads.
AS ABOVE	AS ABOVE
Prawns, yabbies, squid, shellfish, cunjevoi, pilchards, whitebait, fish strips and pieces.	Small minnows, metal slugs, plugs, spoons, jigs and flies.
Worms, grubs, insects, mudeyes, small live and dead fish, shrimp, small yabbies, mussels and dough.	Spinners, spoons, small minnows, small plugs, mini-jigs, wobblers and flies.
AS ABOVE	AS ABOVE
Prawns, squid, squid pieces, cuttlefish, octopi, crabs, pilchards, shellfish, fish strips and pieces.	Jigs.
Medium live and dead fish, mullet, gar, herring, pilchards, squid, fish strips, cubes and pieces.	Trolling heads, Konaheads, squids, big minnows, spoons and jigs.
Small live and dead fish, pilchards, gar, squid, fish strips, cubes and pieces.	Metal slugs, slices, minnows, feathers, trolling heads, squids and jigs.
AS ABOVE	AS ABOVE
AS ABOVE	AS ABOVE
AS ABOVE	AS ABOVE
Small to medium live and dead fish, pilchards, gar, fish strips, cubes and pieces and squid.	Trolling heads, Konaheads, squids, feathers, minnows, jigs and large flies.
AS ABOVE	AS ABOVE
Prawns, squid pieces, shellfish, crayfish, yabbies, worms, fish strips and pieces.	Small slices, spoons, jigs minnows and flies.
Worms, shellfish, small crabs, squid pieces, fish strips.	
Worms, yabbies, shellfish and small crabs.	
Prawns, prawn pieces, mince, dough, squid pieces, bread, fish strips, slivers and pieces.	
Cabbage weed or 'sea lettuce', green weed, streamer weed, cunjevoi, shellfish, crabs, squid pieces, bread and dough.	